Teaching for Inclusion

Eight Principles for Effective and Equitable Practice

Srikala Naraian

Foreword by Dianne L. Ferguson

TEACHERS COLLEGE PRESS

TEACHERS COLLEGE | COLUMBIA UNIVERSITY
NEW YORK AND LONDON

Published by Teachers College Press, 1234 Amsterdam Avenue, New York, NY 10027

Copyright © 2017 by Teachers College, Columbia University

Grateful acknowledgment is made to reprint material from the following:

Naraian, S. (2011). Seeking transparency: The production of an inclusive classroom community. *International Journal of Inclusive Education, 15*(9), 955–973. Reprinted by permission of Taylor & Francis Ltd, http://www.tandfonline.com

Naraian, S. (2011). Teacher discourse, peer relations, and significant disability: Unraveling one friendship story. *International Journal of Qualitative Studies in Education, 24*(1), 97–115. Reprinted by permission of Taylor & Francis Ltd, http://www.tandfonline.com

Naraian, S. (2013). Dis/ability, agency, and context: A differential consciousness for doing inclusive education. *Curriculum Inquiry, 43*(3), 360–387. Copyright © The Ontario Institute for Studies in Education of the University of Toronto, reprinted by permission of Taylor & Francis Ltd, http://www.tandfonline.com on behalf of The Ontario Institute for Studies in Education of the University of Toronto.

Naraian, S. (2015). Love's labor lost: Emotional agency in a school worker's story of family advocacy. *International Journal of Qualitative Studies in Education, 28*(1), 92–111. Reprinted by permission of Taylor & Francis Ltd, http://www.tandfonline.com

Naraian, S., Ferguson, D. L., & Thomas, N. (2012). Transforming for inclusive practice: Professional development to support the inclusion of students labeled as emotionally disturbed. *International Journal of Inclusive Education, 16*(7–8), 721–740. Reprinted by permission of Taylor & Francis Ltd, http://www.tandfonline.com

All rights reserved. No part of this publication may be reproduced or transmitted in any form or by any means, electronic or mechanical, including photocopy, or any information storage and retrieval system, without permission from the publisher. For reprint permission and other subsidiary rights requests, please contact Teachers College Press, Rights Dept.: tcpressrights@tc.columbia.edu

Library of Congress Cataloging-in-Publication Data is available at loc.gov

ISBN 978-0-8077-5857-1 (paper)
ISBN 978-0-8077-5858-8 (hardcover)
ISBN 978-0-8077-7562-2 (ebook)

Printed on acid-free paper

Manufactured in the United States of America

24 23 22 21 20 19 18 17   8 7 6 5 4 3 2 1

DISABILITY, CULTURE, AND EQUITY SERIES
Alfredo J. Artiles and Elizabeth B. Kozleski, *Series Editors*

Teaching for Inclusion:
Eight Principles for Effective and Equitable Practice
SRIKALA NARAIAN

Transition by Design:
Improving Equity and Outcomes for Adolescents with Disabilities
AUDREY A. TRAINOR

After the "At-Risk" Label: Reorienting Educational Policy and Practice
KEFFRELYN D. BROWN

DisCrit—Disability Studies and Critical Race Theory in Education
DAVID J. CONNOR, BETH A. FERRI, & SUBINI A. ANNAMMA, EDS.

Closing the School Discipline Gap:
Equitable Remedies for Excessive Exclusion
DANIEL J. LOSEN, ED.

(Un)Learning Disability:
Recognizing and Changing Restrictive Views of Student Ability
ANNMARIE D. BAINES

Ability, Equity, and Culture:
Sustaining Inclusive Urban Education Reform
ELIZABETH B. KOZLESKI & KATHLEEN KING THORIUS, EDS.

Condition Critical—Key Principles for Equitable and Inclusive Education
DIANA LAWRENCE-BROWN & MARA SAPON-SHEVIN

Contents

Foreword *Dianne L. Ferguson*		*vii*
Acknowledgments		xi
Introduction: Teaching for Inclusion		**1**
Premises of the Book		2
Eight Principles of Inclusive Teaching Derived from Teacher Practice		6
Theoretical Foundations of the Book		12
An Ethnographic Focus: The Research Investigations Underlying This Book		16
Organization of This Book		16
1.	**Teachers-in-School**	**21**
	Building a Classroom Family	21
	Achieving a Transparent Community	25
	Developing a Pedagogical Vision for All Students	28
	Collaborating for Inclusion and Social Justice	32
	Conclusion: Piecing Together the Experiences of Educators	34
2.	**Place and Time in the Grammar of Schooling**	**36**
	Learning in Place, Learning for Community	37
	Time, Place, and Place-Time: The Struggles and Consequences of Individualization	44
	Maneuvering Place-Time for Student Success: Two Stories	48
3.	**Straddling, Resolving, and Transforming Competing Paradigms**	**54**
	Adopting Both Mechanistic and Constructivist Methodologies Simultaneously	56
	Securing a Professional Identity: Working Within and Across General and Special Boundaries	65

	The Ambiguity and Messiness of Inclusive Instructional Practice	69
4.	**Interpreting for Accessibility and Inclusion**	**73**
	Teachers as Interpreters and Facilitators of Stories to Promote Inclusion	74
	Achieving Access Through Interpretation: How Teachers Put Stories to Work	81
	Accessibility as Speaking-for and Speaking-with Students	88
5.	**Working for Community: The Role of Families**	**92**
	Developing Communities for Inclusion . . . With or Without Families	94
	Locating Self, Students, and Families: Distributed Learning and Narrative Complexity	100
	Learning to Listen	106
6.	**Shifting Perspectives: Teachers as Teacher Educators**	**111**
	Teachers Supporting Colleagues	112
	Taking the Long Road: Differentiating Support Needs for Peer Development	118
	Shifting Mindsets: Learning from Elena, Paul, Julie, and Blair	125
7.	**Learning from Teachers' Work: Toward Inclusion as a Pedagogy of Deferral**	**129**
	The Interpretive Stance Toward Teacher Practice Reflected in This Book	129
	New Concepts for Inclusion: The Affordance of U.S. Third World Feminism	132
	Inclusion as a Pedagogy of Deferral	140
	In Sum . . .	144

References	**145**
Index	**155**
About the Author	**163**

Foreword

We have roughly 30 years of research on inclusion, depending on when you start counting. By the middle of the 1980s, inclusion was definitely a special education project driven by a civil rights logic. Through much of the 1990s, most of the research and commentary focused on (1) where the best place was for students with disabilities to learn, (2) the uniqueness of what was entailed in actually ensuring that students with disabilities learned, and (3) a growing list of examples of students being successfully included despite their disabilities. Much of the work during this period assumed a norm that all students had to share in order to learn effectively in typical schools. Thus much of the rationale for special education was to bring students to the normative standards of knowledge and performance in order to *earn* access to typical schools and classrooms.

As the century approached its close, the research shifted to support a broader view of how inclusive schools should be defined. The goal of this shift was to bridge the parallel systems of general and special education to create a single system with not just a diversity of students across a range of attributes, but also a diversity of teachers and other educational professionals working cooperatively. Increasingly, schools and learning reflected a complex interaction between each student's abilities and the environment of the school.

Early in the 2000s, *inclusion* changed from a noun to an adjective, which indicated a move away from equating students' learning exclusively with places toward discovering and describing ways any school could effectively accommodate any student's learning. What ensued was a search for definition among educators: What does it look like? What needs to be in place? What barriers need to be surmounted? How does it work? What resources are needed? How will we know if we "get it right?"

What emerged were lists of characteristics or features of inclusive education, comprehensive frameworks depicting the *processes* of inclusive education and the identification of critical components. Almost a decade into the new century I became curious about what progress had been made since the mid 1990s. When I looked across most of the countries in Europe and North America, I discovered that while some countries had made impressive strides, other countries, including the United States and much of Canada, had made much less progress. And that progress favored only some previously excluded students: "What remains troubling is that the rhetoric of inclusive education for students with disabilities is not matched by enough reality. After [decades], the news is not good enough" (Ferguson, 2008).

Still, all of the research made it clear that moving students to new environments was not nearly enough; it also required fundamental changes in the "core of educational practice" (Elmore, 1996):

> The "core" also includes structural arrangements of schools, such as the physical layout of classrooms, student grouping practices, teachers' responsibilities for groups of students, and relations among teachers in their work with students, as well as processes for assessing student learning and communicating it to students, teachers, parents, administrators, and other interested parties. (p. 23)

So 30 years of research have taught us that using inclusive practices is hard, messy, always being contested, and unfinished. Still, some new directions are emerging. One is focusing more on teachers' relationships with their students and what they need to know about each student's learning. Another is focusing more on teachers' roles as supporters, interpreters, and enablers of learning. We simply need to know a lot more about what constitutes inclusive pedagogy—the hows and whys of teaching.

Teaching for Inclusion and its eight principles for effective and equitable practice offer an important examination of just these things. Naraian offers a close look at exactly how teachers manage many of the things that make pursuing teaching for inclusion so hard, messy, and contested. She acknowledges in principle 1 that inclusion is "unpredictable, multidimensional, and always unfinished." Principle 2 states that teachers need both a holistic understanding of their students and a commitment to social justice to pursue an inclusive teaching agenda. But it is the third overriding principle that points to the fact that any kind of teaching is really about constantly making strategic decisions to foster inclusive practices. Teaching has always been about deciding what to teach, to whom, for what reason, and toward what outcome? Making these decisions about each student in a typical classroom, some of whom have disabilities, others who have other challenges to learning; that is what this book is all about.

Naraian draws from a decade or more of work with teachers, mostly in the classroom, to give us careful narratives of exactly what decisions teachers make. Through the experiences of Jessica, Stephanie, Paul, Julie, Blair, Anita, and Maria, the author creates windows into what makes teaching for inclusion possible. Take, for example, the challenges of time, which there is never enough of for teachers, and place, where students should learn. Additionally, Naraian shows us how the "struggles and consequences of individualization" force teachers to find new ways of understanding that provide them with more and more flexible options for their decisions.

Similarly, Naraian also takes up the many tensions and dichotomies that plague all teachers. Almost more than anywhere else, schools rely on operating within binaries that appear to offer straightforward choices or solutions. Inquiry-based learning and explicit instruction, diagnosis/labeling and strength-based pedagogy, and behaviorism and constructionism—these are just a few of the tensions teachers must negotiate. My own view has long been that it takes a fulcrum to strike a balance and the resolution of such dichotomies lies in finding ways to either synthesize them or find ways to draw on both sides of the tension. Naraian shows us how these teachers find ways to adopt these dichotomies simultaneously, thus rendering them less a struggle than a way to enlarge the possible strategic decisions available to them.

There is much more content of value here in this book. I especially enjoy the author's exploration of teacher identity across "general" and "special" education. But perhaps the most promising new ideas are in the concluding chapter, which explores a potential new conceptual language drawn from the feminism of the Global South. These women find the boundaries or identifiers usually experienced by western women to be shifting and permeable lines across and through which they constantly move.

In the end, Naraian argues quite persuasively for a pedagogy of deferral. Teachers learn through the examples in this book to cross boundaries, straddle competing ideas, partially apply normalcy narratives, all toward pursuing every student's learning needs; collectively, this helps teachers engage in inclusive teaching.

This is an important book that offers new ways to understand what—even after 30 years—we have not yet comprehended. All teachers and teacher educators can only benefit, and take us into the future.

—*Dianne L. Ferguson*

REFERENCES

Elmore, R. (1996). Getting to scale with good educational practice. *Harvard Educational Review, 66,* 1–26.

Ferguson, D. L. (2008). International trends in inclusive education: The continuing challenge to teach each and every one. *International Journal of Special Needs Education, 23*(2), 109–120.

Acknowledgments

There have been innumerable people who have participated directly or indirectly in helping this book take form. Most important in this group are the educators, students, and families who have graciously given their time, with little or no compensation, to help me carry out my investigations. To the students who generously shared their schooling experiences with me, I am grateful for the time and trust they extended to me. To the teachers and other educators who welcomed me into their classrooms and their lives at school, I am humbled by the generosity, professionalism, and care they granted my research. To the families who willingly let me into their worlds, I cannot adequately express my appreciation for the many coffees and conversations we shared as we talked about their children, schools, and learning. Even as this book is grounded in the experiences of all these participants, it can offer a mere glimpse of their depth and complexity.

As a teacher educator, whenever I have yearned for some guidance about doing inclusion, I am inevitably drawn back to my conversations and shared experiences over the years with Dianne Ferguson. When I struggled to understand my place as a disability studies scholar while conducting my research, I recalled the wisdom of Phil Ferguson. And when I was tentative about the potential contributions of my work, I was grateful for the support of Scot Danforth. Collectively, these three senior scholars initiated me into the meanings of inclusion and have generously supported my professional growth along the way. I am indebted to them. Additionally, my membership in the larger disability studies in education community of which they are a part has been a strong foundation for all my teaching and research endeavors. Within this community, I additionally extend my thanks to Susan Gabel for her mentorship. I am also grateful to Dóra Bjarnason for offering me the opportunity to understand the complexity and significance of straddling competing paradigms as a researcher. I owe many thanks to Marleen Pugach, for finding promise in my research and supporting my efforts to advance it.

I am grateful to my colleagues at Teachers College, particularly in the Department of Curriculum and Teaching, for the support they have extended to me. They have enthusiastically championed the research on which this book is based. I have especially benefited from Marjorie Siegel's openness to learn about a disability studies–informed inclusive education even as she has given me the courage to explore fields of study that were new to me. Celia Oyler has always been unabashedly enthusiastic about my research and continually strove to find ways to prioritize that among my other commitments at the College. Cathy Rikhye was instrumental in introducing me to the many players within local schools engaged in the work of inclusion, thereby helping to get my research off the ground.

There have been research assistants over the years at Teachers College who have supported me in doing much tedious work, including conducting routine literature searches and developing reports. I am grateful for their sincere commitment and willingness to endure the unpredictability of following my research agenda. Among them, Mary Ann Chacko has been solidly by my side for many years; her unfailing enthusiasm for my research has been a continual source of comfort.

I have drawn sustenance for the research on which this book is based from my relations with local activist groups working for the advancement of equitable education for students with disabilities. In that group, I owe many thanks to Jaclyn Okin Barney, director of Parents for Inclusive Education, New York City, with whom I have spent countless hours grappling with the frustrations and challenges of practicing inclusive education in urban contexts. Deborah Stein at the National Federation of the Blind has served as my friend, teacher, and mentor since the time I started working in U.S. public schools in the early 1990s. Other local activist professionals from whom I have greatly benefited in understanding the many meanings of inclusion include Mark Surabian and Maggie Moroff.

I am grateful for the support extended by the team at Teachers College Press in bringing this effort to fruition. Brian Ellerbeck's patience, Susan Liddicoat's thoughtful comments, and the collective effort of all in the process of editing, marketing, and producing the book are deeply appreciated. To the series editors, Alfredo J. Artiles and Elizabeth B. Kozleski, and anonymous reviewers, thank you for seeing potential in this effort.

Many members of my family, near and extended, have all in some measure participated in the development of this book. I particularly want to thank my daughter, Maegha, for bearing with the many liberties I have taken over the years with my role as her parent to accommodate the necessity of meeting research deadlines. I am grateful that "inclusive education" has over the years become an indelible part of her vocabulary and her framing of the world. My mother, Annapoorani Sitaraman, remains a singularly important presence in my life; her strength and endurance continually remind me of the many different ways that women all over the world engage with patriarchal systems. To Tom, I say that like you, this book signals a beginning as much as a completion, and I am deeply thankful for the exciting possibilities that both evoke for me.

INTRODUCTION

Teaching for Inclusion

My first experience with inclusion occurred during my years as an itinerant teacher licensed to teach students with visual impairment and blindness in suburban midwestern America during the 1990s. Several of my students were children with multiple disabilities and carried several labels simultaneously, including a label of some form of visual impairment. More often than not, therefore, I was the "related service provider," who provided either monthly consultative support to educators or weekly direct services to the student. While I attended all the conferences related to the student's individualized education program (IEP) and other relevant meetings, I was not expected to participate strongly in the overall programmatic decisionmaking for the student. With some exceptions, I was also rarely in the same building more than twice a week. Given this somewhat peripheral location in the schools, it was not surprising that even as I sensed the tensions among families, students, and educators when working with the concept of *inclusion*, the images of inclusion I came to carry were of teachers and families struggling—sometimes together, sometimes separately—to make curricular and instructional decisions. In teachers' lounges or in quiet hallways, there was a persistent background hum of stories of angry parents, "difficult" students, and outraged educators that seemed to accompany the subject of inclusion. My first understandings of inclusion, then, grew out of the pragmatic wrestling with curricular content, scheduling, materials, distribution of personnel, and peer relationships that characterized these struggles in schools.

Many years later, therefore, as I began to spend extensive periods of time in classrooms as a researcher, it is not surprising that I would become interested not only in what inclusion should/should not look like, but more importantly, in understanding how teachers came to practice inclusion and their rationales for doing so. If teachers are entrusted with the task of implementing a difficult and somewhat nebulous idea, I find it reasonable and just to try to understand inclusion from the ground up, as it were. What does inclusion mean in the lived experiences of teachers as they go about implementing this abstract concept? How can such lived meanings advance the field of inclusive education?

PREMISES OF THE BOOK

My intent to privilege local understandings of inclusion notwithstanding, the meaning of this term is not always self-evident. Although it has been readily taken up within schools, among teachers, schools, families, and scholars, *inclusion* may imply significantly different understandings of disability, schools, and learning.

What Does Inclusion Mean?

As a special education teacher, when I encountered *inclusion*, it meant the physical placement of students with disabilities in general education classrooms. As a researcher working within the disability studies tradition, not only did I come to adopt a broader meaning, I also recognized the distinctions between these approaches and why they mattered. Inclusion as understood within mainstream special and general education scholarship leaves the ability-based conceptual foundations of the general education classroom intact; its focus is to ensure that the effects of the student's disability are minimized in a setting that has been primarily designed for students without disabilities. Therefore, though mainstream special education scholarship has increasingly come to support the inclusion of students with disabilities in mainstream classrooms, it continues to distinguish ability levels between students to determine where and how they should be educated (Anastasiou & Kauffman, 2011; Kauffman & Sasso, 2006). This may also mean that segregated, self-contained spaces may well be regarded as appropriate for educating some students with disabilities.

Inclusion, from the perspective of scholars writing within a disability studies tradition, begins with an exploration of the extent to which schools and classrooms permit students who bring diverse learning profiles (with and without labels of disability) to learn in an equitable manner. Within this meaning of inclusion, disability is not located within the learner but rather resides in the social practices that construct that student as "different." This notion of disability as socially constructed is foundational to inclusive education. For these inclusive educators, inclusion is rooted in a democratic orientation to schooling that acknowledges diversity of student learning profiles as the norm and requires that educational spaces be designed accordingly (Naraian, 2016a). It implies a multisector, whole-school reform effort to create schooling communities hospitable to diverse learners rather than a focus on the remediation of students perceived to be lacking in required skills (Booth & Ainscow, 2011).

For many teachers, inclusion remains at the level of physically integrating students with disabilities in the general education classroom. It occurs alongside predetermined curricular and instructional arrangements that are primarily designed for a mythical "normal" student. Other teachers recognize any given classroom as hosting a range of capabilities; for these teachers, inclusion means trying to reach *all* learners, as well as attending to students with documented disability labels. This book draws largely on the experiences of this latter group of teachers. It is true that they may not present a sophisticated critique of inclusion as popularly practiced. Still, they distinguished between deficit forms of thinking and support structures that enabled success for students who appeared to struggle in schools. Most importantly, they consciously sought to preserve their commitments to student learning in the midst of the pressures of testing, teacher tenure debates, scheduling experiments, and the changing circumstances of students' family lives. In that regard, these teachers offer a wealth of understanding of the intricacies of practicing inclusion that are often missing in broad prescriptions for creating inclusive classrooms.

A note on scope and terminology: I have used the terms *student with disabilities* and *disabled student* interchangeably even though the former is widely accepted as the more respectful method of address and many journals/organizations actually require authors to use that over the latter. The significance of language to index experience in respectful ways cannot be minimized. The activism of individuals with intellectual disabilities within People First movements to redress widespread historical discrimination against this group testifies to the validity of such concerns. However, several disabled activist scholars have also questioned the privileging of personhood in the term *person with disabilities*. Arguing instead for an understanding of disability as valued human experience, they embrace the privileging of disability instead in *disabled person* (Siebers, 2008; Titchkosky, 2011). My interchangeable use of the terms in this book reflects the validity of both positions.

Additionally, though the basis of inclusion is premised on environments that can be responsive to many different types of learners, this book draws heavily on the experiences of students with disabilities and their teachers. Still, the principles derived from an examination of teachers' practices have implications for many categories of marginalized learners. This argument is based on the logic that as a social category, disability remains permeable to all other categories including race, gender, class, sexual orientation, and so on (Siebers, 2008). For instance, an *ideology of ability* can cut across many different types of social experiences. Disability, therefore, can serve as an analytic lens to understand all human experience. In my research, I found that disability as a lens to understand the production of inclusive classrooms can be generative for surfacing many facets of classroom experience that have deep relevance for all learners, regardless of their ability/disability status.

Why Learn from Teachers About Inclusion?

Over the past decade, as my research interests came to focus on understanding how and why teachers did what they did as they created hospitable learning environments for different kinds of learners, I wondered about their everyday decisionmaking:

- How did teachers develop the rationales for their practice?
- Under what conditions were they satisfied with their efforts?
- How did they reconcile their vision of an inclusive classroom with the preparation of students for standardized testing? What dilemmas did such experiences raise for them? How did they resolve such dilemmas?
- How did they make sense of how peers interacted with students with disabilities, and how did that factor into their grouping arrangements or their curricular choices?
- How did their relationships with families influence their classroom instruction?
- What was their relationship with particular types of supports such as technology, and how did they use it to advance their vision of inclusion?

The answers to such questions may seem relatively self-evident to teachers, but surprisingly these questions have not received sustained attention in the research on inclusion. Many authors have synthesized research to generate well-crafted and valuable books on how inclusion should be implemented at the school and classroom levels. Yet, even as examples from teacher experiences are utilized to illustrate those principles, there have been few in-depth case studies of teachers engaging in such work across varied schooling contexts that could begin to address the questions raised above.

Questions of practice are inseparable from questions of theory. The dearth of teacher stories in this nascent field of inclusive education may originate in some part in the critical necessity to first establish the field as a legitimate interdisciplinary tradition in its own right. During the last few decades there has been an increasingly rich and sophisticated body of work in disability studies in education that has come to provide the theoretical foundation for the field of inclusive education (e.g., Danforth & Gabel, 2006; Slee, 2011; Ware, 2010). This scholarship has yielded important insights about the premises of inclusive education:

- Disruption of notions of normalcy and, by extension, the concept of difference
- Avoidance of deficit-oriented approaches to student learning
- Vigilance of, and resistance to, an ideology of ability within schooling practices
- The valuing of the narratives of individuals with disabilities and their families
- The promotion of democratic values in schooling communities (Danforth, 2014; Danforth & Naraian, 2015; Kluth, Biklen, & Straut, 2003; Slee, 2011; Valle & Connor, 2011)

These tenets collectively constitute a broad framework for inclusive practice. This framework has been further supported through pedagogical practices such as differentiated instruction and universal design for learning (UDL). They are premised on recognizing the heterogeneity of typical classrooms and debunking the myth of the "normal" student toward which pedagogical efforts in schools have been typically directed (Baglieri, Bejoian, Broderick, Connor, & Valle, 2011).

Even as the legitimacy of the field of inclusive education as a robust theory-driven enterprise has emerged over heated scholarly debates (Gallagher, 2004, 2006; Kauffman & Sasso, 2006), the directive to teachers engaged in this work has been clear, if implicit: In order to be considered inclusive educators, teachers must take up the framework above within their own schools and classrooms. The successful implementation of inclusion is based on the fidelity with which educators adhere to its tenets. Derived from thoughtful systematic research, these tenets are invaluable in enabling a vision of inclusive schools that we desperately need in order to imagine equitable schooling for all students. At the same time, however, holding teachers accountable to those and only those tenets also serves to exacerbate the "theory–practice divide." It is derived from theorizing inclusion through a critique of how schools have marginalized students with disabilities and their families. In that process, it attaches little value to the contributions of teachers in developing meanings of *inclusion*.

Defining *inclusive education* as a set of nonnegotiable tenets can set teachers up to be perceived in overly reductionist ways; they are either heroically resistant to institutional practices that condone negative understandings of disability or they are passively complicit with the same. Such assumptions of teacher practice fail to do justice to the complexity of schooling conditions within which teacher decisionmaking for inclusion takes place. After all, teachers are required to realize the commitment to inclusion within schooling environments that invariably reflect an overwhelming preoccupation with testing and standardization. Additionally, such notions of resistance or compliance are premised on a restrictive understanding of teacher *agency*. They presume that teachers can simply and unproblematically transport their capabilities to be risk takers and innovators from one schooling context to another. Instead, when investigations of teachers' efforts toward inclusion locate teacher agency within contextual specificities, they can more readily disclose the complexities of this work (Danforth & Naraian, 2015).

This book values teachers' agentive constructions of inclusive schooling that occur within their specific teaching contexts and under larger conditions of student and teacher accountability imbibed by and reflected within schools. It is grounded in educators' narratives of their experiences as well as ethnographically derived data on their pedagogical practices in classrooms. In beginning with teachers' understandings of inclusion, my intent is not to decenter the core tenets derived from the scholarship on inclusive education, a body of work that has struggled to achieve legitimacy against the resistance of the more entrenched mainstream special education scholarship that continues to privilege a deficit-based approach to disability (Anastasiou & Kauffman, 2011; Kauffman & Sasso, 2006). Still, in a climate that is hostile to teachers and at a time when teacher accountability remains a flashpoint in local and national debates on the effectiveness of schools (Au, 2013; Ravitch, 2013), inclusive education as envisioned by committed researchers may seem too out-of-reach to persuade schools and educators to enlist willingly and wholeheartedly in the project. It is precisely to solidify the urgent relevance of inclusive education for schools, therefore, that I begin with teachers' understandings of what it means to "do" inclusion.

EIGHT PRINCIPLES OF INCLUSIVE TEACHING DERIVED FROM TEACHER PRACTICE

This book arose from investigating the work of teachers engaged in the project of creating inclusive communities in schools. During these investigations, I did not hold their efforts up against the core tenets of inclusive education that have already been articulated in the literature. Instead, by listening deeply to their stories and, whenever possible, spending prolonged periods of time observing their instructional practice, I sought to understand the process by which they made decisions about curricular and instructional practice. I learned that as they waded their way through strict schooling mandates for test preparation and/or pressures to produce objective evidence of student learning, they engaged in unique forms of practices that could still enable them to retain their commitment to inclusive schooling. After closely examining these practices, I distilled eight principles for "doing" inclusion that may serve educators in a variety of schooling contexts. A word of caution: These principles are not idealized statements that prescribe what inclusive educators *should* do based on what the teachers in these studies *failed* to do. On the contrary, the principles emerged from an understanding of inclusion grounded in teachers' perspectives of what the process entailed. In that regard, almost all of them offer the novice inclusive educator constructive ways to take up efforts toward inclusion. In a few cases, in documenting some of their struggles (e.g., in working with families), I try to excavate the origins of those struggles and suggest some alternative ways of understanding those dimensions for an inclusive pedagogy.

1. Teaching for inclusion is unpredictable, multidimensional, and always unfinished. Inasmuch as genuine inclusion requires a firm commitment to dismantling the effects of unquestioned notions of normalcy and difference within routine schooling practices, each instance of inclusion may look quite different from another. The agentive decisionmaking of teachers, families, and administrators in the context of specific historically mediated schooling conditions produces inclusions that are always unique to that particular school. In that regard, the shape and form of inclusion remain unpredictable, contingent as they are on the people, histories, and resources that constitute the context in which such efforts take place. This also means that the evidence of inclusion may reside not only within obvious visible markers (e.g., where students with disabilities are seated within the classroom) but more important, in the rationales offered by school personnel when working out the process of implementation. As the descriptions in this book will show, such rationales surface a range of issues that continually expand the limits of each dimension within the practical implementation of inclusion whether this may refer to placement, families, technology, language, or other related issues. It was no coincidence that none of the teachers who participated in the studies from which this book was developed was ever fully satisfied with the accomplishments made in the process of inclusion. Inclusion, it seems, is an ongoing, unfinished process, which is continually marked by old and new struggles and which requires constant maneuvering.

2. Teaching for inclusion is premised on a holistic understanding of all learners and a commitment to principles of social justice. Inclusive education begins with a commitment to equitable schooling practice that can restore the legitimacy of experiences that have been historically marginalized within schools, such as those of students with disabilities. So, even as schooling systems continue to uphold procedures and structures that separate rather than include learners who appear to be different from a mythical norm (Dudley-Marling & Gurn, 2010), inclusive educators are expected to push back against such oppressive practices. All the teachers described in this book were deeply aware of socially unjust practices that disadvantaged many learners, and sought in as many ways as they could to work around them. Coupled with this commitment was a responsiveness to students as learners, which permitted the teachers, whenever possible, to place matters and topics relevant to learners above administrative directives. A stance that combined a commitment to social justice with an open-ended generosity toward students as learners was more likely to produce classroom communities where students engaged each other in respectful ways.

3. Although teaching for inclusion requires a supportive school leadership and school culture, teachers make strategic decisions to foster inclusive practices within the classroom. In all the schools that formed the sites for data collection for this book, principals clearly had important roles to play in supporting teachers to take up inclusive practices. Some administrators made careful choices when assigning students with particular kinds of disabilities to teachers. Others allowed teachers freedom in experimenting with scheduling and curricular decisionmaking. It was evident that teachers respected their administrative leaders and valued the opportunities they made available to them. However, it was also clear that teachers did not themselves attribute all aspects of their instructional and curricular decisions to specific administrative practices within their schools. In describing their decisionmaking process, they were just as likely, if not more so, to draw on their own prior experiences, foundational commitments, and relations with their colleagues to understand inclusion and their efforts to implement it. Particularly at the elementary level, when teachers described the decisions they made to instill inclusivity in their students (e.g., choice of literature, community-building practices, group arrangements), they rarely implicated specific administrative directives or priorities. In fact, even if the school culture was supportive of inclusion, these teachers could identify the flaws and gaps in their colleagues' perceptions of inclusion that often seemed too narrow or superficial. In other words, the commitments to inclusion brought by these teachers informed their everyday practice in the classroom such that, while it thrived under certain schooling conditions, it was not fully contingent on them.

4. Teaching for inclusion entails balancing the limitations of time and placement with an emphasis on high-quality practice. Across all schooling sites, the issues of time and placement remained a recurring preoccupation with educators. The *place* of learning structured their reflections about how students learned, what they should learn, who should teach them, how they should be taught, and who should learn with them. Such questions were almost always accompanied by the perceived effects of *time*. In other words, places implicitly carried particular notions of time as well as the different ways it mattered to student learning. For instance, it was necessary for Stephanie, as a special education teacher, to insist that her grade-level general education colleagues slow things down so that all students in her own collaboratively taught classroom (which had a higher percentage of students with disabilities) were able to master the content. Time and place were inextricably tied within teachers' understandings of how inclusion could be made to work. Teachers worried about the unavailability of time to provide needed supports for students within particular kinds of instructional spaces. Teachers who provided specialized supports took students out of the main classroom to teach them disability-specific skills. Teachers, it seemed, had little control over the ways in which boundaries of places were settled and how people were assigned to those spaces. For instance, a district may require collaboratively taught classrooms to have both a general and a special educator with a predetermined ratio of students with and without disabilities.

What could be controlled, however, was the nature of instructional practice within those already demarcated spaces. As Chapter 2 describes in detail, teachers continually worked to diffuse boundaries that would allow them to preserve a quality of practice that they could find satisfactory. So, for example, when coteachers Anita and Maria contemplated a placement for a student whom they loved but who challenged their pedagogical abilities, they were willing to consider a self-contained placement as long as the instructional practices of the teacher upheld the principles of care, nurturance, and professionalism that they held for themselves. Teachers were also observed creating new spaces of learning within pregiven places that would make it more likely for their students to succeed. Ultimately, the nature and quality of practice delivered by teachers could alter the historically mediated fixed narratives of any schooling place. This meant that inclusion could, to some extent, be decoupled from the issue of placement, leaving room for new imaginings of spaces to implement a socially just pedagogy.

5. Teaching for inclusion necessitates the straddling of competing philosophies and frameworks of learning rather than a purist stance. Few teachers articulated this concept directly in words, but almost all of them demonstrated this in their teaching practice or in the ways they described how they made curricular decisions. The most visible form of such straddling was their use of special education language and practices, even as they engaged in an inclusive pedagogy. Inclusive education scholars have argued for the decoupling of special education from inclusive education in order to abandon practices that continue to use a deficit approach and see students with disabilities as needing to be fixed (Slee, 2011). Across classrooms, however, as teachers attempted to engage in inclusive practice within flawed systems that relied on sorting and separating by ability, special education practice was not easily decoupled from such work. For some, like Stephanie, it might be the emphasis on individualized pedagogy within special education that restored her sense of direction in understanding how to fuse documentation of student learning within her vision of a "transparent" classroom community. For Anita and Maria, it was the combined use of explicit instruction with a focus on student subjectivities that allowed them to work continually against the phenomenon of the school-to-prison pipeline. For Paul, originally a special education teacher, it was the appreciation of the benefits of a constructivist math curriculum that simultaneously allowed him to separate students by ability so that they could more easily attain a respectable high school leaving certificate instead of an IEP diploma that had little relevance in the real world.

In all these instances and more, teachers freely drew on the language and practices of special education even as they used them to develop caring inclusive communities. Sometimes, teachers expressed awareness of the contradictions that surfaced as they spoke. More often, however, such contradictions may have been obscured in the immediate necessity to create opportunities for increased participation of their students. A conscious surfacing of such contradictions through systematic reflection could well have deepened teachers' understanding of their own practice. My own objective, in offering a "rearticulation" of their stories (Collins, 2000; Naraian & Oyler, 2014), has been to permit the disclosure of strategies that have been infrequently reported in the literature, but that can make inclusion a realizable construct for novice teachers.

6. Teaching for inclusion requires an active interpretive stance on the part of teachers to create cohesive classroom communities. The charge to implement inclusion was recognized by most teachers, particularly at the elementary level, as inseparable from the obligation to create a certain kind of classroom community that was premised on principles of care, respect, and responsibility to each other. As they went about this work, most teachers were observed actively mediating students' understandings of each other through dialogue, literature, or direct acts of interpretation. For instance, after an unforeseen encounter with a student with autism who unexpectedly ran into her classroom, Jessica engaged her students in a conversation about the meaning of his actions (see Chapter 4). Such acts of interpretation reflected particular goals on the part of the teachers; these might include the objective of helping students better understand learning struggles (Anita), producing a transparent community (Stephanie), or ensuring that students treated their peers with disabilities with respect (Jessica). In each case, teachers sought to directly influence their students' thinking on the matter of disability through careful verbal mediation. Such interpretive work on the part of teachers had significant effects on the quality of peer relations within those classroom communities. It was not a coincidence that even students with the most significant disabilities were eagerly sought after during cooperative learning experiences in these classrooms. Equally unsurprising was that students themselves began to actively take up the interpretive process as a way to understand and include their peers who could not communicate directly themselves.

7. Teaching for inclusion necessitates enfolding families within the process of educators' own professional growth; this is predicated on teachers' openness to be transformed by families' experiential knowledge. Teachers' relations with families disclosed a contradictory mix of expectations of involvement, genuine interest in their experiences, a well-intentioned concern about their motivations, as well as a dismissal of their significance for the teachers' own teaching. To a large extent, even as teachers made conscious attempts to be respectful of families, they were less likely to draw on families to support their everyday curricular and instructional work. This might well have been an artifact of the communities in which they were situated. For example, family participation was a strong element in Stephanie's school, where parents could be seen wandering the hallways at many times during the day. Anita and Maria, on the other hand, taught in a primarily working-class community, and families were more likely to be visible before and at the end of the school day. Still, in their relations with families, teachers seemed to struggle to find a balance between navigating their management of the classroom and seeing families as a component of that work. As they went about designing the contours of their classrooms whether as *classroom families* (Jessica) or as *transparent communities* (Stephanie), families of students remained peripheral to that process, even as they were required to demonstrate their support of it. It seemed that teachers were eager to invite family perspectives, but less able to use that to bring about fundamental shifts in their own thinking. Teacher narratives as well as data from families collected in the course of these studies indexed the distance at which families were held, as teachers struggled to balance the sorting and stratifying impetus of schooling and curricular mandates with more inclusive ends.

In noting this principle as important for doing inclusion, I draw on current research as well as a deeper examination of why teachers struggled in this process. Research has shown that family understandings of disability have historically differed from professional narratives, offering a perspective that is less likely to be available within typical cultural discourses (P. M. Ferguson, 2002, 2007; Lalvani, 2015). Additionally, the multiple forms of family engagement with schooling have been obscured by normative notions of parent involvement (Auerbach, 2007; Lareau, 1987; Lareau & Horvat, 1999). Even as the significance of family knowledges for teachers' professional growth seemed inadequately explored within their own stories, my role as researcher necessitated understanding the roots of this before identifying it as an important principle for doing inclusion. For instance, teacher competencies as defined by various standards used by teacher education accreditation agencies imply an *individualized* notion of teacher ability that is itself detached from the values, demands, and conditions within which such abilities are realized. Such individualized (and decontextualized) notions of teacher competency suggest that teachers are the sole designers and managers of their classroom communities. As Chapter 5 discloses, such notions obscure the relational work implied in the creation of these communities and the distributed knowledge within them. Adopting the notion of distributed cognition (Lave & Wenger, 1991; Wenger, 1998) allows family knowledges to be more easily integrated within teachers' efforts toward inclusion.

8. Teaching for and growing inclusion requires skills in adult education.
Teachers rarely, if ever, carry out their work in isolation. Across my studies, even as they took up opportunities available within their classrooms to enact their commitments to an equity pedagogy, the teachers were just as likely to want their colleagues to share these values. At the same time, many of them recognized and understood the perspectives of their colleagues even if their stances toward students and learning were different from the teachers' own. For example, even if they were critical of their colleagues' attitudes toward students with certain kinds of disabilities, they could also recognize that they themselves had at some point in time harbored the same thoughts. Others went further and, having arrived at a new level of consciousness, earnestly

sought to bring about similar shifts in thinking in their colleagues. Whatever the scope of their interest and activity in educating their colleagues, teachers remained perceptive of the needs and concerns of their colleagues so that their own efforts at providing professional development in inclusive practices were always designed to reflect those needs. Teachers' understanding of their colleagues reflected a stance of *presuming competence* (Biklen & Burke, 2006) that allowed them to remain nonjudgmental of their practices. Their experiences as adult educators indexes the importance for novice teachers to cultivate skills to understand adults as learners and the significance of reflective practice for taking up the role of teacher educators within their schools.

While principles 1, 2 and 3 are interwoven throughout the book, each of the subsequent principles (4, 5, 6, 7, and 8) is taken up in separate chapters.

THEORETICAL FOUNDATIONS OF THE BOOK

Even as my decade-long research that prompted the writing of this book emerged from several bodies of scholarship, there are three traditions that collectively comprise my theoretical framing of teachers' experiences described in this book. These include disability studies in education, narrative theory, and sociocultural perspectives on learning and human development. Each of these has been foundational to the ways in which I have designed and carried out the research studies from which this book has emerged. In the following pages, I describe some of the key tenets within these bodies of work that have grounded my own learnings.

Disability Studies in Education

The scholarship on disability studies in education (DSE) has remained my intellectual home ever since I began to investigate the meanings of inclusion in schools. It is this interdisciplinary body of work that allowed me to identify and understand my discomfort in the kinds of special and general education practices that I had observed as a teacher and that I continued to explore as a researcher. Disability studies in education is premised on an understanding of disability as an integral part of human variation (Taylor, 2006). Meanings of disability are produced as individuals interact with various institutions in society such that disability is never seen as residing solely within a person (Reid, 2004). In other words, even as the difference of disability may be marked by particular forms of embodiment (i.e., a student who is blind experiences the world differently than someone who may be sighted and intellectually disabled), it is also socially constructed (Gabel, 2005). The particular physical, attitudinal, political, social, economic, and legal conditions under which a person experiences disability imply that its meanings will always be tied to the social context.

This focus on the social context of disability has disclosed an *ideology of ability* (Siebers, 2008) that lies at the heart of educational systems and has led to the proliferation of practices that sort and categorize students based on presumed (in)ability to succeed (Baglieri et al., 2011). The recognition of this ideology has stimulated a comprehensive critique of the epistemological foundations of the field of special education that continues to locate disability as a deficit within the student (Gallagher, 1998, 2004, 2006; Skrtic, 1995). The particular practices of mainstream special education that are premised on diagnosis, labeling, separation, intervention, and treatment are perceived as dehumanizing and upholding visions of normalcy rather than celebrating diversity. A disability studies–informed inclusive education is committed to the full participation of students with disabilities in mainstream communities. Unlike special education, it rejects the presumption that students with disabilities must demonstrate predetermined skills in order to be included in the general education classroom. "Inclusion is not an educational plan to benefit disabled children. It is a model for educating all children equitably" (Linton, 1998, p. 61).

Even as inclusion remains an unquestioned value within this field, scholars have more recently begun to raise questions about maintaining dogmatic ideological positions (Poplin, 2011; Poplin & Rogers, 2005). For example, Poplin and her colleagues describe the work of teachers in a school where direct instruction rather than constructivist forms of teaching were adopted (Poplin et al., 2011). They found that these teachers were still able to create nurturing, inclusive classrooms. Others have raised the necessity for seeking common ground between special and inclusive education to enable better preparation for teachers (Cochran-Smith & Dudley-Marling, 2012). My own position is to avoid binary forms of thinking such as inclusion/exclusion, oppressor/oppressed, and behaviorism/constructivism, which I view as unhelpful to advancing the progress of inclusion. My goal as I enter, observe, and describe classrooms is to uphold a commitment to socially just pedagogy by remaining vigilant of how norms of ability can inform schooling. I simultaneously seek to locate myself within the world of multiple actors in schools since I am convinced that inclusion can never be reduced to a single vision or a single perspective.

Narrative Knowing and Inquiry

The scholarship on inclusive education has, rightly, emphasized the significance of the narratives of students with disabilities and their families, whose voices have been largely suppressed in the history of the education of students with disabilities (Biklen, 2005; Ferguson & Ferguson, 1995). While not seeking to minimize the importance of that shift and the necessity for that perspective, I have deliberately brought the narratives of educators to the front in order to deepen our understanding of inclusive education and strengthen our commitment to it. In this book, therefore, I have privileged the narratives of educators.

The form of narrative inquiry that I have adopted studies "either lived experience as storied phenomenon or the stories people tell about their experiences" (Clandinin, 2007, xiv). In other words, narrative is not only the methodology I have adopted for conducting my research, it also reflects my approach to understanding human experience. I share the perspective of scholars such as Bruner (1986, 1990), Clandinin and Connelly (1996), and Polkinghorne (1988) that people make sense of their lives through stories. People's lived experiences then may be more readily understood through their stories. Such stories register the social, cultural, and institutional context in which these experiences are formed and in that regard have theoretical value for the scholarship on inclusive education. As a narrative inquirer, my intent is not to generate findings that will be predictable across all contexts (Bruner, 1986). Instead, in seeking to understand and describe how educators make sense of their experiences in teaching inclusively, my intent is to develop deeper understandings of inclusive education so that educators in different contexts can relate to the experiences that are described.

Admittedly, the stories that I share in this text collectively constitute *my* research narrative of the experiences made available to me in the field. As I take account of the cultural, political, and social contexts registered within the stories of the participants, my narrative looks for the connections between them that will advance our knowledge of the field. Additionally, it is not my intent to represent a reality "independent of the knower" (Clandinin, 2013); my narrative does not work from the premise that the teachers described in this book are somehow practicing inclusion naively and I need to interpret their practices in more sophisticated ways. On the contrary, as a narrative inquirer, I need to locate my explanations within their worlds. Only then will such explanations remain plausible to them and to the school personnel who will read these accounts.

Sociocultural Perspectives on Learning and Human Development

This book is also grounded in notions of learning and human development that draw directly from sociocultural perspectives originating in the work of Vygotsky (1986; 1978). I understand abilities/traits/attributes as never innate but as always socioculturally mediated (Wertsch, 1991). So, for example, a student's performance in the classroom is never only a reflection of his or her presumed innate abilities. It is always mediated by a range of factors including the tools made available to the learner to express his or her learning as well as the interactional context in which that takes place: that is, teachers' expectations of the student, teachers' beliefs that inform the instructional practices in the setting, and the intellectual resources made available to the learner in that context. This recognition that learning does not take place only in the head of the learner directs our attention to the sociocultural context in which students are expected to learn. What students are/are not able to do or how they do/do not come to understand their own learning is not simply a matter of their innate abilities but rather is inseparable from the many dimensions of the social context.

Additionally, Vygotsky (1978) proposed the concept of the *zone of proximal development*. This refers to the space for learning that exists between what an individual can independently accomplish and what he or she can accomplish under the guidance of a more capable adult or peer. When adults or peers who are more skilled in the use of specific cultural tools employ them within this zone, they enable the individual learner to build on existing concepts in order to learn new ones. The mediational mechanisms that contextualize all learning are, in effect, concretized within the zone of proximal development. This concept has been linked to the metaphor of *scaffolding* (Wood, Bruner, & Ross, 1976), which has come to be understood as "a temporary intellectual support which a teacher offers in order to draw the learner up toward a higher level of understanding" (Fernandez, Wegerif, Mercer, & Rojas-Drummond, 2001, p. 41). Collectively, these concepts support the notion of learning performance as situated within interactional contexts rather than as emerging from processes that take place within the head of the learner. The significance of collaborative learning opportunities within inclusive pedagogy stems directly from such an understanding of the benefits accrued to individual learners in the interactional/interpersonal plane of development (Vygotsky, 1978).

In this book I extend this sociocultural understanding of learning and development to teachers as well as to students. Teachers' learning and performance are also socioculturally mediated in ways that complicate typical concepts of teacher competencies that lie at the heart of evaluation processes in teacher education (Halverson & Clifford, 2006). Indeed, the notion of distributed learning/cognition recognizes that learning processes are spread over a network of human and nonhuman objects that collectively allow for intellectual accomplishments to take place (Lave, 1993; Lave & Wenger, 1991). Evaluating and describing teacher learning, then, must not only look for evidence of teachers' individualized learning but also consider the ways that cognitive processes circulate among people, artifacts, and ideas to produce instructional achievements (Vrasidas & Zembylas, 2004).

Collectively these theoretical frames allow me, as a researcher, to preserve my commitments to socially just pedagogy while situating my understandings of inclusion within the very material contexts in which teachers find themselves every day. In their extensive research on teacher practices, Cochran-Smith et al. (2015) found that teachers were not able to translate their beliefs about equity and diversity into instructional practice. Clearly, the enactment of commitments to equity is deeply complicated by competing priorities within schools. If the assignment to "do" inclusion must be successfully taken up to accomplish the changes that inclusive educators desire in school systems, we need to approach teacher learning in humanizing ways that are cognizant of the conditions under which their work will be carried out.

AN ETHNOGRAPHIC FOCUS: THE RESEARCH INVESTIGATIONS UNDERLYING THIS BOOK

The research that forms the basis of this book was derived from a series of ethnographically oriented studies that were carried out over the period 2005–2013 in U.S. public schools. They included mostly elementary schools within both urban and suburban systems (Naraian, 2008a, 2008b, 2010a, 2010b, 2011a, 2011b, 2011c, 2016b; Naraian, Ferguson, & Thomas, 2012; Naraian & Oyler, 2014). An ethnographic study "focuses on the cultural and social regularities of everyday life" (Merriam, 2009, p. 201) and can therefore afford the researcher a substantive glimpse into the lived experiences of the participants. It is particularly distinguished by its emphasis on the researcher's immersion in the field that can offer an *emic* (insider) rather than *etic* (outsider) perspective. Interviews (formal and informal), documents/records/artifacts, and detailed field notes of observations and encounters constitute the main sources of my data. Overall, data sources used for this book include at least 55 interviews with school personnel, students, and their families; several hundred hours of participant observation (see Table I.1 for an overview of the research contexts of the educator participants who are featured in this book); and documents such as teacher newsletters and student work samples. The conclusions drawn in this book have been synthesized after careful qualitative analysis of data from individual studies, followed by in-depth cross-case analysis (Bogdan & Biklen, 2007).

ORGANIZATION OF THIS BOOK

The chapters that follow describe teachers in the everyday enactments of inclusion illustrating the principles I delineated above. Chapter 1 provides the contextual information for the descriptive accounts in the subsequent chapters. It provides an overview of the schooling contexts from which data were collected, including demographic data, schooling priorities, publicly available information about student performance, and so forth. It also contains narrative sketches of individual educators and/or teams of educators whose practices are described in detail across the chapters. The names of all schools and individuals mentioned or described in this book are pseudonyms.

Introduction

Table I.1. Research Contexts of the Teachers Featured in This Book

Research Sites and Participants	Primary Data Sources*
West Creek Elementary School Suburban 1st-grade general education classroom Included 1 student with multiple disabilities, 1 with physical disabilities, 1 English language learner, and several labeled as *gifted* Focal educators: 1 general education teacher (Jessica), 1 "resource" special education teacher; 1 paraprofessional	Study period: September 2005–May 2006 Approx. 130 hours of participant observation over 5–6 months 13 separate interviews with teachers, therapists, the principal, a paraprofessional, and families of students in the classroom *Research focus: Peer narratives of disability in an inclusive classroom (elementary)*
Midwest School District Urban K–5 classrooms in 4 elementary schools in the district Focal educators: 1 behavior specialist (Julie), 1 social worker (Blair), 2–3 teachers who participated in the professional development (PD) model being implemented	Study period: September 2005–June 2007 Approx. 250 hours of participant observation in schools, district-level case review meetings, and weekly team meetings 10 formal interviews with model implementers, teachers, and district superintendent *Research focus: Chronicling the development of a professional development model to build capacity to support students with challenging behaviors*
Andrews Elementary School Urban Collaboratively taught 1st-grade classroom Included 1 student with multiple disabilities, at least 2 with physical disabilities, several with other labels of disability Focal educators: 1 dually certified teacher (Stephanie), 1 general education teacher, 1 special educator	Study period: October 2008–June 2009 Approx. 70 hours of participant observation over 6 months 17 separate interviews with teachers, therapists, a paraprofessional, and families of students in the classroom *Research focus: The implementation of an inclusive classroom community*
University–School Professional Development Urban PD participants included special educators (e.g., Paul), related service providers (e.g., Elena), parent–school facilitators (e.g., Melanie), and administrators	Study period: September 2010–December 2011 Observations drawn from approx. 35 hours of monthly professional development sessions over 9 months, 3 interviews with 3 PD participants (9). *Research focus: Process of shifting to inclusive practices*

Table I.1. Research Contexts of the Teachers Featured in This Book (Continued)

Research Sites and Participants	Primary Data Sources*
Riverside Heights K–8 School Urban Collaboratively taught 4th-grade classroom Included students with a range of mild/moderate learning disabilities; 2 students used assistive technology in the classroom to support skill development in reading/writing. Focal educators: 1 teacher dually certified in general and special education and in bilingual education (Maria), 1 general education teacher also certified in bilingual education (Anita)	Study period: February 2013–June 2013 Approximately 25 hours of participant observation 3 joint interviews with both teachers, 2 interviews with families of students with disabilities *Research focus: The use of assistive technology to support literacy development of students with disabilities in inclusive classrooms*

*Additional data sources across sites included student work samples, school newsletters, electronic communication with PD participants, and informal exchanges with students and teachers in the classrooms.

Chapter 2 reveals that for both general and special educators, the issue of place of learning and, by extension, inclusion was inevitably accompanied by concerns of time. These two features may be seen as deeply embedded structures within the grammar of schooling that clearly impacted educators' efforts toward inclusion. Working within these structures, educators created a range of places, simultaneously negotiating *place-time* to accomplish their goals. The chapter describes the organizing logic of such places and the extent to which it supported inclusion.

Chapter 3 describes the work of teachers as they moved across multiple instructional paradigms and traditions in order to accomplish important instructional goals. Drawing on the work of Anita and Maria (coteachers), Paul, and Stephanie, it explores the principled ways in which these educators straddled competing instructional paradigms in order to advance their commitments to equitable education for their students. The chapter also examines the effects of the continual movement across conceptual boundaries on teacher identities by describing how this process affected Stephanie's sense of herself and her professional capabilities.

Chapter 4 focuses particularly on two teachers, Stephanie and Jessica, to disclose the significance of teachers' interpretive work for establishing the linkages between *accessibility*, *identity/voice*, and *participation*. Situating this form of practice directly within a form of narrative knowing, the chapter describes how teacher talk mediates the identities of students. Such talk carried the kernels for new narratives of disability, as teachers' deliberate interpretations of student actions allowed peers to engage more readily with a disabled student. Such interpretive work on the part of teachers was deeply linked to teachers' commitments to creating cohesive classroom communities. The chapter offers a distinction between *speaking-for* and *speaking-with* in teachers' interpretive efforts and the outcomes that each accomplished.

Even as the earlier chapter on teachers' interpretive work hints at the kinds of communities they created, Chapter 5 more closely examines the structure of those communities through the lens of family–school relations. The chapter seeks to illustrate that teachers' implementation of community is deeply linked to their relations with families. The chapter argues for a distributed notion of *ability* to recognize how family knowledges can support the development of classroom communities. Drawing on and describing the case of a parent coordinator, the chapter calls for a form of complex listening that can build cultural reciprocity with families.

Chapter 6 engages with the practice of coaching, which many educators committed to inclusive practices took up in their settings. It draws on the rationales for different types of professional development (PD) offered by Paul (a high school special education teacher) and Elena (a speech therapist in a middle school) but focuses particularly on the sustained districtwide efforts of two specialists who were charged with implementing a model for supporting teachers to be more responsive to students with challenging behaviors. The cases presented in this chapter illustrate that within the project of moving schools to more inclusive practices, teachers too must be conceptualized as learners requiring unique supports.

Finally, Chapter 7 reiterates the purpose of the book as the rearticulation of teachers' stories to generate new understandings of inclusion. It turns to writers in the tradition of Third World feminism to make sense of the complexities within inclusive practice. Collectively, the constructs available in this scholarship allow an imagining of inclusion as a pedagogy of *deferral*. Returning to the experiences of the teachers described in the book, the chapter discusses the significance of such a pedagogy for inclusion.

Teachers' practices are never separate from their location along multiple dimensions of social experience including, but not limited to, race, class, gender, sexual orientation, (dis)ability, and linguistic status. Nevertheless, the forms of practice that are stimulated through the intersection of their identities along each or any of those dimensions with their schooling contexts, however important, remain outside the scope of this book. The teachers in this book were selected on the basis of research foci that prioritized certain kinds of classrooms (see Table I.1), although their locations across urban, suburban, elementary, and secondary schooling contexts may have simultaneously reflected some diversity in their profiles. In that regard, the accounts in the succeeding chapters privilege classroom practices as observed and/or teachers' explanations of their practice rather than the trajectory of identity making that is always implicated in teacher work.

This is, therefore, a book for educators developed from the experiences of educators themselves. The intent of the book is to enable teachers and other school personnel to understand inclusive pedagogy when enacted within everyday schooling contexts. By exploring the experiences of educators, the book seeks to identify the many complexities and contradictions of practice, understand how teachers negotiate them, and to subsequently fold these understandings into the process of implementing inclusive education.

CHAPTER 1

Teachers-in-School

Who are the educators whose stories form the basis of this book? This chapter provides an introduction to the main actors—mostly general special educators as well as related service providers—whose efforts toward inclusion disclosed the deeply complex nature of inclusive practice. I offer brief narrative sketches of these actors followed by some contextual specificities about their schools that include demographic data, schooling priorities, publicly available information about student performance, and so forth (refer also to Table I.1). While many educational professionals from these schools participated in the research from which this book is drawn, the educators whose stories are detailed here were some of the focal participants in those studies and their practices contributed significantly to the principles of "doing inclusion" that are detailed in this book. The narrative sketches that follow are not exhaustive; still they disclose the broad commitments of these educators to children, learning, and inclusion. All the teachers were committed to socially just schooling practice, although such commitments differed in intensity and emphasis—for example, high school teacher Paul emphasized caring relationships and the importance of inquiry-based methods that valued students as agentive learners, while Anita worried about the school-to-prison pipeline when working with her 4th-grade classroom. The descriptions of the schools in which they worked offer a window into the conditions that permitted them to realize, to a greater or less extent, such commitments.

BUILDING A CLASSROOM FAMILY

Jessica

> *I want them to love coming to school.*

Jessica committed to being a teacher very early in her life, noting that she had "always wanted to work with kids." She reveled in the extensive opportunities for student teaching offered within her academic preparation. A young White woman who had been teaching for 3 years, her decision to take the position of a 1st-grade teacher in an elementary school instead of a teacher at a satellite school for students identified as *gifted*, was based on her desire for developing strong connections with her students. She sought to enlist her students in her own love for learning and to regard it as an enjoyable experience. She regarded their social–emotional growth as a prerequisite for academic learning. Speaking of her professional goals, she noted: "I think the biggest one is that I want this to feel like a family, like a school family. Where the kids can come and know that this is a safe place and it's OK if you make a wrong guess . . . that nobody is going to laugh." She sought to make herself more accessible to students, often through humor whereby they "could see [me] as a person instead of as their teacher."

Jessica acknowledged that she wanted all her students to reach the mandated benchmarks, but recognized that was not necessarily a realistic goal. "And so I look at each child and figure out what is reasonable for them." As she tried to understand each child's needs, whether they were "diagnosed" or not, she struggled "to hit them in that perfect spot that is going to get them to the next level." She yearned to reach the most challenging of her students, acknowledging her own unpreparedness to adequately support students with difficult behaviors. Even when their actions were hard to understand, she stated earnestly, "I want so much for this person to feel happy at school." She actively developed her own competence to reach learners for whom traditional strategies did not appear to work. She took additional coursework at the local university to learn to create inclusive classrooms and to understand the perspectives of families of students with disabilities. The latter especially "made her heart ready" to receive a student with significant disabilities in her classroom. She noted that one important challenge in successfully including students with a range of disabilities was to decipher what their IEP goals might look like in the classroom.

In describing her own memory of inclusion as a young 3rd-grade student, Jessica clearly distinguished the experience of her past from what she sought to accomplish in her classroom. Recalling her first encounter with a boy whom she realized now had had cerebral palsy, she described how he ended up on that first day "having a seizure and urinating on the floor." Describing the ways she and her peers instinctively recoiled from him, she acknowledged that they had had no understanding of this boy as a fellow student, "that he learns too." They remained instead totally uncomprehending of his presence in the room. It was not surprising then, that in her own classroom, she worked actively to mediate students' understanding of each other in many different ways. This might take the form of particular kinds of instructional grouping arrangements that offered opportunities for students to work with partners with diverse learning profiles. For example, she modeled appropriate forms of interactions with Harry, a student with significant disabilities who used an augmentative communication device, and actively discouraged peers from "petting" him or treating him in infantilizing ways.

Most important, she actively used children's literature to spark discussions about difference and disability. Such discussions, as we will come to understand in subsequent chapters, sent a clear message to students that brooked no argument. She kept a watchful eye on how peers interacted with each other, including students with disabilities, in the classroom, and did not hesitate to express her disapproval over statements/actions that she felt did not reflect the inclusive ethos that she sought. So, for instance, she might pull aside a student who had displayed inappropriate interaction with a student with disabilities and have a private dialogue with him or her about the issue. Her objective was to help students acquire the skills to interact respectfully in situations that they might not have encountered before.

Jessica's principal rated her as one of the star teachers in the school. The principal had deliberately chosen her as the teacher for the particular mix of students with disabilities who had been placed in her classroom in September 2005. Jessica was aware that many adults—teachers and parents—wondered about the benefits of including students with significant disabilities and attributed this response to fear or simply lack of experiential knowledge of the student. For her part, she maintained generally cordial relations with the families in her classroom, inviting them to participate in periodic celebrations of student work. But it was quite clear, as she herself admitted, that she did not require their participation or involvement to keep her classroom running smoothly.

All in all, by the end of the school year (and when data collection at this site came to an end), Jessica expressed delight at how her class had "congealed" into a unit. Noting all the ways that students in her room spontaneously reached out to their peers with disabilities, she was struck by the fact that inclusion was actually working. She recalled her initial nervousness about having a student with significant disabilities in her classroom. But as she looked back at the year, she expressed satisfaction at how much progress students had made and her own sense of accomplishment; she felt that she had been successful.

West Creek Elementary School

The school where Jessica taught, West Creek Elementary School, was located in a largely middle-class affluent suburban district of Oakland in a large metropolitan area of the Midwest. The suburb itself was established as early as 1853 and boasted many historic sites, quaint neighborhoods, and community parks. The median household income at the time of the study in 2005 as reported by the city was $65,340 with more than 90% of the population (approximately 27,000) classified as White. West Creek Elementary was one of 5 elementary schools in the district during this period. Established in 1956 when it began, with seven classrooms and sprawled over 10 acres of land, it now housed 29 classrooms, two gymnasiums, a computer lab, and a library among a host of other facilities. It also boasted a playground that could be accessed by wheelchair users.

The demographic makeup of the school as reported in the Annual Report Card for the school on the State Department of Education website during the time of the study indicated that over 75% of the students were White, with about 21% considered Black. Latino and Asian students made up the remainder of the school population. A deliberate decision had been made by the school board to increase the number of minority students in the school, which had led to the admission of students who voluntarily transferred from the inner-city area. The school was also the designated "accessible" elementary school in the district at the time of the study. So, all elementary students with physical disabilities in the district attended West Creek. This had been the first year that all elementary schools had begun to enroll students with all types of disabilities, including students with "extreme needs," since the board had required that they attend their home schools. Overall, the principal felt that the teachers in her building had come to accept the inclusion of these disabled students, whether they might have initially wanted to or not, and they just needed to be supported through it. "I think it's the pressures of everything, and that's just one more pressure, see, that they didn't have to deal with before. That's all it is. Not that they don't want the child, I don't think per se. It's just one more thing."

The school, like many others in the district, had embraced a program of Positive Behavioral Interventions and Supports (PBIS). With the help of PBIS trainers and facilitators, the school had collectively generated four "universals" for the building: "Be safe, be happy, be respectful, be responsible." These principles were echoed not only through classroom conversations, they were visible as printed guides posted on the hallways and in the bathrooms. The process of integrating these PBIS principles had not been free of challenges. Teachers had initially questioned the premise of beginning where the learner was located. Eventually, however, the principal reported that teachers did come around to this new systemic approach and understood that when responding to student behaviors, *fair* did not mean *equal*. Elaborating on the specific goals at West Creek, the principal listed the primary goal as making sure that students succeed academically; the second goal was sustaining communication with the community and the families; and the third goal was having high expectations of behavior.

Many of the traditions within this building—Ice Cream Social, Trivia Night, Family Fun Night, book fairs—reflected the traditions of this predominantly White middle-class community. The separation of families of color from those that managed the Parent Teacher Organization (PTO) was quite distinct as evidenced in the turnout at these events. As the principal pointed out candidly about the PTO, "It's all White women who don't work, pretty much." Much of the community-building effort by the PTO was instituted along lines that might not necessarily encourage participation from all members of the school community. Describing with outrage the deliberate withdrawal of interest by the PTO members in recruiting minority families from the city, the principal remarked regretfully, "I would love to hear more of a voice from the parents of our city children. That's 25% of our children."

Nevertheless, the school had instituted a strong emphasis on community that was welcomed by teachers. The staff members I interviewed expressed deep satisfaction with their work environment and appeared to be strengthened by it. It was not uncommon to hear the following statements: "I really enjoy it and a lot of the reason is because of the people that I work with." Or, "I love it. This is a great place for kids." The teachers seemed to appreciate the community-building emphasis of the school that was continued within individual classrooms, such as Jessica's.

ACHIEVING A TRANSPARENT COMMUNITY

Stephanie

> *Somebody once said to me, a special ed teacher is just a really well-trained, a really good teacher. But I do feel like having a dual certification background gives you a broader toolbox for dealing with all the children that you have.*

At the time of the study, Stephanie, a young female of Asian origin, served as a special educator in a collaboratively taught 1st-grade classroom of students with and without disabilities within a large urban school district system in the United States. During the course of the year (and during the study), her coteacher left for a few months on maternity leave, and Stephanie was asked to take up the general education role, while another special educator was brought in as her partner. Although she was dually certified, this move was still rather unusual given prevailing administrative bias toward placing such teachers in special education roles. After more than 2 years with her previous teaching partner, this change would become a valuable opportunity for Stephanie to craft a professional identity wherein she could freely experiment with special and general education forms of practice as she went about realizing her commitments to caring classroom communities. Her prior sense of being stifled by her general education colleague, who had assumed greater control over the curriculum, gave way to a sense of liberation with the supportive presence of her new coteacher, who strengthened her special education roots while affording her the space to grow. Recognizing the institutional privileging of general education knowledge over special education, she hoped that new special education teachers would advocate more strongly for themselves with their administrators.

Stephanie's experience in teaching middle school students in the same K–8 school for 2 years before being assigned to this classroom had taught her to avoid adopting an authoritarian role with students. Instead, she sought to create a "transparent" community where "everybody's welcome, and even though everybody's different, we just work together, we have fun together." She wanted students to feel emotionally secure to express themselves within her classroom. Realizing that this goal was crucially related to her own practice, she strived to invest it with the kind of transparency that would bring her closer to her students, while simultaneously facilitating their learning. "And so I find that the more I talk about how I process my learning or how I process situations, I think it gives them the language, and a little bit of connection to me as a learner, and then they are able to better understand themselves, and then hopefully one day to start to express a little bit." This emphasis on language was a crucial component of her toolkit for instruction. She considered it important that students understand the purposes behind her actions, whether they related to undertaking disciplinary procedures or implementing curricular experiences. She built on her understanding of the role of "teacher talk," acquired within her own preparation as a teacher, to eagerly take up opportunities for classroom discussions on a variety of matters. She did not hesitate to abandon a lesson in mathematics, for instance, if she felt that the moment required attending to social–emotional conflict in the classroom.

Her support for including students with a wide range of disabilities in the general education classroom was enthusiastic; she found it unfair that student growth had to be measured only in terms of attainment of grade standards. She sought to establish a strong relationship with Trevor, a student with a computer-based augmentative communication device, so that she could more effectively plan for his academic growth. She recognized ruefully that the kind of "inclusion" program currently in place in her school was suited to some students with disabilities, particularly those whose intellectual achievement could be readily measured by the school. But she welcomed the presence of students with more complex disabilities such as Trevor, noting that the kinds of experiences offered to students with disabilities in this school setting were different from contexts that emphasized the acquisition of more functional skills. She carefully observed the ways in which students interacted with their disabled peers, stepping in to mediate when she thought they were inappropriate. For example, not only did she worry about their use of the descriptor "wheelchair kids," she might just as likely permit other students in the classroom to use Trevor's device to communicate if they felt unable to speak. Though some might find this easy sharing of personalized technological supports troubling, her approach seemed directed at "normalizing" participation differences in the classroom.

Stephanie engaged readily with the families in her classroom, welcoming their overtures of involvement, whether it was to organize celebratory parties for the children or to advocate for their child's needs. Generally, however, their involvement seemed to be typically determined along class and race dimensions, with White middle-class families more likely to be strongly visible in the classroom than working-class families and/or families of color. Except for the occasional invitations extended to families to speak to the group about specific cultural events, families did not play an active role in the everyday implementation of schooling. Stephanie even perceived herself as needing to "rein in" some of their behaviors, particularly in the context of the prejudicial behaviors she noted among families, which she found worked against the spirit of community she was trying to instill in her students. She thought that the child-rearing practices reflected in her school community diminished the resilience of children. Her inclination was to see her students as capable of assessing themselves as learners, as naturally empathetic to each other, but as deeply dependent on adult modeling. She often mentioned adults (whether families or other teachers in the building) as constituting one of her biggest challenges to implementing an inclusive community (this will be explored in greater depth in Chapter 5).

Andrews Children's School

Andrews Children's School, where Stephanie was a teacher, was a K–8 public school within an urban school district that spanned a wide metropolitan area of several million people belonging to diverse racial and ethnic socioeconomic groups. The school was established in 1994, and at the time of the study (2008–2009) it had already become noteworthy as one of the few schools within the school system that included students with significant physical and communication disabilities. Typically, such students in the district had been (and still are) served in separate educational facilities that offer limited interactions with nondisabled peers. Andrews has been described in school reviews as being at the "forefront" of inclusion, because of its capability to draw and support students with complex physical and communication challenges. It is not surprising that, unlike many other schools, it did not maintain self-contained classes. However, while the significantly disabled students that it did receive might carry many different labels, they were still expected, with supports, to accomplish grade-level benchmarks. In other words, one was unlikely to encounter students with "severe" or intellectual disabilities in this setting.

As part of the process of shifting to more inclusive models, schools were encouraged to maintain classrooms where special and general education teachers collectively taught groups of learners formed using a predetermined ratio of students with and without disabilities. Andrews had at least one such cotaught classroom in each of the primary grades. Such classrooms were characterized by an unusually large number of adults who might serve in the capacity of paraprofessionals or as various kinds of therapists who "pushed into" the classroom—that is, provided services in the naturalized setting of the general education classroom rather than in a separate location within the building. Families of students in the school were often eager for their children (without disabilities) to secure a location within such classrooms, not only for the additional supports they presumed were available, but also because they welcomed the opportunity for their children to interact with peers with disabilities.

At the time of the study, there were 695 students enrolled at Andrews, 46% of whom were White, 25% Black, 22% Latino, and 7% Asian. English language learners constituted 2% of the population, while 5% of the school was constituted by students labeled as receiving special education services. Public records also showed that the estimated percentage of students in this school who were from families receiving public assistance was 21–30%. The school displayed a strong family presence—families were encouraged to come into the classrooms when dropping off their children; many lingered to stay for the Morning Meeting, which was typically the first activity of the day. A typical morning would find the school teeming with family members as they brought their children in, chatted with each other, and/or exchanged pleasantries with the teacher. A similar scenario would take place at the end of the school day when children were picked up.

Like West Creek, the family community in this school, too, appeared to adopt (at least at the time of the study) norms that were typical to White middle-class families. Teachers might place sign-up sheets for families to volunteer for various activities that supported the everyday functioning of the classroom, such as sharpening pencils, vacuuming carpets, making copies, and so on. Families willingly took up the responsibility for planning parties and celebrations in the classroom. Schoolwide fund-raising activities drew on events like the silent auction culminating in adult parties at various popular locations in the city frequented by middle-class patrons.

DEVELOPING A PEDAGOGICAL VISION FOR ALL STUDENTS

Paul

> Math is a caste system. Either you get the number line or you don't. And if you don't get the number line, you're not going to move ahead.

Paul was a White male special education teacher at a high school in Bell City, a large metropolis in the United States that subsumes several hundred schools within the public school system. During 2010–2012 the high school Bell City Academy of Arts and Culture participated in a pilot program initiated by the city's board of education to support students with disabilities in their home schools. Educators within these pilot schools were encouraged to participate in professional development activities that, it was hoped, would collectively build the capacity of the schools to create inclusive environments where students with disabilities could progress toward the same educational outcomes as their nondisabled peers. As a member of a pilot school, Paul took up the opportunity for such PD offered through a university–school district partnership. He was assigned to a PD strand that centered on strengthening family–school connections where I was the lead facilitator. It was in the context of this PD that Paul's efforts toward inclusion emerged.

Paul's entry into the teaching profession occurred after a long and productive career in banking, where he had initiated hugely successful marketing practices. Relinquishing a "sexy job at Citibank" to become a Teaching Fellow, he joined his newly adopted profession as a special educator in a self-contained classroom for students labeled *emotionally disturbed*. He cultivated his pedagogical style in this setting where limited resources and a general schoolwide hostility toward his students seemed to make him more determined to create experiences that would support their active learning. Even after his serendipitous move to a high school (whose principal was Paul's friend from his school days), Paul's assessment of himself as being effective in teaching "reluctant learners" carried over into his experience in high school classrooms where students with disabilities were integrated with their nondisabled peers: "I am more drawn to needy kids, I guess. I don't know how else to say it." At the new school, he assumed the lead teacher role in a cotaught math class and also taught a 10th-grade math section by himself. While he actively took up and reveled in the opportunities to develop and restructure the mathematical curriculum at the high school and work with nonlabeled learners, his satisfaction remained incomplete because he was not "as much of a special ed teacher" as he would have liked. He had also declined offers to assume key administrative or coaching positions because, as he noted, "I have to be there with the kids."

Paul's sense of himself as an effective teacher arose from his determination to make mathematics accessible to his students. He was aware of the deep complexities within math curriculum where a single math concept such as fractions simultaneously invoked the concepts of division and ratio/proportion, requiring students to recognize such interchangeability in a seamless manner as they solved problems. His approach included not only PowerPoint slides, which he spent "hours and hours and hours and hours" creating, but also "tricks," "rap songs," and "hands-on funky projects" to reinforce connections within the curriculum. Paul recognized that cultural myths of possessing a "math gene" or being a "math person" contributed to a "math caste system" that made it difficult for students to acknowledge their lack of proficiency in mathematical concepts. Indeed, one important reason for his excitement in the new inquiry-based curriculum that he was implementing in his math classes was that it created an atmosphere of trust to self-identify gaps in knowledge and remedy them.

Paul's deep understanding of mathematical conceptual knowledge permitted him to recognize the ways in which "rich, engaging" activities could enable learners with differing capacities and skills to experience success in the classroom. Yet, even as Paul remained optimistic that regardless of presumed intellectual ability "any kid" *could* participate in rich and thoughtfully designed mathematical experiences, he was more skeptical that students who posed behavioral challenges, such as those with labels of autism, could be effectively included in general education classrooms. He recognized that among all ability differences encountered by teachers, the one that most seemed to "train wreck" their plans centered on behavioral issues. As he experimented with constructivist approaches that could enable greater student success in high-stakes examinations, he struggled with understanding how inclusive classrooms could encompass *all* types of learners.

Paul's curricular efforts and pedagogical style drew on collaborative relationships. He appeared to have a strong working relationship with his coteacher ("we gelled fantastic") with whom he felt supported in taking the risk of attempting a new inquiry-based math curriculum. It was clear, too, that besides his immediate congenial relationship with his coteacher, his approach to teaching and learning itself incorporated the importance of peer learning and peer support. His approach toward his coparticipants during PD meetings was always respectful, humorous, and clearly intended to recognize their contributions as valuable. Paul also welcomed deep relationships with his students but was under no illusions that their parameters could be indefinite. While he did not place constraints on the topics that students might bring to him, he did let them know that "if you tell me anything about you threatening to hurt yourself or hurt someone else, I go and tell."

Paul's satisfaction in his work was due in considerable part to the supportive context facilitated by the school principal, Larry, who tried to harness the specialized skills of his faculty. Larry conferred many opportunities on Paul, significantly expanding his role in the school. Besides his teaching responsibilities, Paul coordinated the school schedule and served as the data specialist creating the disaggregated tables required by the No Child Left Behind Act (NCLB) and tracking student scores that would be tied to teachers' tenure decisions. Paul relished these opportunities even as he fully recognized the potential for misuse that inhered in them. Still, it was clear that such responsibilities were tied to his overall sense of connectedness to the school community.

Bell City Academy of Arts and Culture—Paul's Perspective

In a collaborative project that we undertook together after the study was completed, Paul offered a detailed written description of the school where he worked. To preserve Paul's anonymity, I have withheld details of this project.

The following description draws heavily from his narrative about his school. The quoted excerpts are drawn from our collaborative work.

Opened in 2005, Bell City Academy of Arts and Culture was a relatively small school with just over 300 students who were predominantly Latino and Black. It was a "high need" urban high school that served students considered "at risk." The label *high need* indexed the fact that over 60% of the school's families fell below a certain income level, qualifying their children for the city's free breakfast and lunch program. Paul noted that *at risk* meant that students struggled in school showing "low grades, low promotion rates, and poor graduation rates." He felt that the "unique" element of this school was its intensive arts program, which offered students the opportunity to major in drama, art, music, or dance. Students were given the opportunity to perform in multiple shows each year, work with some of the city's most talented artists and producers, and attend many professional artistic performances each year. Paul noted that the school did not require any auditions or pretesting for student eligibility for admission. Instead, they gave preference to students who resided within the neighborhood in which the school was located. Still, alongside a large percentage of students from the immediate neighborhood, students from all parts of the city also attended this school.

Thirty percent of the student population in Bell City Academy of Arts and Culture were designated *special education* students. Paul saw this as an "unusual characteristic" because, according to him, most schools in this city had approximately only 6–10% of their students identified as special education. This large population of special education students presented "a unique challenge" to Paul's school and his colleagues. At the heart of the matter was to find ways to differentiate instruction so that it could be accessible to all learners, "while at the same time maintaining an appropriate pace of instruction to ensure that students master all the content necessary to pass mandated standardized state assessments—clearly, a very difficult balancing act." He added that this challenge had "made us all better teachers, however, forcing us to hone our pedagogy, share best practices, and creatively find effective methods of teaching students of all ability levels."

In our conversations during the study, Paul spoke highly about his principal, Larry, whom he had actually known many years prior to applying for a position in this school. He reported that Larry sought to foster a general climate of collaboration and inquiry within the building, hiring "people that are into shaping what's around." He encouraged any attempt initiated by the teachers for innovations in curriculum, schedules, and so forth, and supported opportunities for collective problem solving and growth. With such institutional support, Paul was able to develop his pedagogical vision, draw on his extensive prior experience in managing data, and simultaneously participate in the deeper structural processes within the school.

COLLABORATING FOR INCLUSION AND SOCIAL JUSTICE

Anita and Maria

> *I think [Anita] and I know a lot about different things. I might know more about [the] specifics of [the] kinds of labels of disabilities and things like that. But I think she knows just as much as I do of good practices.*
>
> —Maria

During the period of data collection (February–May 2013), Anita and Maria were coteachers in a 4th-grade dual-language classroom with 9 and 8 years of teaching experience, respectively. Both Latina women, Anita was the general education teacher while Maria served as the special educator (though she was dually certified in both general and special education). Both teachers were qualified in bilingual education and had been at the school for 4 or more years. This was their second year as collaborative teaching partners. Even as each brought unique biographical experiences that would influence the ways they interpreted curriculum and interacted with students and colleagues, they shared some common priorities that were reflected in their pedagogy.

Both teachers drew heavily on commitments to inclusion and social justice. Stating earnestly that "I really *really* believe in inclusion," Maria saw it as an opportunity that "teaches all kids a lot more about themselves and how to cooperate and work together." She was unable to understand why teachers worried about "high kids" being "brought down" when they were included with students with disabilities. Indeed, both teachers were often skeptical that their colleagues understood the meaning of *inclusion* especially when they continued to make snide remarks about students with disabilities. The remarks of their general education colleagues about why a student was not placed in an alternative or more restrictive setting directly contradicted Anita's approach. She was more likely to wonder instead why a student with an IEP in her classroom even needed a label. For her, inclusion was a model that mimicked real life. Deeply driven to work against the "school-to-prison pipeline," Anita was only too aware of the limited opportunities for social and economic mobility within the largely working-class community in which these students were embedded. It was this knowledge that fueled her pedagogy: "The biggest way you can promote social justice is that you teach somebody how to read and write. What else is there in this society?"

A strong desire to collaborate was another element that fostered their relationship when implementing inclusion. Even as Anita felt that she had found the perfect partner for collaboration, Maria recognized that both of them felt a collective responsibility to *all* students. Each of them worked with students in small groups in the classroom that included both students with and without labeled disabilities. There was no arbitrary separation of students or curriculum between the teachers. Maria was observed on several occasions leading the math session as much as she might lead a literacy or science lesson. While she might take the lead on IEP-related paperwork, she still described the process of writing student goals as collaborative. It was not surprising that, for Maria, inclusion was about "being able to cooperate with someone and collaborate with them in [the] classroom." Additionally, this collaborative ethic appeared to be a generalized value in the school, where teachers freely approached each other to solve problems they encountered with students in their classrooms.

The community of educators in this school drew on similar cultural origins as the families of students in this school, which both Anita and Maria saw as beneficial for their growth. For Maria, who entered the U.S. public school system as a student with no knowledge of English, the opportunity to "promote biliteracy and biculturalism" offered by this school through teaching in both English and Spanish was very appealing. Anita felt welcomed in a school culture where she felt she was "on the inside." She believed that there would be many "more things you have to mitigate if it's a culture different from your own in which you are teaching."

Both teachers experienced the stress of mandated testing and test preparation as inimical to the process of creating the kind of inclusive classroom community they desired and to their capacity to be effective as teachers. They worried about the effects of testing on their students, often feeling helpless to protect them. During the month when the teachers were engaged in serious test preparation, Anita remarked helplessly that it was a "horrible" time for them. They tried to push back against "the sense of the test being so powerful" that it might completely overwhelm them, influencing the ways they spoke to students or thought about them. The teachers struggled collectively to resist the "dark cloud" of testing and to maintain an environment "where it's still safe, where it's still playful, where it's still fun." It was clear that both teachers equally discounted the significance of such testing. While Anita dismissed it as a "crapshoot" that could not provide a genuine assessment of student growth and learning, Maria worried that such measurements of learning disadvantaged students with disabilities in decisions regarding their placements.

The Riverside Heights School

The Riverside Heights School in which Anita and Maria taught was a preK–8 public school in a large urban school system within the United States. The School Quality Report issued by the district showed that during 2012–2013 the school had a total enrollment of 463 students. Situated within a largely working-class community, 96% of the student population were Latino and

3% were Black. Additionally, 88% of the students were eligible for free or reduced-price lunch. The report also noted the positive environment within the school as well as the inclusive culture of learning that promoted high expectations with supports and engagement with families. Indeed, while its record of student academic achievement was evaluated as "meeting target," school environment was assessed as "exceeding target." Publicly available information indicated that families were supportive of the school, with more than 90% noting that they would recommend this school to others. More than 80% of the families responded to the annual school survey. Interestingly, unlike at Andrews Children's School, one was less likely to run into groups of families within the building, in the mornings or during other times of the school day.

The school was a "dual-language" school, which meant that on 3 days of the week, students were instructed in Spanish and for the remaining 2 days in English. During the period immediately preceding the districtwide standardized tests, teachers were permitted greater flexibility so that they might insert literacy instruction in English even on days that were scheduled for instruction in Spanish. According to the same School Quality report, during the 2012–2013 school year, 17% of the students were recorded as "with IEPs," while 43% were considered English language learners. Teachers seemed to overwhelmingly support their principal as an effective leader for the school. Anita and Maria both spoke positively of their relations with the administration and seemed to feel supported in their instructional efforts.

The building itself was surprisingly spacious, with a large gymnasium and wide hallways and a rooftop playground. Unlike many schools in the city that had responded to the directive from the district administration to retain students with disabilities by creating self-contained classrooms, the school did not maintain such classes. Instead, students with disabilities were educated in collaboratively taught classrooms that included students with and without disabilities and were supported by a general and special education teacher. However, at the time of the study, such classrooms were not quite so readily available in the middle school section of the school, complicating placement decisions for students with disabilities in 4th and 5th grades.

CONCLUSION: PIECING TOGETHER THE EXPERIENCES OF EDUCATORS

The educators described in the preceding pages were some of the many participants in the studies who shared their stories with me and whose practice I either had the opportunity to observe or understand through extensive conversations. These teachers were distinguished from other participants because of the length of time, opportunity for interaction, and range of objectives that characterized my experiences with them. Over a 7-year period, I spent 3–9 months in each of the classrooms of Jessica, Stephanie, and Anita and Maria, clocking 3–10 hours per week in each of those settings and conducting 2–5 interviews with each of them. While I did not observe Paul in his school setting, I was afforded a period of 9 months of working closely with him in a PD opportunity that I facilitated and that allowed me access to his perspectives. Additionally, I was able to conduct 3 interviews with him over a period of 9 months. The extensive data I obtained from these procedures meant that I was able to obtain a rich and generative glimpse into these teachers' everyday practice. It allowed me to readily distill several key ideas that have come to inform the content and structure of this book. My hope is that the introduction of these actors within the particular contexts in which they worked will allow the reader to make better sense of their efforts to advance inclusion, which I detail in the following chapters.

There were also other educators whose experiences were instructive in very specific ways and whose struggles also inform the content of this book. For these educators, I felt that I had insufficient data to speak to the breadth of their roles in implementing an inclusive pedagogy within the classroom. However, the data I was able to obtain of their experiences spoke to a slice—a really important slice—of the project of doing inclusion. For these educators, I have embedded their stories and their schooling contexts within my analysis of their experiences in the context of inclusion (see Chapters 5 and 6). My engagement with these educators was no less lengthy than the others. For example, Elena and Melanie participated in the same 9-month PD opportunity as Paul that I facilitated, as well as in three separate interviews during that 9-month period. Along with coresearchers, I followed Julie and Blair for 2 years in the district where they worked, spending many hours in the field as I shadowed them, participated in weekly meetings with them, and conducted interviews with them and the teachers they served (Naraian et al., 2012).

Collectively, all these educators illustrated the experience of struggle that lies at the heart of any attempt to understand and dialogue across difference (Holland & Lave, 2001). Their struggles point less to an oft-repeated notion of inclusion as "difficult" as much as to the open-endedness, unpredictability, and continuous nature of inclusive processes. Implicit in their efforts and accounts was not only the commitment to supporting student growth in both academic and nonacademic areas, but an energy to continually recognize and address the never-ending list of barriers that they encountered in this process. Their resolution of these challenges never fully satisfied them but seemed to leave them more strongly equipped to take on the next set of dilemmas. In that regard, they embodied the desire for change that motivates many teachers—novice or veteran—and that sustains a commitment to schools, students, and learning.

CHAPTER 2

Place and Time in the Grammar of Schooling

I have math goals for Trevor, but I just don't have the time. And then when I spend so much time with Trevor, I feel guilty because I know that Rafael needs something too, and I know there are things that need to be going on for Rafael and Kevin.
—Stephanie

When I brought up the fact that he [the student with disabilities] was shutting down so much during testing; that he still crawls under desks sometimes; or he's selectively mute at times where he just won't respond, . . . the psychologist asked, "Why isn't he in a twelve to one-to-one [a restrictive segregated classroom]?" I was like [disbelief on her face]: Well, I don't know about that.
—Maria

An intractable dilemma for inclusive education scholars has been that the implementation of inclusion in schools has often entailed a narrowed focus on the *placement* of students with disabilities in general education classrooms. In other words, schools frequently worry more about granting students with disabilities physical access to mainstream settings and experiences than taking concerted efforts to ensure their full participation within those spaces. The educators described in this book were deeply aware of the learning opportunities created when students with disabilities were included in general education environments. However, there were clearly some structural aspects of schooling that complicated their efforts to be successful in this project. In order to recognize teachers' efforts toward inclusion, one has to first understand the operation of these structures. An examination of these structures can more readily disclose the dilemmas in "doing" inclusion and the skills displayed by these teachers to maneuver within the structures.

In particular, educators across my studies identified the lack of time to accomplish instructional goals with their students as a significant challenge to their capability to practice inclusion. Whether administrators, general or special educators, or related service providers, all seemed to hold *time* partly responsible for inadequacies in their efforts to include students with disabilities within general education experiences. Additionally, interwoven with their frustrations with time were their assumptions about the *places* where such time was spent. Places in school appeared to signify certain types of learning experiences that required particular kinds of learners and/or barred others from the same. These entwined themes surfaced frequently in teachers' accounts as they tried to rationalize their decisions when trying to create equitable opportunities for their students. Collectively, they shed some light on the stubborn, unhelpful linkage between place and inclusion that has dogged inclusive education efforts; that is, *inclusion* must mean the placement of students with disabilities in general education classrooms.

Tyack and Cuban (1995) offered the concept of the "grammar of schooling" to describe the practices that "structure schools in a manner analogous to the way grammar organizes meaning in verbal communication" (p. 85). Such practices may include the ways that schools organize time and space, sort and divide students, or break up knowledge domains into subjects. They suggest that teachers, who are socialized into this grammar, draw on these practices without being formally conscious that they are doing so. Not surprisingly, it has remained extraordinarily stable over time. Analyzing the work and discourse of educators in my studies affirmed place and time as significant elements within this grammar, bearing directly on teachers' efforts to implement inclusion. In the following pages, I show how the concepts of *place* and *time* pervaded teachers' thinking about students and learning. The project of inclusion that they undertook was inevitably embedded within these concepts, as were the dilemmas they encountered and the solutions they developed to address them. In that regard, their practices reflected their creative manipulation of place and place-time to support their commitments to students with disabilities. It soon became evident that such maneuverings were driven by a focus on high-quality practice rather than by pregiven fixed narratives of places.

I begin this chapter by laying out how place and time came to inform teachers' understandings and practice of inclusion and the professional identities they evoked. Spatial theorists have argued that the investigation of place necessarily implicates time so that the concept of *place-time* may more closely reflect the ways in which their intertwining produces particular kinds of place identities and narratives (Massey, 1994; Soja, 1996). Though the following account is informed by such intertwining, for the purposes of disclosing the relevance of these structures for inclusion, I first take up each structure separately.

LEARNING IN PLACE, LEARNING FOR COMMUNITY

In this section, I describe the multiple ways in which places and learning are linked to produce certain kinds of student and teacher identities that then impact the ways inclusion comes to be implemented.

The Demands of Place on Students and Teachers

Across studies, schools came to signify a series of places with boundaries that permitted some to be *in* them, while others remained *out*. In other words, places implied different kinds of learning experiences that simultaneously evoked different types of learners. Maria's quote at the beginning of this chapter, for instance, reflected her revulsion at the potential effects of a restrictive segregated setting on her student. The kind of learning experience offered by *that* place seemed to be out of sync with the needs of her student. But teachers were also likely to assume that places themselves exerted some demands on who could or could not be placed within them. When Anita hoped that Marcelo, a student with learning disabilities, would acquire self-advocacy skills, she acknowledged that such skills would be required by the general education classrooms in which he might be placed in the future, and where there would be less teacher support than his current collaboratively taught "inclusion" classroom. The characteristics of different places required students to possess certain competencies.

Still, there was little if any consensus among general and special educators about the types of student competencies required by these places. Stephanie argued against the eligibility criterion for inclusion that was operative in her school: "These children [students labeled as *disabled*] don't cleanly fall into the category of having physical disabilities and being intellectually average—that's such an unfair requirement." Similarly, a general educator like Anita could respond to a student with moderate speech and language difficulties in her classroom with a baffled "Why does he need an IEP?" while other educators in her school equally wondered why he wasn't placed in a self-contained classroom. Clearly, there was no universally accepted method for gauging the fit between student competencies and characteristics of place to determine if students should be inside or outside specific places.

Teachers' own conceptions of whose learning mattered were also entangled with the requirements of place for specific types of learners. For instance, when Jessica argued that the inclusion of Harry, a student with significant disabilities, was important because it benefited his nondisabled peers, she was implicitly suggesting that if he could not produce such benefits, then some other place would be more appropriate for him. This means that for students with significant disabilities, their placement in general education classrooms not only depended on others' perception of benefits derived from their presence, but that the benefits *they* might accrue from this was somehow less relevant than those of their nondisabled peers.

Additionally, the places that separated different types of learning and learners made particular demands on teachers. Teachers could be nervous in receiving certain kinds of students as exemplified in Paul's statement: "When teachers completely integrate classrooms, they are saying, 'Oh God, we are going to get another blah blah blah,' and the kid's name they usually say is a behavioral issue kid and not a learning disabled kid." Moving students successfully across boundaries required specific competencies that teachers might not possess. These boundaries therefore demarcated different knowledge communities (e.g., general and special), separate professional identities (e.g., general and special) and consequently, different educational priorities. For instance, special educators were painfully aware that the general education classroom privileged the knowledge and status of general educators leading to inequitable relations in collaborative teaching, a phenomenon that has been reported in the research on coteaching (Bessette, 2008; Scruggs, Mastropieri & McDuffie, 2007; Strogilos, Nikolaraizi, & Tragoulia, 2012). At the core of such relations was the issue of working with a stigmatized group of students. This might be illustrated in the attitude of general school personnel who "hated us because they were all afraid of our kids" (Paul). Or it might be reflected in diminished opportunities for professional growth when school leaders stubbornly associated special educators with self-contained settings and were unwilling to grant them greater independence within general education spaces. In any case, the default place of inclusion—the general education classroom—brought with it both opportunity for professional growth and tensions evoked by belonging to competing professional communities.

The preceding paragraphs illustrate that places clearly have the capacity to exert demands on both students and teachers. Viewing it thus permits us to recognize how teachers negotiated those demands in their efforts to be inclusively oriented and preserve their own sense of self-competence. How did they respond to such demands? Why did they do so? What effects did these responses produce?

The Creation of Place-Within-Place

As educators maneuvered general and special education knowledge domains and spaces when seeking inclusive opportunities for their students, they continually sought to make the boundaries between such places much more porous. They created place-within-place options; this might take the form of a learning center in the school that was made available to *all* students in the building including students with disabilities. Or it might mean delivering specialized services to students alongside their nondisabled peers in the general education classroom. Or it could mean creating flexible learning spaces within the school or classroom with students arranged in various configurations.

These place-within-place options were generally anchored in one of two primary premises: *student connectedness* or *student learning need* (Naraian, 2016c). While the notion of student connectedness can be understood as related to the call for creating cohesive classroom communities (Sapon-Shevin, 2007), the notion of learning need is more complicated. Recent research has argued that learning needs do not reside within the learner as typically understood but are instead socially constructed (Dudley-Marling, 2004; Sleeter, 1986). This is aligned with sociocultural perspectives that understand learning as always culturally and socially mediated rather than as located solely in the head of the learner. Inclusive educators have drawn on such research to argue for schooling arrangements that can offer flexibility in curricular and instructional approaches thereby making school spaces hospitable to diverse types of learners. Still, successfully identifying students as possessing some need or another is often the cornerstone of effectively functioning school systems. It is currently not uncommon in various parts of the world to distinguish learners who have "special educational needs" from those who do not. There remains, therefore, some theoretical tension within the concept of *learning need*. But even as scholars problematize this usage, it continues to have currency among educators in schools. Each organizing logic for the creation of places—student connectedness and learning need—set in motion particular forms of practice.

Student Connectedness. Some teachers—namely, Stephanie, Jessica, Anita, and Maria—approached the work of inclusion as interconnected with the formation of a cohesive classroom community that could support the academic and social–emotional development of all the students. This meant that besides supporting students with disabilities, the places they created within classrooms for disabled and nondisabled students to come together were equally designed to meet the community needs of general education students. These teachers made the development of nondisabled students' learning integral to their inclusive pedagogy. For instance, Anita and her coteacher Maria, having carefully selected a classroom reading text about a student with significant disabilities, were observed to lead classroom discussions that could promote student understanding of the consequential impact of adult and peer responses to disability. They sought to "broaden the band of normal" (Anita) for the students such that they could recognize the diversity of learners in their own class as reflective of the real world. Prioritizing such peer relations, Stephanie too would not hesitate to abandon a lesson in math operations and focus instead on facilitating students' capacities to build relations with other members of the community. She would engage her 1st-grade students in extended discussions about an event that may have triggered a dispute or unpleasant situation, inviting them into a dialogue about it. Jessica, who used a range of children's literature to help students describe and understand differences among themselves, shared this emphasis on timely discussions to foster an inclusive mindset in the classroom.

This logic of community, which implied a focus on developing student connectedness, also meant that teachers were continually trying to find ways to support students, even with the most significant disabilities, to achieve the same academic outcomes as their nondisabled peers. They were not always successful. For instance, Jessica, with the adaptations developed by the special education teacher, could engineer an activity where Harry (introduced previously as a nonverbal student with significant disabilities) used an augmentative device to demonstrate his participation during some math activities. However, as the activities grew in complexity, Harry found himself increasingly in the sole company of his paraprofessional working on nonacademic activities. Stephanie was somewhat more successful in gauging the literacy capabilities of her own nonverbal student with significant disabilities, Trevor. She did not hesitate to demand greater use of his computer-assisted communication device and require him to meet the same standards as everyone else, even to the extent of having him stay after school like some other students to complete his work.

Student Learning Need. Other place-within-place options for learning operated differently. For instance, special educator Angie, who cotaught with Stephanie for a few months in her collaboratively taught "inclusion" classroom, commented on the efficacy of pulling students out of the main classroom space at different times because "they all have extremely different needs." Commenting on the fact that they were all at different levels, she argued that she "would pull them out three separate times," if necessary, to ensure that their inclusion in the mainstream environment still produced desired learning outcomes. Similarly, Kristine,* another special educator who facilitated the inclusion of Harry and other students with disabilities at West Creek Elementary School, supported students in a learning center within the school that was open to all students, but which was premised on certain needs such as when "somebody is having a behavioral problem, a meltdown, or they just need to get away." For these teachers, the concept of student learning need was foundational to the creation of learning spaces to support inclusion.

When teachers emphasized learning need to create place-within-place options to break fixed general–special boundaries and stimulate greater inclusivity, it had particular effects. For instance, the focus on student learning need seemed to simultaneously require teachers to describe their students in hierarchical ways. As Angie, a dually certified teacher, worried about meeting the widely divergent needs of students, she commented on her struggles within this classroom: "So it's in some ways more difficult because we really have to provide a higher level for some children over the top, but we're really slowing it down not just for the middle, but really for the lower-end kids." The special education background of both teachers in the team (Stephanie and Angie) meant that, according to Angie, they could "catch the lowest group up while not impeding the progress" of the "higher-level kids." At West Creek Elementary, Kristine mused over the curricular support that she

---

* Angie and Kristine were both special educators who worked with Stephanie and Jessica, respectively. I did not gather sufficient data about their practice to afford them a stronger place within this book.

provided the students who came down to the learning center. She developed a generic curriculum that was "just very basic stuff" with "lots of board games and lots of things we can do with letters and numbers and those types of things."

Interestingly, the teachers who pursued the creation of new kinds of places based on the nature and intensity of student learning need were mostly special educators. Contrary to what they might have hoped, these efforts toward inclusion seemed to solidify rather than weaken the boundaries between general and special education.

The Intertwining of Community/Student Connectedness and Learning Need

Even as these two foundational premises—*student connectedness* and *student learning need*—created different kinds of places for inclusion, educators could not keep them wholly separate in their decisionmaking. At the administrative level, Laney, principal of West Creek Elementary School, explained her rationale for distributing students with disabilities across different classrooms. She tried to make the number of disabled students assigned to different teachers "pretty equal as far as meetings to attend." However, "more significant-needs students would be with the two teachers who were *all for inclusion*" (emphasis added). In other words, the demands placed on teachers vis-à-vis students' learning needs would be fairly distributed so that they did not seem overly burdensome on teachers. Teachers may even be protected from having "tough kids" in their class for successive years. But the complexity of certain kinds of disabilities might equally require only those teachers who could also foster a community where these students were welcomed. The linkage between the responsibility to meet students' specific learning needs and a commitment to foster community was clearly recognized within school planning.

Teachers themselves could not disentangle these threads within their own planning and practice. Stephanie was committed to creating a transparent and inclusive classroom community where students could feel safe and respected. She was also aware that her role and responsibility as special educator in this collaboratively taught classroom included the instructional programming of students with a range of learning needs; this might include both significant disabilities as well as students without labels who were considered at risk for academic failure. Distinctively separate as the orientations of individual need and community connectedness might be, the process of securing inclusion wherein all students could succeed within the space of the same classroom necessitated that they be considered together. So, even as Stephanie sought to represent students to each other in ways that could support greater connectedness between them, classroom dialogues on the "fair" distribution of resources among students inevitably included a discussion of different needs that students might bring.

Students benefited when these principles were intertwined. For instance, Stephanie noted that one of her students with disabilities might not be fully able to achieve the learning benchmarks required by the general education space, but "that is not to say that he cannot do the work without the right access." In other words, even if the needs that stemmed from a student's disability might adversely impact his achievement of grade-level outcomes, the onus lay on the instructional context to provide the entry points for him to participate. Considering the logic of connectedness and learning need together allowed, therefore, for the issue of *accessibility* to emerge as a necessary component of promoting inclusion. In this regard, teachers drew on technology to enhance the accessibility of classroom experiences. Jessica promoted the use of the augmentative communication device used by Harry during whole-group events such as choral recitation or Morning Meeting. This allowed Harry an opportunity to "speak" (albeit in a programmed manner) his contribution to the group activity, likely permitting his peers to view him as a legitimate participant within their community. Maria, in her quest to improve the literacy skills of Marcelo and other students with disabilities, sought out and found a simple assistive technological device in the school that she used systematically with them. The impact on the students' academic and social–emotional growth encouraged her and Anita to place a request with the school system for an assistive technology evaluation so that other tools might be available to them that would be even more efficacious in supporting skill development.

Beyond generating physical accessibility for students with disabilities to curricular materials or classroom experiences, teachers were aware that such forms of accessibility were necessary to influence peer perceptions of their capabilities. Still, Stephanie also pointed out that "all this access should not be confused, because we don't know technically, literally, what Trevor's voice really is" because one could not know "what the inside voice is really saying." Her concern lay in the ways in which such unmediated use of technology would impact how students with disabilities might be perceived by their peers: "I think for them [peers] to see technology as something that would replace the person and the inside voice would be a detriment because then it becomes too easy to understand." In other words, the use of technology may be justifiable to meet Trevor's communication needs; however, its significance had to be weighed against its capability to support genuine understanding between him and his nondisabled peers.

Not surprisingly, such intertwining of the principles of *student connectedness* and *learning need* also produced dilemmas, since the objective of addressing the latter might easily conflict with the former. For instance, offering individual students extended time to meet individualized learning needs could easily lead to their removal from the group. While a teacher like Stephanie or Jessica might still prioritize the benefits of classroom connectedness and create opportunities within the general education classroom space for those needs to be met, others like Angie might argue that "if they were pulled out on a one-to-one basis, they might be moving even quicker." Interestingly, Anita resolved this dilemma by adopting the position that by recognizing learning needs, one did not negate an inclusive ethos; rather, doing thus supported the foundation for inclusive classrooms, because it "mimics more of what real life is." She could then create book groups based broadly on reading proficiency (that is, different learning needs), but also offer significant choice to students within those groups.

For many of these teachers, it seemed that the key issue raised while considering both student learning needs and student connectedness centered on the availability of supports for students, that is, the nature of instructional practices within a place of learning. When Anita and Maria worried about Sam's future placement, they were deeply aware of the lack of supports available in the options that were being considered for him and knew this would constrain his ability to represent himself as the multidimensional learner whom they had come to know. When Stephanie ruefully admitted that her classroom was likely most suitable for a student like Kevin for whom physical accessibility was the strongest need, she was signaling the difficulty of providing supports to students with a range of intellectual needs in successfully accomplishing learning outcomes.

Applying the logic of student connectedness and simultaneously balancing academic goals with social–emotional goals for all students, meant greater opportunities for transforming classroom pedagogy. It stimulated a range of instructional arrangements, curricular materials, content-area strategies, and extensive professional collaboration to achieve a range of educational objectives. For instance, Stephanie illustrated how "the special ed part is informing what we do to the general curriculum," when the strategies used to provide curricular access to some students (with disabilities) could just as readily be utilized for all students. On the same count, the special education emphasis on documenting the learning of individual students ensured that *all* students and teachers in the inclusive classroom were held to high expectations. Across sites, it was evident that teachers were in a continuous process of refining their practice as they pushed against surface meanings of *inclusion*, against given professional boundaries and against the pregiven fixed nature of classroom places.

TIME, PLACE, AND PLACE-TIME: THE STRUGGLES AND CONSEQUENCES OF INDIVIDUALIZATION

Unlike the potential flexibility afforded by places in schools, the issue of time offered much less scope for creativity in the process of fostering inclusive practices (Naraian, 2014). On the surface, most educators appeared to subscribe to a linear conception of time, a typical phenomenon in education

(Gray, 2004). Such a linear conception means that time in schools is *quantified, measured, managed, consumed, organized, distributed, planned for,* via socially normed temporal structures such as the school year, school day, and class periods to accomplish educational outcomes. For example, as IEP documents frequently attest, educational goals for students with disabilities may require that after a fixed period of time, a student "will be able to spell 4th-grade-level words with 90% accuracy, 80% of the time," under specific learning conditions such as "with/without prompting." When students are unable to achieve such precise outcomes, they are placed *outside* time as "slow" or "fast" learners, creating a space for delineating the "normal" or the "special" child (Gray, 2004).

Typically, in schools the designation of children as particular types of learners requires an individualized approach to children's learning needs. The concept of *individualization* is codified in the IEP, which lays out the nature and parameters of specialized supports and services and accommodations required by a student. Individualization is accomplished by describing the ways in which *time* is organized for *this* student:

- How much time in what kind of place?
- How much time for therapy?
- How much extra time for tests?
- When will services begin and end?
- When will the plan be reviewed?

Individualization, then, becomes a means by which special education programming can control and *decelerate* time (as dictated by general education practices) for *this* student. Such engineering of time is inextricably bound to available practices within different schooling spaces. In the following sections, I lay out the ways in which educators across my studies worked with the notion of time when seeking inclusion. Again, my rationale is that a careful appraisal of the structures within which educators worked can disclose the particular creative manipulations they devised to advance the project of inclusion.

The Incompatibility of General and Special Education Time

Even as *time* held a "naturalized" location within generalized education discourse across the research sites, the construct of individualization meant that, in practice, special education time and general education time remained somewhat at odds with each other. For instance, all teachers, general or special, were situated in the discourse of adequate yearly progress (AYP) brought by the accountability regulations of NCLB that were intended to hold all students, including those with disabilities, to high academic standards. AYP was predicated on a predetermined linear concept of time; it presumed that growth could be understood as significant only when measured yearly and that successive yearly measurements would (or should) signal the cumulative achievement of individuals and schools. These broad expectations of time, in turn, influenced teachers' priorities in their everyday instructional practices as they worried about what students were learning, how much learning they were able to show, who was falling behind, and what measures they needed to take to improve learning outcomes in the classroom. It was not surprising that teachers worried about the inevitable failure of an inclusive community as peers of students with disabilities came to inhabit different place-times. Jessica commented on peer responses to Harry as they began to engage in intellectually complex tasks: "As they are progressing in their academics, I think for some of them it kind of slows them back and they don't want to take that pause." That pause may also need to occur when a student with an augmentative communication device requires a committed listener who can wait till the voice output is delivered to provide the response that will complete the conversation.

The differentially experienced place-times within general and special education also influenced the ways inclusively oriented special educators negotiated curricular decisionmaking with their general education colleagues with whom they collaborated either in grade-level discussions or within a cotaught classroom. For instance, Stephanie noted that she would repeatedly have to inform her colleagues that "our kids are not there; we have to keep at this" insisting that they "slow it down" so that it was about "what *they* [the students] need versus what *we* [the teachers] need." Another special educator, who sought to support Michael, a student with physical and intellectual disabilities, within a general high school setting, complained about the impossibility of teaching important life skills that required extensive blocks of time within the rigid scheduling frames made available to all students.

This incompatibility between the place-time of general and special education was again disturbingly reflected in the concerns of Laney, the elementary school principal, who wondered about the relevance of the extraordinary efforts undertaken in her building toward inclusion when it remained a negligible priority in the district middle school. In other words, the "success" of an elementary inclusive community was partial at best and illusory at worst, since it could not be continued within future place-times, namely, in later middle and high school spaces. Such projections of place-times had implications for the kinds of decisions that were made in the present. So, despite an eminently successful year experienced by Jessica with the inclusion of a student with significant multiple disabilities in her classroom, the professional community in the school collectively recommended more restrictive educational place arrangements for him during the following year.

Place-Time and the Logic of Learning Need

The incompatibility between general and special education that informed educators' conceptions of place-time stemmed from the understanding that some students needed more time to learn (Naraian, 2014). This is a common enough notion and has even produced modifications of the assessment requirements enforced by NCLB (Zigmond & Kloo, 2009). However, coupling the concept of *individualization* with the belief that time needed to be slowed down for some learners also brought about the creation of other kinds of structures that thickened the boundaries between general and special education. Once again, the logic of student learning need permitted schools to reapportion time through specialized, separate (and presumably more efficacious) spaces for learning designed specifically for students with disabilities. However, a concerted emphasis on the logic of student learning need also narrowed the capacity of school spaces to accommodate diversity in student ability. Instead, what was offered were alternate (often segregated) places that had independent instructional goals and purposes and that could remain progressively disconnected from the mainstream.

The narrowing of curriculum within these restricted spaces was particularly reflected in the emphasis on functionality within the educational programming for some students, particularly those with significant disabilities. So Kristine, the special educator who supported Harry in Jessica's classroom, could argue for the importance of teaching him nonacademic skills that would allow him to "count pills" or participate in schoolwide recycling, all of which led him successively away from mainstream classroom experiences. The emphasis on developing "functional" skills arose historically from the concern to develop a planned systematic curriculum that would be relevant for students with moderate to significant disabilities (Browder & Spooner, 2006). Still, such a functional emphasis was itself intertwined with the inflexibility of time as it was experienced in schools, which served as a strong rationale for instruction in separate places.

Sometimes, the tensions in place-times of general and special education were more generative. For instance, Stephanie was also able to report that the insistent contribution of the special educators to the grade-level team had led all educators (general and special) to begin questioning the pace and content of the curriculum itself. She noted that within their team, there was "this push and pull" between the curricular items that needed to be covered versus "let's slow it down just a little bit and it's okay to probably skip certain things." These teachers recognized that doing so might impact "the way our room looks," but it was important to "go at the curriculum a little bit more." By referencing the "the way our room looks," Stephanie might have meant the ways in which students were arranged in the classroom or perhaps a reduced attention to making the physical space visually attractive while increasing attention to meeting student needs. Whatever the case, she was clearly noting her satisfaction with the ways in which her role as a special educator had influenced general education practice among her grade-level colleagues.

Time and place, therefore, emerged as strong predictable structures within the grammar of schooling that almost always informed the decisions made by teachers in efforts toward inclusion. As they worked within these structures, teachers inevitably encountered and took up the logic of learning need. The logic of need itself emerged in part from the emphasis on individualized pedagogy, which in conjunction with place and time left intact the divisions between general and special education. In the next section, I draw on the experiences of some teachers to illustrate that a focus on providing quality supports to students can diminish the relentless force of time as well as blur boundaries between general and special education.

MANEUVERING PLACE-TIME FOR STUDENT SUCCESS: TWO STORIES

Coteachers Anita and Maria at the elementary school level and Paul at the high school level struggled to secure suitable places of learning for their students. Across research sites, this process of considering placement for students in one type of classroom or another was frequently accompanied by an intense, even painful soul-searching, a deep reflection, an awareness of the political and material conditions in which decisions had to be made, and above all a strong compulsion to act on behalf of students. The place identities that teachers imagined were inevitably entangled with their efforts to consider the significance of time within various places. In the following paragraphs, I offer a summary of the dilemmas encountered by Anita and Maria and then Paul as they contemplated issues of place and place-time (Naraian, 2016c).

Anita and Maria on Middle School Placement for Sam

As Anita and Maria went about infusing a broad array of instructional approaches to create a classroom that would embrace all learners, they struggled to understand how to most effectively support Sam, labeled as *learning disabled*, who clearly was not achieving the same academic and social–emotional goals as most of his peers. They willingly afforded the time, consideration, and flexibility that his unique learning performance demanded within the protective confines of their classroom. But they were simply unable to "decode" him. His actions left them baffled because there did not appear to be anything predictable about when he might "shut down" or when he might be cheerful and engaged. The only certain knowledge they could claim about him was to recognize signs of frustration when he was unable to "get it." Otherwise, they remained nonplussed by his constantly changing emotional state as he went from being almost catatonic one moment to nonchalant and unperturbed the next. Additionally, he required significant support to complete tasks in the classroom. While both teachers supported all the students in various combinations of small groups, Maria was observed on several occasions providing one-on-one support to Sam to complete a given task. Yet they also delighted in his funny, quirky personality, finding much humor in some of his actions in the classroom. He was always treated as an equal participant during whole-group discussions. He had amicable relations with his peers, who seemed to garner as much enjoyment from him as he did from interacting with them in the classroom, cafeteria, or playground.

The dilemma for Anita and Maria, as 4th-grade teachers in a K–8 school, arose when they began to plan ahead for Sam's following year and for his subsequent middle school experience. Their description of Sam engaged only indirectly with the concept of *learning need*. When describing his level of maturity with peers, Anita was more likely to say "that is *his* way of socializing," fully aware that his peers seemed rarely uncomfortable with his form of play. They did recognize that his emotional maturity might be qualitatively different from his 4th-grade peers. For instance, he was known to react to tests with uncontrollable anxiety that might entail crying, throwing objects, and crawling under a table. They recognized that it was the expectations of the environment (particularly when having to take a test) that placed Sam under so much stress that it might leave him unable to demonstrate his learning in any meaningful way. Their main goal for him was to recognize his rising levels of frustration and to be able to draw the teacher's attention to it before he "shut down." Increasingly, they had begun to see evidence that when he worked in a small group, he was much more self-directed and able to experience greater levels of success.

Still, when the school psychologist, after learning about his age-inappropriate behaviors, wondered aloud why he was not in a small self-contained setting, they were outraged. Sam's apparent need may have seemed to map neatly onto a readily available placement option for *that* professional, but for these teachers it was clearly a much more complex issue. Certainly, the mere proximity of a teacher in a small setting created conditions for him to feel more capable and produce satisfactory work. However, it also needed to be a setting that could recognize that he was a competent learner who could engage in knowledgeable interactions; Maria, however, stated flatly, "I have not seen any great self-contained classrooms." Furthermore, any school within the public school system in which they were situated would inevitably require some kind of quantitative evidence of Sam's capability and, in that regard, would always fail him, because despite environmental modifications, he still experienced testing as inordinately stressful. For Sam to be successful within the place-time of *any* classroom, he would require additional supports. They recognized that the supports provided within their own classroom were not fully adequate for Sam; yet the unfavorable, generic place-identity of a self-contained classroom rendered the additional supports available in that setting negligible.

Still, even as they resolutely resisted the idea of recommending a small self-contained setting, they were unable to completely eliminate that choice. They were not certain that the current type of collaboratively taught classroom had been wholly successful for Sam, but they were also aware that the school currently did not have the resources to provide Sam additional supports in this setting. Though Anita and Maria were committed supporters of inclusion, they still could not bring themselves to deliberately include services on the IEP that they knew their school could not make available because that would position it as "out of compliance." They were far too embedded within their school community to take up such a subversive option. Not surprisingly, weighing the demands of a singly taught middle school classroom with 33 students and the affordances of a small-group setting, they tilted, albeit reluctantly, in the direction of a self-contained special education classroom as Sam's future placement.

Paul on an Inquiry-Based Math Curriculum for All Students

Although a certified special educator, Paul's facility in mathematics education opened up many unexpected opportunities for him at his high school. Following his experience as a special educator in a self-contained classroom, not only did he become the lead teacher in a cotaught math classroom, he also planned the high school math curriculum in ways that would ensure that incoming students with disabilities could be placed within general education spaces rather than in self-contained rooms. Paul's perception of himself as an effective teacher was inseparable from his commitment to making mathematics accessible to his students. With his colleagues, he used each instance of systemic change to reevaluate the math curriculum and pedagogy. One such instance of systemic change occurred during the adoption of new learning standards by the school district. Given the emphasis on problem solving within these standards, Paul persuaded his principal to invest in a project-centered math curriculum that could scaffold the process of critical thinking while simultaneously allowing students to enter the problem in a variety of ways. Paul's excitement inspired by student responses to this inquiry-based curriculum was illustrated in his comments: "It was so awesome to see the kids unfold this . . . " and "Oh my god, it's wonderful! I am getting a sense that the learning is real-er!" and "It's so exciting. It's really, really, *really* exciting!" Clearly, the activation of student learning generated its own conditions for professional satisfaction. But it was also Paul's deep understanding of mathematical conceptual knowledge that permitted him to recognize the ways in which "rich, engaging" activities could enable learners with differing capacities and skills to experience such success. The exercises within the inquiry-based curriculum, he argued, "have such a depth to them that it is instant differentiation." All students, whatever their skill level in the mathematical concepts, could participate in a way that was valid, establishing an atmosphere of greater trust and risk taking. In a school where 30–50% of students entering 9th grade read at a 5th-grade level, this curriculum permitted him to utter with conviction: "Any kid can enter [the curriculum] at critical thinking; every kid is doing some critical thinking."

Paul understood student learning as shifting rather than fixed, and as multidimensional rather than narrowly defined. This was reflected on more than one occasion, as he described "teaching kids to move beyond frustration" or "socializing" them into the shift from the lower standards of middle school to the more rigorous demands of high-stakes examinations. Counterintuitively, it was also reflected in his descriptions of the system that he and his colleagues had created for a more inclusive mathematics instruction. Beginning with the belief that all students, regardless of disability label, would (and should) take the state-sponsored high school examinations required for graduation, he and his general education colleagues sought to generate a fluid process that was intended to be simultaneously noncategorical as well as directed at supporting student needs. When students entered high school, they were assessed for mathematics ability (not IEP goals) and placed in different groups. However, these groupings were not fixed. "If come January, some of these kids are rocking it, we move them upstairs and say, 'You know what? Try and take the [state math exam] and if you fail it, do another semester with us next year.'" The teachers developed and implemented high school experiences such that students took as much or as little time as they needed (1, 2, or 4 semesters) to prepare for the math exam.

The complex rationale for student distribution across classes emerged from Paul's understanding of the importance of establishing "safe" environments for risk taking in math learning; the necessity to compensate for middle school practices that prioritized IEP goals over mastery of skills; the worthlessness of an IEP diploma that meant "nothing, nothing, nothing" in the real world; and the importance of a curriculum that could allow all students to engage at their own skill level and simultaneously develop critical thinking. In his account, the teachers in these classes were only weakly distinguished as general or special educators, since the classes themselves were open to all students. Paul was acutely conscious that these procedures for class composition and curricular management might be construed as tracking, since it was based on students' skill level. But it was also accomplished without affecting their standing in other content areas and it converted an externally imposed mandated requirement for graduation into an opportunity to revitalize the curriculum within all educational spaces. He preferred to refer to this system as a form of "flexible" tracking.

Reflections: Invoking Teacher Agency Within Place-Time

If the dilemma confronted by Anita and Maria arose from the certain impossibility of finding the most suitable place for Sam (after all, how could he or any other student escape the inevitability of tests?), it may have been the creative maneuvering of existing school structures to work *with and against* such impossibility that marked Paul's experience. The emphasis Anita and Maria placed on Sam's emotional state permitted them to embrace him as a valued learner. It simultaneously became the yardstick by which the self-contained classroom was left as the default choice. They could envision and desired a far more generous and supportive environment for him, but in the absence of that, they settled for what might be least likely to afford him emotional stress.

Paul took no less pleasure in the emotional lives of his students and securing strong relationships with them, but his entry into inclusive practice occurred through the provision of certain kinds of curricular experiences. In focusing on students' success as learners, he challenged the given boundaries of classroom spaces, and the demarcation of professional boundaries including the roles assigned to teachers. At the same time, his efforts continued to be stimulated by his awareness of the different skill levels (i.e., learning needs) that students brought in math and his dissatisfaction with the arguably impractical practice of placing students with widely varying skills within the same classroom in a high school setting.

Paul's likely accomplishment was undoubtedly strengthened by the strong collaborative relationships he developed with his colleagues during this process. Indeed, his embeddedness within his school and his recognition of the skills brought by his colleagues allowed him, in part, to engage in risk taking with scheduling and student configurations. Ironically, it was a similarly strong connection to their school community that left Anita and Maria *unable* to meaningfully shift projections of place for Sam. Recognizing and empathizing with the administration's inability to procure needed resources to secure a different configuration of services that could benefit Sam, they felt unable to force the issue by recording other forms of support on his IEP since that would inevitably have rendered their school "out-of-compliance."

Doing inclusion is unpredictable, multidimensional, and always unfinished. The experiences of Paul and Anita and Maria suggest that educators take up the conditions offered within their schooling contexts to foster new narratives in many different ways and with different results. Research has shown that agency is not just a stable internal property that individuals (in this case, teachers) simply transport from one context to another (Holland & Lave, 2001). On the contrary, teacher agency emerges as the affordances of a particular schooling context intersect with the unique biographies of individuals (Priestly, Edwards, & Priestly, 2012). For instance, Paul felt immensely supported and encouraged by the culture of risk taking and initiative within his building. The principal, Larry, appeared to foster a general climate of collaboration and inquiry within the building, hiring, as Paul pointed out, "people that are into shaping what's around." Larry encouraged any attempt initiated by the teachers for changing curriculum, schedules, and so forth. The intellectual freedom afforded in this context allowed Paul to broaden his pedagogical vision as well as draw on his extensive prior experience in managing data. With his principal's encouragement, he could utilize the skills he brought as a successful data analyst, take risks in maneuvering the curriculum and methods of instruction, as well as implement a complex schoolwide schedule that could permit the flexible use of place configurations.

At the elementary school, Anita and Maria certainly felt deeply connected as "cultural insiders" both to their colleagues in the school and to the students who came from largely working-class Latino families. This shared cultural context strengthened their sense of urgency to work intensively with students so that even as they dismissed high-stakes tests as nothing more than a "crapshoot," they still did not hesitate to adopt instructional approaches that would directly help students acquire specific skills needed to succeed in such assessments (described further in Chapter 3). In this regard, their inability to propose instructional places for Sam other than what was available within their school may owe in some part to the *status of (dis)ability* within their reflections around the needs of this student community. The teachers—like the school—seemed to hold disability and linguistic status as two discrete experiences that needed to be addressed separately. If (dis)ability remained separated from linguistic/cultural marginalization within teachers' commitments to equity, it may also have remained separated within the ways they conceived of their own roles as advocates for their students. Located within a responsive professional community that overwhelmingly recognized the marginalized linguistic/cultural status of its learners, they could regard disability as requiring something other than what this community could give. The rationale implicitly required of Anita and Maria by the school—namely, lack of personnel is a justification for not including certain services on the IEP—was therefore taken up by them with no hesitation, but indeed with sympathetic understanding.

Whatever the outcomes of their engagement with place and place-time, these educators rejected fixed narratives of places that suggested only singular ways of thinking about experiences within them. In other words, the nature of practices within places could alter meanings of learning/ability/disability that they might historically have come to represent. It was not surprising that Anita and Maria could reminisce nostalgically about a teacher who conducted a wonderful self-contained classroom that would have been perfect for Sam. Places therefore could have different identities constructed by actors within them (Massey, 1994). However, the extent to which teachers were able to successfully manipulate those place-narratives lay at the interface of a range of situational factors and their own internal resources that could not be readily predicted. Additionally, as each of these cases illustrates, such efforts, rooted as they were in widely varying school contexts, would always reflect differing levels of (dis)ability analysis.

CHAPTER 3

Straddling, Resolving, and Transforming Competing Paradigms

To understand the complexities of the everyday work of inclusive pedagogy, it may be helpful to remind ourselves of its beginnings. Inclusive education emerged from a critique of special education practices that used a deficit understanding of disability, imposing rules of normalcy on all students. A disability-rights lens helped draw attention to the widespread *ideology of ability* that pervades schooling systems as they sort, categorize, and rank students (Siebers, 2008). It is logical to presume that instructional practices that support inclusion must work in sync with this perspective.

When scholars began to question the conceptual and organizational foundations of traditional special education (Gallagher, 1998, 2004; Skrtic, 1995), the lived experiences of students with disabilities and their families were an important element of their theorizing. This meant, too, that they were more likely to take up methodological approaches that privileged interpretivist and qualitative research designs rather than methodologies that drew on quantifiable data (Ferguson & Ferguson, 1995). In other words, such research was less likely to rely on test scores and other numeric outcomes to explain phenomena and more likely to focus on the conditions for learning that emerged from specific practices. In this regard, it placed greater emphasis on issues of identity, positioning, and self-understanding that grew out of participation in schools.

Not surprisingly, the views of human development and learning that have come to inform the educational approaches in the field of inclusive education are often at odds with mainstream special education paradigms. Traditional special education practices have been criticized for relying on a mechanistic approach that is perceived as dehumanizing to students with disabilities (Heshusius, 1989). Yet this paradigm (reflected in practices such as direct/explicit instruction) continues to have currency with mainstream special educators as they describe, assess, and implement programming for students with a range of disability labels including *learning disabilities, autism, emotional disabilities,* and *multiple/significant disabilities* (e.g., Browder et al., 2007; Haager & Vaughn, 2013; Horner & Carr, 1997). Inclusive educators, however, place a contrasting emphasis on constructivism to inform their pedagogy, which is a logical outcome of the values and commitments of the field of disability studies that privilege the experiences of individuals with disabilities and their families over professional discourse (Biklen, 2005; P. M. Ferguson & Nussbaum, 2012). Whether it is adopting sociocultural perspectives on literacy or taking up inquiry-based approaches to mathematics, inclusive educators assume that practices that are learner-centered rather than teacher-directed allow for deeper, authentic learning on the part of students with disabilities.

Many special educators, however, argue that students with disabilities bring innate challenges that hinder mastery of routine learning tasks. They view constructivist approaches that de-emphasize their deficits as unhelpful to their learning. These special educators instead uphold the importance of explicit, intensive, and systematic instruction for helping students with disabilities achieve important educational outcomes across content areas including literacy and math (Ritchey, 2011; Troia & Graham, 2002). Indeed, with its focus on helping students acquire specific skills and strategies, explicit instruction has been identified as one of the instructional practices that makes special education "special" (Vaughn & Linan-Thompson, 2003).

These different perceptions of disability and learning have placed special and inclusive educators at odds. The latter remain ambivalent, if not deeply suspicious, about the role of mechanical and ability-based practices such as direct instruction within inclusive pedagogy. Still, as educators continue to learn about how diversity of learning profiles in schools can be best supported, some researchers have begun to question the significance of this debate. When Poplin et al. (2011) investigated teachers' instructional practices in low-performing urban schools, they found that traditional, direct instruction was the dominant approach. But they also found that teachers' commitment to and respect for their students made them effective educators. Poplin et al. critiqued the overreliance on constructivist approaches for students with disabilities and proposed that inclusive educators rethink their orientation to forms of teaching such as explicit instruction (Poplin et al., 2011; Poplin & Rogers, 2005).

Across my studies, I found teachers consciously and unconsciously working through and across multiple paradigms as they developed their professional trajectories. Noticing how some teachers straddled, navigated, and transformed these competing ways of thinking about students and learning, I studied the compelling rationales they brought to this process. How do teachers make sense of these competing approaches in schools as they work toward inclusion? What guiding frames do they use as they strive to be inclusive in their orientation to learners, yet committed to their professional roles in schools that are increasingly focused on meeting narrow standards of achievement? Investigating these questions simultaneously draws our attention to the identity processes that are always implicated in teacher practices. In reaching across professional boundaries to enact inclusion, how should teachers identify themselves: as special educators, inclusive educators, or (when dually certified) general educators . . . or, all three (Naraian, 2010a)? What are the effects of taking up particular kinds of practices in schools on teachers' professional understandings of themselves? This chapter takes up these questions.

ADOPTING BOTH MECHANISTIC AND CONSTRUCTIVIST METHODOLOGIES SIMULTANEOUSLY

The debates between mechanistic pedagogies (such as explicit instruction) and constructivist pedagogies are typically carried out in scholarly venues, but they were never quite absent within the classrooms that were studied for this book. Educators in these studies may not have used the same terminology or adopted similar arguments in discussing the merits of their different approaches, but they were clearly aware of the root differences between the approaches they took up. They were not wedded to a single approach, and they were not immune to the tensions that arose from using competing methodologies.

Explicit instruction may be understood as a set of instructional practices wherein students receive explicit description and explanation of content, observe teachers modeling thinking, memorize key vocabulary, practice, and receive feedback till they are able to generalize the content to other settings (Archer & Hughes, 2011; Knight, 2002). It relies on specific elements including the logical sequencing of skills, the breaking down of complex skills and strategies into smaller instructional units, step-by-step demonstrations, providing a range of examples and nonexamples, and giving both immediate and corrective feedback. The form of pedagogy observed in some of the settings described within this book and/or described by educators included some of these elements, some of the time.

Constructivism, on the other hand, is a psychological theory "that construes learning as an interpretive, recursive, nonlinear building process by active learners interacting with their surround—the physical and social world" (Fosnot, 2005, p. 34). A primarily learner-centered approach, it is premised on the individual's struggle to make meaning, leading to progressive shifts in cognitive structures that ultimately constitute development. Examples of constructivist instruction within these schooling sites included inquiry-based or problem-based learning opportunities, active collaborative learning opportunities, and student-centered discussions. Most of the teachers described in this book actively took up such constructivist methodologies.

Explicit instruction has been critiqued for fostering a mechanistic, even reductionist form of practice that removes the complexity and ambiguity within learning experiences, rendering them less than meaningful to students (Heshusius, 1989; Knight, 2002). It is also seen as supporting a "banking" form of education, and in the absence of genuine dialogue with students, views them as lacking in agency and as being unable to construct new knowledge (Freire, 1970/2000). Explicit instruction may lead to isolated skill acquisition without generalization of learning (Archer & Hughes, 2011; Knight, 2002). On the other hand, by prioritizing students' own construction of meaning, constructivism has been critiqued as being inattentive to the foundational skills that students need to develop proficiency and independence in learning content-area knowledge (Knight, 2002). Still others have also acknowledged the possible lack of preparedness of the learner to know how to participate in constructivist inquiry-based methods (Schwartz, Lindgren, & Lewis, 2009).

In practice, it may be that these approaches are not so distant from each other, nor are teachers generally committed to only one and not the other. Research has shown that when using explicit instruction, teachers may still draw on a social constructivist perspective that frames the student in holistic ways (O'Neill, Geoghegan, & Petersen, 2013). They also did not appear to emphasize the transmission model of learning typically associated with direct instruction. As the data from my studies showed, teachers often engaged in an eclectic approach drawing simultaneously on multiple traditions. While this may carry an inherent risk of producing contradictions within one's approach, plurality of method seemed to be much more reflective of teacher work than a purist stance of adhering to a single approach.

Principled Eclecticism: Anita and Maria

The focus brought by Anita and Maria to their students was not on remediation of individual deficits, but on development of skills and dispositions they considered important for citizenship in an inclusive, democratic community. In that regard, they were deeply aware of the role of the social environment in producing particular kinds of student learning performances. For example, they were empathetic to Sam, a student with disabilities, when he responded with extreme fear and anxiety to tests, recognizing that his needs as a learner were determined by the social and cognitive demands of the learning situation. (This was, of course, in contrast to the school psychologist who used the same information to question the placement of Sam in a mainstream classroom; see Chapter 2.) But they also emphasized a concerted focus on skills as benefiting Sam whether in the distant future or in the classroom he might attend the following year. The approach to literacy instruction adopted by Anita and Maria, then, reflected a planned synthesis of multiple approaches (Naraian, 2016b).

Literacy Instruction for Real Reading. Anita and Maria developed a notion of *real reading* that would come to determine the blend of approaches they took up within their classroom. They described it in the following way:

> *Real reading* means that you leave 4th grade with a realistic goal that we talked about, which is: Can you write a paragraph? If you can write a paragraph, we are very confident that later on, you will learn to write an essay. We look at real reading as what you will carry beyond 4th grade. That you are not asking yourself, "Am I reading at a [certain] level?" But you are talking about "When I don't know a word, what do I do? When you ask me a really hard question, do I go back to the text?" . . . So if a kid can say that and be metacognitive about what they are struggling with, I think for us, that defines success. (Anita)

Such a conception of *real reading* triggered an instructional practice that drew on a blend of systematic instruction of skills interwoven with a learner-centered emphasis on supporting their social–emotional growth and participation in the classroom.

Almost all skill activities in reading and writing were systematically broken down by Anita and Maria and formulated as a series of steps that students were asked to follow. For example, after the teachers provided a clear oral and written description of the task of responding to a question about a text, they might write the steps on a poster as follows:

1. Read the question, and write the topic sentence.
2. Write details to support the topic sentence.
3. Check the facts you have written to make sure you do not repeat yourself.
4. Ask yourself, do the facts make sense?

They strived to remove all ambiguity within the step-by-step process they offered. They did not presume that the students would generalize after having completed one set of steps collectively with the group. In repeating the sequence of steps for each part of the question, they seemed to err on the side of redundancy in order to more readily disclose and identify the pattern of thinking and response called for by specific tasks. They did not assume that their students would intuitively recognize this process. All the steps that were identified for each of the various literacy tasks were written on a separate poster during the lesson and then later hung on the wall in the classroom along with posters on other writing topics, so that students could refer to them whenever needed.

While the teachers were clearly committed to such an instructional process that was explicit and systematic, their practice equally conveyed a commitment to have students participate in that process rather than remain passive recipients of it. For instance, during a lesson on writing a short answer response, students would begin by calling out different suggestions. As a group, they collectively evaluated each suggestion, with Anita facilitating their progress in identifying several additional steps that were important; that is, one detail does not equate one sentence, details should be different from each other, check details to avoid repetition, and so forth. In other words, students collectively participated with the teacher in formulating the steps to a writing skill, which were then transferred to a poster that was later hung on the wall for future reference. It was not uncommon for students to be seated on the rug during these discussions for a 30- to 40-minute period of time.

Throughout the duration of the study, I did not observe a single whole-group instructional session where Anita and Maria did not have the full and willing attention of their students and where students were not actively raising their hands to participate. There were the occasional moments when students might fiddle with each other's hair, or exchange knowing glances and smiles with each other. But for the most part, supported by varied seating arrangements (students selected from a range of options including chairs, the rug, or ergonomically designed stools), use of multiple forms of presentation (oral, visual posters, and document readers), or frequent turn-and-talks to neighboring students and predetermined reading/writing partners, students remained engaged in the lesson. Students with disabilities were expected and encouraged to participate via supportive class routines that permitted all students to take turns in sharing. Sam, whom I had often observed as being in a constant state of bodily movement during small-group activity, generally remained focused and able to demonstrate sustained attention to the teacher leading the whole group. In other words, when explicit instruction was coupled with active participation, all students seemed to perceive its benefits as real to their own growth.

Alongside such explicit instruction, the teachers seemed to place an emphasis on creating a responsive context where the core value was to preserve a community of learners. When carrying out preparatory activities for the standardized tests, they tried to clarify to the students that the type of reading they had to do was different from the "other" kind. They used analogies such as preparing for a marathon as a way for students to orient themselves to test preparation, and they allowed students time and space to express their questions and anxieties about the tests. Teachers clearly recognized that students' academic performance was always linked to environmental factors that could have a positive or negative influence on their learning. For instance, the section on the wall titled "Writer of the Week" displayed a range of student work: Even a written product of just a few sentences might, according to the teachers, serve as a good example of evidence from the text and merit such public display, just as much as a more extended piece of writing that illustrated a strong short answer response. Placing them both in this section suggested that the ability to be a successful writer could take many different forms. Students, then, took up such valuing of different forms of literate texts in their own responses to peer work. When Maria, on his request, read Sam's story to the class from his assistive technological device, several students expressed their interest in giving him "compliments" even though his story was significantly shorter and sparser than the one that they had just heard from another student.

Real Reading as Linked to Real Outcomes. These teachers saw their work in the classroom as directly linked to the social and economic progress of the community in which they and their students were embedded. When asked what her greatest motivation for her teaching was, Anita responded, "The school-to-prison pipeline . . . this is real. This is serious." The "real" struggle in supporting students effectively was recognizing that young adults from the socioeconomic group represented within this school were mostly engaged in menial jobs. Literacy instruction for these 4th-graders had serious long-term consequences, and teachers' planning for it, therefore, was grounded in outcomes that would be enduring, community-oriented, and meaningful. This focus on students as future citizens meant that though they worried about students' display of skills on standardized tests, the teachers also sought to develop the students' understandings of diverse communities.

For instance, within their literacy program the selection of the book *Out of My Mind* (a novel by Sharon Draper about a student with significant communication disabilities struggling for acceptance and inclusion) was deliberately made to promote an inclusive classroom culture. One of the essential questions the teachers took up within their planning was "How and why are physical differences viewed differently from academic and language-based differences?" Other questions included: "What does it mean to be in an inclusion classroom?" "What does it mean to academically struggle?" The use of explicit instruction in making the process of reading and writing unambiguous, therefore, did not signal a watered-down approach to curriculum. As they prepared to explain meanings of *inclusion* to the students, the teachers discussed the analogies that would be most suitable for this particular group of students. Describing it eventually to the group as "when children of all abilities can participate," they facilitated a lively discussion that took up the different angles from which students approached the experience of disability as illustrated in the book they were reading. They used student understandings of the text to acknowledge that considering different perspectives may sometimes lead to confusion but also "expand what we mean by normal" (Anita).

Still, they were realistic enough to recognize that this one book could not be a game changer in terms of its effects on the students. However, they did see it as fostering a different way of understanding difference. "So, maybe [they] will leave this classroom thinking, 'Why don't I get to know a person first before I judge them?'" (Maria). When they grouped students in the classroom for book clubs, they drew on both ability levels and interests of students. As Anita rationalized, "I think it mimics what is in real life." They hoped students would develop an enjoyable relationship with books, recognizing that the ability to give sustained attention to a book and carry on a conversation about it with their friends was a valuable outcome for their students.

Eclecticism Grounded in Real Instructional Practice. Despite the potential risk of internal contradictions within an eclectic approach, researchers have increasingly emphasized the importance of adopting a flexible approach over theoretical orthodoxy, and have called for a "responsible eclecticism" (Jaruszewicz, 2005), a "principled eclecticism" (Lingard & Gale, 2010), and a "critical flexibility" (Yanchar & Gabbitas, 2011). Each of these ways of describing an eclectic approach calls for drawing on multiple methods and traditions, but more important, they all require teachers to critically examine the assumptions they bring to the teaching–learning process. When teachers reflect on the values and purposes behind their instruction, they are better able to ensure that their use of differing methodologies does not unwittingly bear contradictions. A "critical" eclecticism is premised on such reflection and can help maintain the internal consistency of one's practice. Yanchar and Gabbitas (2011) add that when practitioners continually clarify the conceptual premises and goals of their practice, the methods they use are themselves transformed so that they are not, as in this case, simply constructivist or explicit instructional methods. They have now acquired a new dimension that transcends those distinctions because it reflects the sense-making of the teacher/practitioner.

Thus Anita and Maria were able to resolve the competing aims of explicit and constructivist pedagogy by grounding their efforts in instruction that they conceived of as *real*. Their goals were specific: They were concerned for the long-term futures of these students and their communities; they wanted to introduce students to the range of human differences; and they hoped to inculcate positive relations with books. Collectively, this was their expressed rationale for their approach to literacy instruction that reflected a vision for both the short term and the long term. In other words, they employed a narrowed focus on the needs of the moment—increased skills in specific forms of literacy practices—alongside a more globalized understanding of the functional skills necessary for students to take up their roles as citizens of their communities. This kind of *dual vision* provided the foundation for recognizing why different methods were effective for their students at different times.

Other teachers may arrive at a different conception of literacy instruction that will enable them to craft a unique form of socially just pedagogy that draws on other traditions. The forms of practice that each one takes up will be informed by the particular schooling conditions within which they find themselves. For example, shared cultural backgrounds with both the families and other educators in their building, which enabled Anita and Maria to feel like insiders, stimulated them to take or avoid risks that teachers within other communities might or might not. In Anita's case, it allowed her to feel safe enough to say, "I don't have to second guess about how I'm going to phrase something or how it's going to be interpreted" when having conversations with families. Their embeddedness within this community made it reasonable and logical to draw on both explicit instruction and constructivist methodology to support long-term student growth.

Dialectical Engagement: Paul

Paul's engagement with mechanistic and constructivist forms of learning and pedagogy emerged in the context of his self-reported narratives of his instructional practice. A central theme within his stories was the coexistence of competing philosophies within his commitments to students and school. Even while working with a regimented reading program alongside a project-centered, inquiry-based mathematical curriculum, his approach was not to coerce them into some notion of harmony with each other. The scripted planning of the former certainly did not sit easily with him, but he remarked, "I don't have to reconcile them [the two different approaches] . . . . I mean, eventually I will, but I don't have to do that this year. I can just let it be, let it flow." He seemed to hold these competing pedagogical approaches separately, albeit within a coherent and stable whole. In doing so, he illustrated a continual movement between *local* and *global* factors, not dissimilar to the kind of dual vision that Anita and Maria seemed to display. This meant that, on the one hand, he could be fully immersed in issues of curriculum, mathematical pedagogical content knowledge, supportive relationships with students, assessments of student (dis)ability and competence, as well as opportunities for professional collaboration in his teaching—that is, the local practices that collectively established the conditions in which students learned. On the other hand, he could also draw on a more globalized awareness of the conditions of schooling that included the cultural context of mathematics education, the unforgiving requirements of high school graduation, the significance of scheduling, as well as the tenuous position of teachers in relation to tenure (the last, in particular, acquired through other significant professional roles assigned to Paul including special education liaison, data tracker for tenure decisionmaking, scheduler, and data analyst).

A Dual Vision in Discourse. If the dual vision of Anita and Maria was enacted through their pedagogy, Paul's dual vision was made evident in the ways he talked about his pedagogy, his students, and his school. Paul's movement through local and globalized understandings necessitated the adoption of positions and approaches that often represented conflicting views of learning and human development. Paul's prior experience as a corporate executive seemed to permit him to step outside his everyday pedagogical work to examine it from an administrative perspective and bring a more globalized view of schools. For instance, it prompted him to see that a special education grouping of 12 students to one teacher may have been successful ("we have kids from that program who are currently in college") but was simply not practical. It also left him with a clear recognition of his role as the "person in the middle" who had to manage those who ran the system ("whether it's Citibank, the Catholic church, or the education system"), while he delivered services to his "clients"—the students who came to school. This view of being "in the middle" seemed to reflect his instinctive awareness of the contradictions that characterized all aspects of human experience. Whether it was in describing the effects on his parents of his early career moves (they realized that that "their little hippie was becoming a corporate dude!") or in describing his colleagues as dedicated educators who constituted a certain kind of group ("it's like the best democrat and the best republican"), he seemed to be very much at home in acknowledging and using opposites in the same breath or idea.

Nowhere was this awareness of the contradictions in human experience more clearly reflected than in the language he used to describe students. Such language shifted between thoughtful analyses of student learning and teacher competencies to popular expressions that conveyed narrow, one-dimensional understandings. So, on the one hand, he might speak earnestly about students needing to feel safe and his responsibility to build a climate of trust, so that their learning could unfold and that even the "child with the 62 IQ" is "fully engaged, fully participates, and can contribute fully to his group." He insisted that he could never become one of the "bigwigs" in management and that he needed to "be there with the kids." He remained aware of the complex social histories of his former students in self-contained classrooms and was cynical about how much their performance really mattered to district officials. On the other hand, he would also simultaneously slip into descriptions of students as "ones and twos" or "kids in the slower section" or kids who needed to be "remediated" or the importance of matching pedagogy to type of disability. Each time he used such terms or descriptions, however, he simultaneously acknowledged that it was "politically incorrect" or "a confrontation against inclusion" or noted sarcastically, in the same breath "a nice way to describe kids, huh?"

Additionally, Paul's facility with using different types of languages to describe students meant that he could confidently wield a quantitative discourse when describing the effects of a building initiative, to say, "We are running 2.6, which means we are more than 260 percent over the projections in math performance." Yet, in the very same breath, he could emphasize that the "real impact" had been in the creation of a "safe" environment where "kids that struggle with math are not afraid to say, 'I don't know how to add fractions.'" He could speak to the importance of measurement and accountability yet also note that indicators of outcomes may be too narrowly defined. In pedagogical matters, he clearly recognized *tracking* as a "dirty word" even as he supported a flexible version of it to promote students' chances of success in the state-sponsored exams described in Chapter 2. Or, though he raved over the new inquiry-based curriculum, he recognized that its approach was still premised on proficiency in prerequisite skills ("When they come in and they can't count by ten, it's a little difficult") and so simultaneously sought more rote exercises to improve their mechanics in math understanding. His use of language to describe the complexities of the work he carried out was always informed by contradictory or oppositional perspectives.

His vision of math instruction was fueled by the desire to provoke deep engagement from students with the curriculum. This process entailed a dual focus on inquiry-based pedagogy and rote or mechanistic forms of learning that would permit students to experience greater success in their learning and raise their status within the student community. So, when Paul and his colleagues created the "flexible" tracking system, which would strengthen student skills while building their competence to take the state-sponsored examinations, he also recognized that teachers who had the "math gene" might not always be cognizant of the scaffolds needed by those who did not have an intuitive understanding of mathematics. It was therefore necessary within this modified tracking system, to implement an inquiry-based curriculum that could both deepen student engagement and foster mathematical thinking.

Speaking of math as a "caste system," he could then say without flinching at the inherent contradiction in his words that his practice "creates this really *safe* environment for these kids to be *remediated*" (italics added). Paul's use of *safe* suggests an interest in learner-centered notions of learning just as *remediated* simultaneously implies an externally driven focus on deficits within the students. This straddling of competing views of the learner might well have acquired a new dimension in the context of his actual practice in the classroom, as was the case with Anita and Maria. Just as their commitments to their students arose from a belief in real reading, Paul's management of competing perspectives on students and learning may have similarly transformed them into something new and equally complex (Yanchar & Gabbitas, 2011). In the absence of observational data on his classroom practice, I can only speculate that a different metaphor of practice might have emerged from his instructional decisionmaking that would then inform and define the trajectory of the just and equitable pedagogy that he pursued.

The Benefits of Dialectical Engagement. Paul's reflective posture that coupled critique of schooling systems with specific forms of action imbued his "stories of school" (Clandinin & Connelly, 1996) with a continuous sense of self-renewal. In other words, the straddling of competing philosophies seemed to stimulate him to take up creative forms of action that continued to feed his commitment to his students. He did not appear to experience any fragmentation or disillusionment as a result of this process. On the contrary, it provoked him to think more deeply about issues of inclusion where he could consider both the needs of students and that of teachers. So he might wonder whether inclusion could be best supported by having teachers whose professional preparation would correspond to all the different types of learning needs presented by students. Or, despite understanding the fundamental premise of inclusion, he might acknowledge, with some empathy, teachers' resistance to students who displayed challenging behaviors in the classroom. In either case, Paul's wonderings are not necessarily indicative of a faulty or misguided understanding of inclusion. Rather, they reflect one moment within Paul's unfinished process of negotiating the inevitable contradictions that emerge from the practical implementation of inclusive practices.

The notion of *dialectical engagement* is derived from negotiating two different historically mediated approaches, neither of which may be fully sufficient by itself to understand a particular phenomenon, in this case inclusion. A dialectical engagement draws on each of the oppositional positions and, through a systematic method of reasoning, accomplishes a synthesis that can then, as in this case, afford an understanding of schools that is generative. Paul's dialectical movement within his pedagogical practice was enabled throughout by his inquiry-driven approach as well as by his tacit commitment to marginalized students. It was via such engagement that Paul could take up new forms of practice, while preserving a continuity of self in the face of change and uncertainty. After all, he had little control over distant events such as district decisions to hold or not hold high school leaving examinations biannually. (Holding them biannually allowed students to assess their content-area learning without fear of penalty). His dialectical engagement allowed him, however, to take up new challenges within his pedagogy in the classroom and in collaborative work with his colleagues.

SECURING A PROFESSIONAL IDENTITY: WORKING WITHIN AND ACROSS GENERAL AND SPECIAL BOUNDARIES

Teachers' encounters with conflicting paradigms were not restricted only to the realm of instructional practice. The backdrop to teachers' instructional work was the complex story of professional identity making—what identity category should they claim? And do they have a choice? For instance, a dually certified teacher must specifically don the identity of a special educator if that is the role assigned to her. In their various administratively designated roles, teachers may grapple with specific ways of thinking about the parameters of those roles:

- What makes a special educator different from a general educator? Who decides?
- What overlaps, in any, exist within their roles? Who determines those overlaps?
- Can a special educator be an inclusive educator?
- Is a general educator automatically an inclusive educator?

This preoccupation with identity surfaced in a variety of places—in teachers' relationships with colleagues, administrators, students, and families; in the curricular decisions they made in the classroom; as well as in the opportunities they pursued for their own professional advancement and growth. Inevitably, their identity work invoked a movement across professional boundaries that seemed to implicate competing ways of viewing teaching and learning. In this section, I examine Stephanie's story to illustrate this movement within identity-making processes (Naraian, 2010a).

Figuring an Identity for an Inclusive Classroom

Holland, Lachiotte, Skinner, and Cain (1998) offer the construct of "figured worlds" that provide the contexts of meaning in which individuals come to understand themselves and to take up forms of action. Figured identities are derived from the rules imagined by actors—how individuals should engage with each other in the context of the activities that inform that world. As the descriptions in Chapters 1 and 2 suggest, Stephanie generally *figured* herself as an educator entrusted with the responsibility of creating a just world where student-citizens adopted multiple perspectives to develop the ideals of tolerance and respect. In practice, this meant that she tried to translate the notion of *difference* into a working concept of *community*. This goal might mean provoking students to consider how they might adjust their responses when working with different partners; enlisting support from students to modify an activity to allow greater participation of peers with physical disabilities; choosing deliberately to avoid the use of assistive technology if she felt it interfered with the development of authentic social relations among students; or openly resisting attempts of some parents to marginalize other families within this classroom community. In these and other ways, Stephanie demonstrated the seriousness with which she took the charge to create an equitable classroom. Her role as an educator mattered to her.

Her efforts to build and implement community took place within a collaborative teaching model that prescribed particular relations between general and special education. Within this relation, Stephanie (dually certified) was the assigned special educator. The classroom space, where she sought to implement a cohesive community, ironically came to serve as a contested ground where Stephanie struggled to craft the professional identity she sought. It stemmed to a large extent from the fact that her coteacher's general education background seemed to automatically afford her a permanent superior status. Stephanie noted:

> Jeanine [general education teacher] teaches all the curriculum except for one curriculum area that I've told her I loved and I would love to teach myself, which is writing. So I've been teaching writing all these years. But that's really the one area that I actually [plan] and feel like I can, in some ways, say, "We should do it this way."

She added with some resentment that Jeanine informed her at the beginning of the year that she wanted to take over "all the general ed pieces." Jeanine was delineating roles clearly in a way that positioned Stephanie as a "second-class citizen," someone who could offer support like a paraprofessional but could never take charge. Stephanie yearned to have a sense of ownership over all students and felt eminently capable and professionally qualified to do so, given that she was dually certified in both general and special education. However, the general assumption that accompanied taking on the role of the special educator was that "you are here for the IEP kids, and so you should be there focusing exclusively in some ways on the IEP kids."

Stephanie understood that such devaluing of her perceived professional affiliation was a systemic phenomenon that pervaded not just this building but the culture of educational practice in general. Stephanie commented on the unexpected effects of a special education license on the career prospects of dually certified teachers. Other educators, including administrators, seemed to automatically assume that a dually certified teacher would not seek anything other than a special education position. In Stephanie's view, the purpose and role of the special educator's presence in the collaborative team-taught classroom was unclear not only to families, but generally within the profession itself. This implied that the significance of dually certified professionals was even less visible or apparent to administrators, rendering inconsequential the collective worth of their preparation as teachers. She advocated strongly for dually certified teachers to be assertive in establishing their priorities and skills to administrative leaders. It was not surprising, in this regard, that Stephanie herself made an attempt with her administration to request an assignment as a general educator within a collaboratively taught classroom. Equally unsurprising, her request was denied.

Borrowing on Special Education Discourses for an Inclusive Identity

During the course of the school year, Stephanie's general education partner left on maternity leave, and Angie, another dually certified teacher (also functioning currently in the capacity of a special educator in the school), was brought in to constitute the team. Stephanie took over the lead role from this point, functioning for all intents and purposes as the general educator in the classroom. Following the pregiven district model meant that *a special educator* (who was *dually certified*) was now serving as a *general educator* and collaborating with a *special educator* (who also happened to be *dually certified*). The new roles and relations brought about by these changes had hugely empowering effects on Stephanie. While it certainly allowed her greater freedoms in curricular planning that she had been denied before, it also did so in the context of a genuine collaborative relationship with a special educator. Emboldened by the personal rapport that she could share with Angie, Stephanie took risks in prioritizing her own goals for the students rather than those of Jeanine's. Acknowledging that Angie's unfamiliarity with the classroom could have partially accounted for this, she nevertheless delighted in a collaborator's response to her ideas with a "why not?" instead of the resistance that she was used to encountering with her previous partner. More important, however, it was the shared professional background they brought as special educators that she seemed to have rediscovered and which allowed her to rethink how learning should take place within her transparent inclusive community (Naraian, 2011b).

This shared background meant that they could approach children's learning in similar ways. She described Angie and herself as "universal thinkers" whose goal was to have children become "master learners" by themselves and who did not see themselves as "information disseminators." In fact, even the very layout of the classroom could be reconsidered from this perspective. Stephanie pointed out: "My thing with making the room look nice has always been whatever we put up should be something that is absolutely useful to the kids. If they're not going to look up there and use it at any given point, I should not be putting it up there." It was not surprising that she commented that Jeanine would never have tolerated the way their classroom looked now.

The very language they used as two special educators reflected alternate goals for their students. Stephanie explained: "It's not so much the technical terms, but it's the understanding of why we need to do certain things in a certain way, and not just jump and say, 'Let's just teach them, let's move on.'" Instead, it was important for them to consider the "little progressions that kids need to make in order to get to a bigger concept" and not hesitate "to spend some time on the little details, to make sure that they can get to that big point." Stephanie's acknowledgement that this was a different way of thinking of curriculum, teaching, and how students learn points to the inherent difference between generalized and special education pedagogy. General educators typically adopt an approach that is driven by curriculum coverage for the whole group contrasting with the special education emphasis on individualized instruction (addressed in Chapter 2). Revisiting and strengthening her special education roots meant that she could legitimately focus on the learning and growth for all the students in her classroom and adjust the pace of the curriculum to suit these goals, regardless of the questions raised by the general educators on the grade-level team. Indeed, it appeared to have eventually raised her standing among these same educators, who admitted that she was becoming much more influential in planning for curricular progress. Drawing on a common purpose she shared with Angie, she could focus on "what they [the students] need versus what we [the teachers] need."

The sense of comaraderie that Stephanie experienced with Angie also meant that they were more likely to make space for reflection. Such reflective moments might occur at the end of the day or even during the course of the day as events unfolded. In either case, it sparked more opportunities for discussion, evaluation, and modification of instructional practice and assessments of student learning. As Stephanie used her renewed awareness of her special education roots as a resource to understand and address general education standards and priorities, she began to talk more about accountability and the documentation of student growth. This meant a reevaluation of her own priorities, the most significant one being her extraordinary emphasis on student social–emotional growth over academic learning. She wondered if practices such as role-playing or even her extensive scaffolding on interpersonal relations might actually have done her students a disservice. She commented that despite these efforts, students did not appear to have "internalized the kindness." She speculated that excessive adult mediation of student conflict may have produced the unintended consequence of student inability to solve problems independently as well as student indifference to academic learning as a primary goal of classroom life. Grateful that the opportunity to work with Angie had triggered this shift in priorities, Stephanie remarked that she was now more concerned about questions like: "Why is there a child who still cannot read words like 'cat'?" or "Should there be any children at that point in 1st grade?"

Stephanie believed that her changed practices actually served to make her teaching more transparent. She critiqued her own former "make-everybody-feel-good" approach that put a "blanket" over everybody as being equally "smart" and allowing this to take precedence over "empowering children to know who they are as learners." Instead, by slowing down the curriculum, breaking it down more, and affording learners devices such as rubrics to monitor themselves, she felt that students had come to derive greater ownership over their learning. Simultaneously, by not "micromanaging" their interpersonal growth, they could still be encouraged and trusted to become "reflective learners." So her original commitment to create "great citizens" still prevailed, but now she had discovered a better way to make that happen, by instilling "hope" while encouraging self-reflection.

THE AMBIGUITY AND MESSINESS OF INCLUSIVE INSTRUCTIONAL PRACTICE

Stephanie's identity work as much as Paul's initiatives, as well as the real reading instruction of Anita and Maria, collectively register an important facet of inclusive education—it can be "messy" in the contradictions it surfaces and the tensions it evokes. And it is precisely because such contradictions have to be addressed differently in different settings that it is also to a significant extent unpredictable. In working with and through these contradictions, these teachers were simultaneously engaged in an energized, creative practice that they clearly did not fully know how it might unfold. What can their experiences and their stories teach us about the concrete realities of making inclusive education happen?

All these educators were operating within in-between spaces where there was no clear formulaic way by which they could determine what steps they should take to maintain an inclusive orientation. Yet it was not the absence of a formula that they worried about. In other words, their musings on inclusion did not reflect a yearning for directions on what it *should* look like. On the contrary, their practice reflected inclusion as an unfinished process that they continually manipulated as they noticed and processed new information about student learning. In their hands, inclusion remained a dynamic, breathing, changing concept rather than an abstract, static idea that they were somehow trying to implement in reality. The "reality" of inclusion was their perceptions of student learning, their collaborations with colleagues, their interactions with families, and their engagement with administrators, all of which contributed to their understandings of how inclusion was happening in their classrooms.

Teachers were not uncomfortable with the ambiguous nature of these spaces. In fact, their ability to take up practices from multiple, competing traditions or work across boundaries reflected their unspoken recognition of the inevitability of such border-crossing work. The release from extreme categorical positions—behaviorist or constructivist, special or general—seemed to have offered a space within which teachers could find opportunities for creativity. Whether it was in the "flexible" tracking initiated by Paul in his school, or the "real" reading emphasis brought by Anita and Maria, or use of special education discourse to support Stephanie's "transparent" community, these teachers used the resources available to them to create unique pathways for student learning that could satisfy their goals for equity. Their stances were less likely to be polarized and more likely to be conciliatory, such that they seemed to at least recognize the perspectives of colleagues with whom they disagreed.

One might even argue that the space of their work in schools did not permit them to take up a polarized stance. For instance, the administrative pressure for accounting for student growth meant that Stephanie could not simply rely on a feel-good approach where "it doesn't matter if learning happens [laughs] as long as the kids are happy and they can advocate for themselves and they have a good set of learning skills going forward in life." Inasmuch as she still held these goals to be important, administrative priorities facilitated by a rediscovery of special education emphases helped her adjust her vision for their learning that *she came to uphold on her own*—it was not something she felt coerced into taking up. For Paul, too, the requirement to use a regimented, explicitly structured reading program with individual students became an opportunity to understand the benefits this provided his students, even as he simultaneously invested his energies wholeheartedly in developing inquiry-based activities that would allow an entry way for students with a range of learning differences. For Anita and Maria, given their location within the linguistic and cultural community of their students, distinctions between competing traditions were barely visible; their holistic long-term approach to their students entailed a creative response that could satisfy both immediate academic goals and their vision for their students' futures.

Yet, naturalized as their practices may have been, the reconciliation of competing ways of thinking is not realized without some danger. It is harder to remain vigilant to questions such as "inclusion into what?" and "different from whom?" (Graham & Slee, 2008) when attempting to respond creatively to situations and pressures that are presented as high-stakes matters. Indeed, such questions seemed quite remote in relation to more immediate demands of documenting student growth for accountability, successful completion of high-stakes examinations, or collaborative teaching dilemmas. Inclusion as situated in the midst of these competing claims might easily deflect attention from the norms of ability that inform practices. For instance, Stephanie clearly upheld a notion of ability as fluid rather than fixed; yet her struggle for ownership of the general education curriculum left her less reflective of how norms of ability still informed her efforts to create a transparent community. Had she reflected on this element, she might then have been able to recognize how both general and special education procedures produced student failure. How might this affect her relations with future coteachers? (At the end of the study, I learned that she and Jeanine would no longer be coteaching in the same classroom.) As she continued to blur professional roles, could an additional focus on ability-based practice afford her new ways of negotiating relations with her colleagues?

The instructional practice of Anita and Maria, too, did not always sit easily with the aims of a critical pedagogy. The texts they used in their literacy instruction, for instance, rarely, if ever, addressed the marginalized histories of the student community and/or the political context of their lives. The teachers also admitted they would not introduce curricular texts that they perceived would be controversial within this "conservative" family community. In some ways, it seemed that their role as "cultural insiders" appeared to have left them *less* able to take certain risks in their educational decision-making. On the one hand, they were committed to securing a placement for their student with disabilities (Sam) that would be most responsive to him as a learner. On the other hand, they were unwilling to jeopardize their position within this school community to push the administration to sponsor placement decisions that were in Sam's best interests. The creative agency illustrated elsewhere in their pedagogic practice was not matched by the advocacy required to confront an administration that was otherwise deeply hospitable to their needs.

As for Paul, even as he remained committed to the successful participation of students with disabilities and deeply conscious of the inequitable premise of tracking, his concern for the pragmatic work of inclusion left him grappling with "includability" of some students. It may be possible to teach *some* abilities in the general education classroom, but teach them *all*? To put it differently, he, like many other educators, was still locked into a notion of *inclusion* as *place*. The call to attend inclusively to disability and, by extension, disrupt norms of ability, seemed to immediately conjure up the *place* where that was supposed to happen, namely, the general education classroom. Indeed, the stubborn linkage between *ability norms* and *place* seemed to have a dual effect; it made it difficult to work against the former while solidifying the latter as a necessary concept in inclusion. In other words, as long as educators considered *inclusion* to mean placement in the general education classroom, it was difficult to identify and break down norms of ability.

Ultimately, the use of competing traditions by itself, while appearing to be necessitated by the everyday conditions of schooling, may not, counterintuitively, have significant consequences for the *inclusive* status of the pedagogic work of teachers. The combined use of both constructivist and mechanistic forms of learning does not detract from the inclusive nature of the pedagogy. Rather, as we learned from the experiences and stories of these teachers, decisions about the use of competing traditions were motivated in part by their commitments to students' learning and their futures. They also seemed necessitated by the complex conditions within schools. Such work, then, may be considered a part of the professional toolkit of teachers in their quest for enacting an equity pedagogy in the classroom. As practice that is grounded in the material realities of schools, it simultaneously offers a creative site of opportunity for teachers to accomplish forms of inclusive schooling.

CHAPTER 4

Interpreting for Accessibility and Inclusion

As increasing numbers of students with disabilities receive their education with their nondisabled peers in inclusive settings, the issue of *access* has surfaced as an important refrain within efforts to increase their participation in schools and classrooms (Thousand, Villa & Nevin, 2007). All educational activity, special or general, is fundamentally about access (Titchkosky, 2011). All learners need to be able to access the many different experiences offered within schools in order to develop the skills and knowledges that will produced desired educational outcomes. Yet societal response to the phenomenon of disability has made the issue of access visible in a somewhat narrowed way. The question that is typically placed under consideration is this: Is this event or location accessible? The tacit assumption is that such events and locations should contain certain elements that will grant specific groups of individuals (mainly with physical or sensory disabilities) access to the information that is otherwise readily available to those without such disabilities.

As Titchkosky (2011) observed, the very notion of *access*, as it has come to be used, implies that environments are not designed with all individuals in mind. Similarly, access for students with disabilities typically refers to accommodations that are made so that they can participate in the same experiences as their nondisabled peers. Professionals and families may ask, do these students have access *to* the general education curriculum? Yet this notion of access deflects attention from the nature of the general education curriculum itself and *for whom* it has implicitly been designed. In other words, who counts as a student?

Legislative efforts to recognize the diversity within student populations and to hold schools accountable for providing appropriate education rely on notions of access. As the goals of achieving *equality of access* to education (which was the primary intent of PL 94–142, Education for All Handicapped Children Act, 1975) have shifted to ensuring *equal outcomes* for all students (Yell, 2012), meanings of *access* have come to be more securely situated within classroom practices that can support increased participation of students with disabilities. Lave and Wenger (1991) describe *learning* as changing participation in changing communities of practice. In other words, any assessment of students' learning must consider opportunities for participation made available to them within multiple contexts of schooling. This means that we require a notion of access that can accommodate students' participation in the wide-ranging physical, intellectual, and social life of their educational communities (Jaeger, 2012; Naraian & Surabian, 2014). This chapter attempts to broaden our notions of access beyond the delivery of curricular materials and experiences, that is, *physical* access (Jaeger, 2012). While not minimizing the importance of such material accommodations to the learning of students with disabilities, I will look more closely at other instructional processes that may be equally necessary for access to full participation for all students.

The linkage between access and participation also implicates notions of *voice*. In other words, an equitable pedagogy that provides access must stimulate structures of participation whereby student voices can emerge in meaningful ways. This idea is rooted within the foundations of inclusive education, which seeks the empowerment of historically marginalized groups, including students with disabilities and their families, whose voices have been largely obscured. A pedagogical approach that sought to foster student voices might include specific instructional practices such as differentiated instruction, an emphasis on collaborative learning, inquiry-based experiences, and other forms of universally designed planning (Valle & Connor, 2011). Many teachers across my research sites attempted to implement various forms of these practices in their efforts toward inclusion.

TEACHERS AS INTERPRETERS AND FACILITATORS OF STORIES TO PROMOTE INCLUSION

One component of teacher practice that emerged as critical to the project of inclusion was the *deliberate and systematic interpretation of student actions to peer groups*. Teachers I studied sought to directly influence their students' understandings of difference through verbal mediation. Analyzing the purposes of such interpretive activity and its effects on students and their peers offered additional ways to think about access. Teachers' interpretive work, particularly with students with complex and/or significant disabilities, made strongly visible the linkages between *accessibility, identity/voice,* and *participation*.

The Relationship Between Teacher Talk and Student Identity

> I find that the more I talk about how I process my learning or how I process situations, I think it gives them the language, and a little bit of connection to me as a learner, and then they are able to better understand themselves, and then hopefully one day to start to express a little bit.
>
> —Stephanie

Why is teacher interpretive discourse significant? Whom does it serve? How? We should begin by first acknowledging the ubiquity of teacher talk. Teachers are almost continually *directing, explaining, questioning, answering, suggesting, agreeing, requesting, persuading, inquiring, commenting,* and *solving*—almost all of which requires some form of verbal engagement with students. Mercer (2002) suggests that it is primarily through talk that teachers create a shared understanding, "a continuing, contextualizing framework for joint activity" (p. 143), that enables them to assist students to reach higher levels of development. Such talk inevitably comes to play a significant role in the development of student identities within the classroom. Indeed, researchers have investigated teacher talk to reveal the many and diverse ways that student identities are mediated during routine events in the classroom (Cazden, 2001). Through their talk, teachers generate "models of identity" that are taken up by students in different ways and that position them variously within the student community (Wortham, 2006).

The identities of students with disabilities are equally mediated by such teacher talk. P. M. Ferguson (2003) even argues that the identities of individuals with intellectual disabilities are *contingent* upon the narratives disseminated by others around them. In other words, the ways others interpret their actions enable individuals with disabilities to participate in different ways. The histories of many individuals with autism reveal that when others interpreted their actions as meaningful and valuable, they were able to disclose the breadth of their capacities (Biklen, 2005). When others understood their actions as deviant or meaningless, they were stifled, sometimes for many years, unable to reveal themselves in authentic ways. Interpretive activity in the classroom has important consequences for all students, including students with disabilities who have little control over how they can represent themselves to others. Since teachers clearly have control over the nature and type of talk in the classroom, it follows that students' ability to disclose themselves—that is, their *voice*—is inevitably entangled with teachers' interpretations of their actions.

The intertwining of student identities with contextual factors such as teacher talk and participation structures has strong theoretical roots. Identities are always culturally and socially situated and mediated by relations of power (Gee, 2000–2001; Holland, Lachiotte, Skinner, & Cain, 1998). Drawing on Bakhtin, who asserted that a single utterance always implies multiple authors (Holquist, 2000), such conceptions of identity imply that voice does not reside within a person but emerges at the interface of the personal and the social. Additionally, a single utterance always implicates many other voices of speakers, near or distant. When peer students respond to the loud vocalizations of a nonverbal student with a "Shhhh!" and a finger on their lips, they are voicing themselves *and* adults in that setting (and beyond) who have typically responded to student disturbances in a similar manner.

This notion of *voice* as plural and socially situated has important implications for inclusive classrooms. First, it suggests that a student's identity development (i.e., the emergence of voice) is never separate from the ideas, beliefs, and resources that circulate within that classroom. The same student may display different levels and intensities of learning in different classroom settings. Second, it implies that a student's identity formation occurs through relations with peers, teachers, and other members of the classroom community. Third, the notion of voice as plural and changing—voicing—emphasizes the *process* of self-expression rather than some static, abstract concept. Students' identities (and by extent, their participation) are continually evolving as they perform within different sociocultural contexts. Collectively, these implications urge teachers to focus not only on what students are saying, but where they are saying it, with whom, when (i.e., what they are doing), and what they are *not* saying.

The Significance of Teacher Talk for Peer Understandings of Disability

As suggested above, peers add a critical dimension to the task of achieving accessibility and inclusion. Across my research sites, the ways in which students, particularly with significant disabilities, came to reveal their growth and learning was always linked to the ways in which peers in the classroom understood and/or related to them. In other words, peer learning, and by extension peer identity development within the classroom context, was crucial for students with significant disabilities to emerge as capable, agentive, and worthy of membership in the community. For instance, in Jessica's classroom, peers would frequently raise Harry's hand during a group activity and state, "Harry wants to say something," even if Harry, who did not have a reliable means of communication, had not indicated in any way that this was true. Still, with Jessica's willing participation in allowing the student to speak for Harry, the student would then proceed to state an idea, albeit in a false, high-pitched voice as though ventriloquizing for Harry. Jessica and Harry's peers were collectively imagining Harry's response to the event at hand to sustain his status as a member of the classroom. Other peers, like Andrea, might stop by his chair during a class writing exercise and muse aloud, "Harry, how do you spell *name*?" without seeming to expect an immediate response from him. As the descriptions in subsequent pages will show, the teacher's interpretive work in this classroom fostered a climate in which students could make comments such as these that represented their disabled peer as a capable member of their classroom. This in turn allowed Harry to engage with his peers in continually expanding ways. Whether seeking physical contact with a specific classmate or using his augmentative device appropriately during a planned choral recitation, Harry benefited from peer interpretations of him to then express or *voice* himself.

The scaffolding of such peer interpretations/narratives of disability by teachers revealed itself as a critical component of classroom practice. As the studies showed, teachers accomplished such scaffolding in different ways and with different results. The following episode illustrates one teacher's interpretive work:

> Jessica had just gone up to the board and begun talking about upcoming activities in the classroom. All of a sudden, a tall boy ran into the room giggling loudly. He went straight to the corner of the room where the books were located and picked out a book randomly, still laughing. He was pursued into the room by a tall, heavyset man who strode purposefully toward him and proceeded to take him firmly by the arm. Jessica, who had first appeared startled, recovered herself to say calmly and politely, "Hi," and the man responded with equal equanimity, "Good morning, Mrs. Hilton." He quietly asked the boy to return the book he had taken and then led him firmly from the room. None of the students in the classroom had reacted with more than a glance at the boy. It had all happened very quickly, and Jessica had been careful not to express any exaggerated reaction. When they had left, the students simply turned to look toward Jessica and waited for her to resume speaking. She looked approvingly at the group, and her first response was to make an announcement that she was going to give the class a Shining Star (a schoolwide incentive program) "for being so good and so focused on what we were doing." As she seated herself again in her rocking chair after the uninvited visitors had left the room, Mark asked her who that boy was. "That's Adam," said Jessica. "I know that he has a brother just like him. Adam has something that is called autism. Autism is when your mind does not work the same way that ours does." She now began to probe the students on their reactions to Adam.
>
> *Jessica:* What do you think he was doing? [No response from the class].
> *Jessica:* Do you think he was in control of his body?
> *Class* [in unison]: No.
> *Jessica* [nodding]: Just like we are not sometimes, right?

Class: Yeah.
[Melissa has her hand raised by this time].
Jessica: Yes, Melissa.
Melissa [haltingly]: My neighbor is a boy who has autism.
Jessica: What is his name?
Melissa: John.
Jessica: And do you play with him?
Melissa: Yes.
Jessica: And is he cool?
Melissa: [nodding her head].

The discussion clearly ended, Jessica returned to the assignment of various jobs for the week.

Jessica was clearly committed to framing disability as a part of everyday life in school. She expected students to accept this implicitly; there was a certain finality to the interpretation she offered to Melissa about her experience. The message, then, was sent clearly and uncompromisingly to both Melissa and the rest of the class: *It didn't matter that Adam was different. His difference, however incomprehensible it might appear to be at first glance, was really not disconnected from our own everyday experience. And so, his difference was to be unquestioningly accepted under the rules of living as a family.* By articulating an important belief system within this classroom community, Jessica's interpretive work created the conditions that could allow easy relations between students with and without disabilities. Students were being socialized into accepting difference in the classroom.

However, Jessica also relied on a transmission model of learning that was less likely to encourage collaborative inquiry into the event. There was insufficient opportunity for dialogue that could stimulate students to wonder about the relation between Adam's disability and other forms of differences in school. If Jessica had encouraged dialogue, students might have asked: Why wasn't Adam in a classroom at that time like everybody else? Where did he learn in the school building, and why? Why was there an adult with him in school, but not with Melissa (a student with physical disabilities)? What if he didn't want an adult with him all the time? In other words, the interpretive work carried out by Jessica to create new stories about disability had to simultaneously recognize *peer* students as learners, who needed tools to make sense of the forms of disability they encountered. Even if Jessica might have felt compelled to move ahead quickly after the interruption, what might make her scaffolding of peer students more effective? In the following pages, we will come to understand why this would be important for the project of achieving greater accessibility.

The Practice of Interpretation: Drawing on Narrative Roots

If interpretation should be understood as an intentional form of practice, there may be some principles that teachers can consciously apply when using it. When we turn to its theoretical roots, we can identify some tenets that can guide the interpretive work of teachers. In its reliance on explanations of actors-in-context, teachers' interpretations may be considered a form of *narrativizing*. Each time we offer an explanation to ourselves and others about the individuals or events we encounter in our daily lives, we are engaging in a form of narrativizing. We continually plot events and characters in narrative form as an intrinsic part of our everyday lives though we are hardly aware of the process. These stories imbue our daily realities with meanings that are uniquely constructed by us. Each of us creates and narrates our own stories drawn from other stories that we receive.

Narrative is not premised on reflecting the "truth" of an event. Instead, it is the *plausibility* of an explanation rather than its correspondence with some aboriginal truth that confers credibility to that explanation. The purpose of narrative is to be "trafficking in human possibilities rather than in settled certainties" (Bruner, 1986, p. 26). Narrative invests all its characters with agency; they are all actors with intentions and goals, and must be perceived as such. This is especially significant for many students with disabilities, particularly those whose communicative efforts—that is, their *voicings*—do not occur in standard ways, whose actions are routinely "explained" in the literature, but whose self-stories are just as routinely ignored. Additionally, narrative does not rely on an all-knowing omniscient narrator; the very element of tentativeness rather than certainty that lies at the heart of narrative acknowledges the multiple perspectives that are generated by different prisms, each of which captures a part of a reality.

Interpretive work in the classroom can accomplish such narrativizing. In order to do so, the stories (explanations) offered by teachers to explain an action or event should possess three qualities:

1. The actor(s) described in the story is a conscious, reflective, thinking being with goals and purposes.
2. The story draws on a very specific (often shared) sociocultural context in which the action takes place such that listeners can receive it as a plausible explanation.
3. Instead of authoritative statements, the explanations/stories are deliberatively tentative, allowing for the possibility of multiple perspectives.

Collectively, these qualities of narrative give credence and guidance to the interpretive work of teachers in the classroom to support the emergence of alternate understandings of disability and learning.

The potential of interpretations to have the desired impact ultimately rests on how they are received and who receives them. In other words, the manner in which these stories are told will impact how they are retold; that is, the new stories that emerge. In these classrooms, the telling/delivery of interpretations within routine conversations deliberately enlisted students to view differences in their classroom in specific ways. Frank (2010) notes that stories can work "to make characters available as generalizable resources that listeners use to engage in work on their own character" (p. 30). Each interpretation of student action to the group offered the narrative resources by which students could generate other narratives about themselves in relation to their peers, disabled or nondisabled.

For instance, Mark, one of Harry's peers, was observed within Jessica's classroom to move through a process of self-understanding during the course of the school year. Early in the year, his teachers reported that Mark made remarks along the lines of: "But Harry will not be able to ever do that . . . ." or "How come Harry gets to use these and we don't?" or "I don't think he really understands this . . . ." Mark's remarks differed from the others in that they appeared to question the premise that Harry should be accepted as just another student in the classroom. Yet, after a few months, the adults in the room reported that his interactions with Harry had grown more "positive." He was observed to be a consistent member of the group of boys who would receive Harry every morning at school. When the group gathered before Thanksgiving to express appreciative thoughts about each other, Mark was heard to corroborate another student's description of Harry as "special" by saying, "Yeah, so what if he can't respond. He can still laugh." Mark's evolving understanding took place in the context of the narratives of learning differences that were made available within this classroom. This continual spread and infusion of stories within other stories is a reminder that students (like all individuals) not only think *about* stories but *with* stories (Frank, 2010).

Teachers' interpretive activity therefore becomes crucial to the project of generating new narratives about disability, learning, and schools, and in that regard remains a political endeavor. For instance, in Jessica's class, students' ways of describing disability were largely idiosyncratic, in that they were based on their personal experiences. So it was not uncommon for a student to describe a disabled person as "he is not like us," or as Andrea described Alice (a student with Down Syndrome), "she is like Harry, but she can walk and she can talk." They were utilizing their own bodies as a point of reference to understand something that they perceived as unfamiliar. In their interpretive efforts, teachers in the classroom never used the term *disabled*. Yet the power relations implicit in the term *disability*—the meaning of the word implicates relations between people in a community—can offer a rich forum for engaging in dialogue about how differences arise and the ways they impact the lives of all members in that community.

ACHIEVING ACCESS THROUGH INTERPRETATION: HOW TEACHERS PUT STORIES TO WORK

Both Jessica and Stephanie consciously sought to mediate student understandings of disability within their 1st-grade classrooms. They accomplished this through a range of instructional arrangements that included creating routine opportunities for students to help each other, use of literature to inculcate values of tolerance and respect for difference, collaborative learning experiences, and classroom celebratory events that welcomed adults, families, and even students from other classes. However, the facet of their teaching that remained integral to their expressed desires to create a community of diverse learners lay in the ways they linguistically mediated student understandings of difference. A careful analysis of the teachers' conscious work in this area disclosed that each teacher's interpretive work was interconnected with their unique implementations of community. Stephanie's efforts to represent students were intended to normalize student actions in a way that could foster the transparent community that she sought. Jessica too drew on a similar commonsensical notion of personhood as a means of strengthening the family ethos of her classroom where differences were accepted. Peers with disabilities, these teachers seemed to say, were, first and foremost, persons just like their nondisabled classmates.

Descriptors such as *person with disabilities*, which are widely accepted today, seek to establish an individual as a person *first* before being recognized as a *disabled* person. Scholars have critiqued such explanations; they argue that *subtracting* disability from the individual in order for him or her to be recognized devalues the experience of disability (e.g., Michalko, 2002; Siebers, 2008). Still, the notion of personhood seemed to have served as a ready resource to support the inclusionary efforts of educators like Jessica and Stephanie. Additionally, it was evident that for both teachers, such efforts were strongly linked with the behavioral norms that they used when implementing their inclusive communities. This reliance on behavioral norms, as we will see, often complicated their interpretive work in securing greater peer understanding of disability.

Normalizing Difference for a Transparent Community: Stephanie

The larger narrative that directed Stephanie's interpretive efforts in the classroom was an imagined transparent community where student voicings could happen with ease (Naraian, 2011b). She was committed to creating an environment where students felt safe to engage in authentic self-expression. Not surprisingly, along with her coteacher, she not only sought to build awareness of learning differences among peers but also invited and modeled strategies to engage with such differences when they surfaced during collaborative learning activities. She worked actively to ensure that students in this classroom did not come to regard any of their peers with visible disabilities in ways that might set them obviously apart from the classroom community. She also engaged students in critical conversations around social conflict with their peers to help them develop empathy and thereby create an emotionally safe space for her students. This meant that an important priority was representing students to each other in ways that could sustain their status as valued and important members of this community.

Stephanie's linguistic mediation to accomplish this goal was integral to her routine practice in this classroom. So, for example, as she waited for the class to get ready for an activity, she might announce the *number* of students who did not appear ready to begin work but she would never call out their names. When she asked Jolene to sit aside as the rest of the group was lining up for recess, Stephanie assured the group that Jolene was "not in trouble." When students declined without reason to participate in the morning greeting, she accommodated the vagaries of their moods by accepting their responses and offering a normalizing explanation to the group about their silences, while simultaneously suggesting other ways they could still participate.

Representation as Interpretation of Difference. Stephanie's representation of Trevor, a student with multiple disabilities who did not use standard forms of communication, occurred in the context of her goals for such a transparent community. Not only was he expected to be part of classroom routines and activities, she also actively scaffolded the process of his participation. In her interactions with him, she modeled an acknowledgement of the valued role he played in this community. She always waited to hear his response to her question before moving on to the next person. Whatever the form of morning greeting, whether a song performed with vigorous actions or a simple rhyme, his participation was always expected and coordinated with other adults in the classroom.

Stephanie was also observed on several occasions offering interpretations to the group about Trevor's nonverbal responses. For instance, when his aide, Felipe, was coaching Trevor softly about his "share" for the day, Stephanie normalized this activity by reminding the group "you know when you really want to share something and then you forget it?" On another occasion, when Trevor burst inexplicably into uncontrollable tears at the end of a storytelling session, Stephanie normalized this response by reminding the group that "sometimes our emotions get the better of us." Making obvious the multiple ways in which people engaged with a variety of experiences was important in Stephanie's view not only to help peers relate to Trevor but also to help them understand themselves as learners.

Trevor's representation by Stephanie as a student engaged in curricular tasks reinforced the goals of the community in this classroom. Through the creation of a "responsive literate context" (Kliewer & Biklen, 2007), she earnestly sought to establish the connectedness of Trevor within this classroom. She facilitated an academic "model of identity" (Wortham, 2006) for him, requiring him to participate in routine classroom academic activities. Not surprisingly, students took their cues from her moves. The following event during a lesson on writing strategies offers a glimpse of how her representation of Trevor as a "typical" student came to be taken up by a peer student.

> Trevor was positioned directly opposite Stephanie so she could display the book more closely to him even as she addressed the whole group. After highlighting strategies like the use of ellipses, she paused on the page where the words *crunch munch* were written. She asked the group to "turn and talk" about that page. It seemed an impromptu move, possibly more as a way for Stephanie to concentrate briefly on Trevor. She turned in her chair and began to interact closely with Trevor. After a few minutes, marking the end of the turn-and-talk, she turned back to the group and said, "Trevor really likes the word *crunch*." As the other students talked about the book and the words, Marianna volunteered, "Like Trevor, I like the word *crunch*."

The desire for a transparent community that stimulated Stephanie's deliberate efforts to represent students to each other in careful ways meant that she was not always supportive of the efforts of other adults, such as families and administrators, to represent students with disabilities in ways that she perceived as dishonest. For instance, she disagreed with descriptions of the large sled, which would transport Trevor in his wheelchair on the ice, as "Trevor's skates." She expressed the same disapproval of the administration's representation of his computer-based augmentative device as "his pencil." She was concerned that when Trevor's abilities were misrepresented, it did not convince other students because "in a child's mind that's not true, that's not the honest thing." She explained further:

> Sometimes I think we are just trying to make everything sound so nice and make the general ed kids feel comfortable . . . which is okay in the beginning. But I think it's also okay to be a little bit honest and just say, well, you know, Trevor could technically write with a regular pencil, like you and me, but it's just very hard to read. It's very hard for Rafael to write with a regular pencil. That's why he tries using a computer and that's why even people who are bad spellers do that. I think it's okay to say things like that.

Representing student difference did not require a pretense narrative that paid scant respect to peer students' abilities to understand complex experiences. It did not align with the kind of transparency that Stephanie sought in the creation of her classroom community.

Upholding Norms of Care Within Interpretive Practices. Stephanie's interpretive work in this classroom community inevitably drew on the classroom rules that were central to the everyday regulation of student actions. The rules, posted clearly on a classroom wall, documented five cardinal principles by which students were to regulate their actions in the classroom:

1. Take care of yourself.
2. Take care of others.
3. Take care of the environment.
4. Be safe.
5. Do your best work.

Individual and group accountability was assessed on the basis of these rules, especially the first two. It was not uncommon therefore for Stephanie to invoke the "rules" of care as she publicly interpreted the activities of the students in the group. For example, Stephanie might point out to the group that "Maria was taking care of herself" and others by waiting quietly and patiently in line as the class readied itself for recess, or that a student "took care of others" by not calling out of turn. On the same count, she would also point out that the art teacher took care of them by giving them extra time when they needed it, and that as a group they needed to take care of *him* by making sure they arrived at his art class on time. As she held all students accountable to these rules, students with disabilities were not shielded from its effects. For instance, once, when Trevor was positioned on the stander (a positioning device to support students with physical disabilities), he seemed to perhaps intentionally drop a wipe placed on his table to the floor. After this had happened a few times, Stephanie, more convinced with each passing moment that these were intentional acts, brought her face close to him and instructed him that if it happened again, he would have to bend down and pick it up himself since it was the rule in the classroom to "take care of your environment."

Stephanie also did not hesitate to represent herself in a way that could serve the interest of a transparent community. While going over the rules in class, Stephanie noted that she might mistakenly ask a student to "get up and return when ready." [This was a directive given when students were clearly distracted or unable to focus on the group task. It signified that the student should get up, walk around the room, and return to the group, the expectation being that this physical interlude might serve to break the course of inattentive behavior.] She added: "Even if I make a mistake—and I am going to make mistakes—there are days when I am going to pick on people because I am not perfect." Her suggestion was that the student should let her know, because "that gives me a chance to apologize to you, because I want to." Stephanie's interpretation of her own actions, however inattentive it might be to issues of power between teachers and students, may still be understood in relation to her overall desire to achieve a transparent community and to help her students "get into my head." In representing herself as she did above, she sought to apply to herself the norms to which she was holding students accountable, at least as much as the inherently unequal relationship could permit; she could at least apologize.

Accepting Difference to Sustain a Family: Jessica

Jessica's defining practice was her unambiguous commitment to the creation of a "family" within the classroom. Recognizing that social growth and academic learning were deeply linked, she insisted on a code of behavior that aligned with this goal, allowing little room for violations of any kind. A fundamental premise of Jessica's family narrative was the notion of "*we are the same, we are different*"; that is, "despite our differences, we are really all the same." It was not surprising that through deliberate interpretive work, she socialized peer students in this classroom into understanding Harry as first and foremost a person and a student, just like them. An effective backdrop for her efforts within the classroom were schoolwide practices that embraced the notion of positive behavioral supports and an emphasis on building relations with the larger community of families.

Tools for Acceptance. Helping students become comfortable with the idea of difference and encouraging its acceptance as part of a family-like environment were Jessica's principal aims for her students. For instance, she might read the book *Moses Goes to a Concert* (by Isaac Millman) to introduce deafness as a form of difference. Then, after sharing a story about her own father, who could lip read, but who was deaf and did not know sign language, she encouraged students to share their various experiences with deaf friends and family. As illustrated by the previously described incident with Adam, the boy with autism, the purpose of these "tellings" was not necessarily to help students understand the nature of such difference, but to accept its presence within a family. Consequently, while students might identify the deaf individuals in their families, Jessica was less likely to facilitate a discussion during these moments that built on student questions about deafness and, implicitly, normalcy.

Instead, accepting such differences within this family narrative meant recognizing that different people had different needs. Jessica did not hesitate to have conversations with her group of students to promote greater understanding and respect for the specialized tools or behavioral supports that some students may require. These efforts to interpret or explain Harry were often framed around a "how would you feel if . . . " type of question, which sought to connect the commonplace experiences of the students with the uncommon routines of those who appeared to be different. In other words, despite the external visible trappings of difference, she sought to emphasize the inner commonality of childhood that could bind them together, as illustrated earlier in her response when Melissa volunteered that her neighbor was a boy with autism.

Jessica's approach to student nonnormative behaviors inevitably drew on her own experiences with them when she was in school. Recalling her fear when she had encountered a classmate with cerebral palsy, she remarked: "We looked at him like, 'what is he doing?' There was no understanding of . . . that he learns too." In the absence of a conscious mediation of that experience, the connection to him as a student like everyone else had remained obscured to her and her peers. It was not surprising, therefore, that for her own students, Jessica sought to provide them with the linguistic and intellectual tools that could empower them when faced with actions from their peers that seemed incomprehensible or out of the norm. She noted:

> I think kids at this age are so accepting anyways naturally that to give them some background on why it was happening made them more understanding and made them kinda want to help. You know, "I know you are angry. Why don't you go to the safe place?" So, teaching them the kind of language they can use, so that they feel more in control of the situation. I think it helped settle everything out, and bring us together.

Inclusion and the promotion of inclusive communities required that peers be empowered to respond to difference in respectful ways.

Jessica accomplished her commitment to create an emotionally secure space in part through literature. She did not hesitate to draw on such literature to communicate norms of behavior for the classroom that required acceptance of differences among people. She described a particular student, James, who avoided any kind of contact with Melissa, a peer with disabilities, and would not touch her or sit next to her. When, on one occasion, he refused to extend her the customary greeting required of all students, Jessica deliberately set out to reorient him and assimilate him back into the norms she had set for the classroom. She reported:

> So later in the day, I read a book called *You Are Special* by Max Lucado. . . . Basically, the moral of the story is that if others say mean things it's like giving a gray dot, but if you don't listen then it can fall off . . . the gray dots are the negative things. So, during choice time, I pulled him over and I tried to explain it in that framework, "What do you think you did to her [Melissa] this morning? Was that a gray dot or a gold star?" So he said, "Oh, I think it was a gray dot," and he had questions about her and cerebral palsy and didn't understand what it was. I think he actually thought it was something he could catch. And so we had this big discussion, just the two of us, about how it's from birth. So,

once we talked about that, he came in the next day and started helping her do stuff. It was so exciting.

Her description of her own meditational work with this student was telling: "So later that day, I really crushed it. I made him . . . He didn't have to touch her, but at least go up and look her in the face and say, 'Good morning, Melissa.'" James's violation of the code of acceptance was not going to be dismissed without an explanation. As one of the students in the classroom, Melissa deserved the same respect as everyone else, which he had initially denied her. Jessica's interpretive work in this instance not only sought to give voice to Melissa's experience, it vigorously sought to communicate to James the inappropriateness of his response. This then eventually led to a more dialogic moment where James could express the doubts that he had about her condition and that underlay his apparent rejection of Melissa.

Jessica's commitment to deliver an interpretation of Harry as a student of equal standing within the classroom was also made visible in her own interactions with him. She greeted him spontaneously and unfailingly in the room. She incorporated him into the conversation as an agentive member: "I think Harry spelled that word correctly" (when he was with a partner), or "Let's give Harry a hand," or "Harry is not here with us today." Or she might use his name in an example that she wrote on the white board. She reminded students when their actions, however well intentioned, infantilized him or did not adequately respect him as a person. Indeed, her own statements, such as the ones above, sought to establish his equal standing in the classroom and may have allowed peers to take risks in their own interpretive work with Harry. There were numerous occasions when peers partnering with Harry might lift his hand and say something like "Harry thinks that . . . "

The Role of Norms in the Family Story: Not unlike in Stephanie's classroom, this willing, even determined, embrace of differences within Jessica's "family" community remained intertwined with a normative framework that interpreted some actions or behaviors as more desirable than others. In the episode described earlier when Adam, the boy with autism, ran into the room, Jessica enforced the norms of appropriate school behavior as she unhesitatingly rewarded the class with a Shining Star immediately after he had been hastily removed from the room. She was acknowledging the good behavior of the class in response to Adam's unannounced arrival in the classroom. The class's reaction had been incredibly muted, embodying a lack of response to Adam's giggling, uncontrolled entrance. By rewarding the class for not reacting to Adam, Jessica unwittingly threw into relief the behaviors that were not desirable, namely, Adam's actions, which flouted the rules of "normal" classroom behavior.

Another instance of implicitly maintaining normative rules of classroom behavior typically occurred when students turned to Harry to admonish him with a serious "Shhhh!" if his "speech" (a loud and extended "Ahhhhhhh!") interrupted the proceedings of a whole-group meeting. Jessica for the most part ignored these exchanges, implicitly sanctioning peer responses to Harry's vocalizations and upholding the norm of silent student behavior when the teacher controlled group instruction.

In either case, one might argue that the very narrative of acceptance circulating in Jessica's classroom enabled such peer response. It allowed students to display "good" behavior in the face of something out of the ordinary in the first instance, and to remind Harry as an equal peer about the rules of membership in the second. Yet Jessica's actions in rewarding the class for their "normal" classroom behavior or in not mediating peers' understanding of Harry's vocalization, might equally have suggested that *differences could be ignored even as they were being acknowledged*. Clearly, it was not easy to reconcile an acceptance of difference with the application of behavioral norms in the classrooms.

The operation of academic norms, too, seemed unavoidable. Although Jessica was committed to Harry's inclusion in the classroom, she was less able to address the disparity in cognitive levels evident between Harry and his classmates. She did recognize the wide learning differences that were inevitable within the classroom and was anxious to meet the needs of all students, even those who had not been "diagnosed." In fact, the challenge she willingly assigned herself was to identify "where everybody is at and then try to hit them in that perfect spot that is going to get them to the next level." However, she also seemed to suggest that Harry's "diagnosed" needs appeared to fall outside the pale of normal differences that could be expected in any classroom. So, from her perspective, the disconnect between Harry's cognitive level and the increasingly "academic" nature of the future grades in elementary school foreclosed the possibility that the general education environment could offer him "real" benefits. The academic norms of a typical general education classroom, she seemed to suggest, could not account for the learning that could be expected from a student with significant disabilities, such as Harry.

ACCESSIBILITY AS SPEAKING-FOR AND SPEAKING-WITH STUDENTS

The sincere interpretive work of teachers like Jessica and Stephanie clearly enhanced accessibility for their students with disabilities. What cautions can we derive from their experiences that may be helpful to their and others' future efforts at interpretation? One way to frame the complexity of this work is to distinguish two different stances within interpretive activity—a *speaking-for* or a *speaking-with* (Naraian, 2011a). The purpose of *speaking-for* is to disrupt stereotypical or uncritical responses to nonnormative behaviors in the classroom. Much of Stephanie's representation of Trevor's and Jessica's explanations about Harry or Adam clearly fell into this category. Through such speaking-for, teachers tried to allow student voices to emerge and promote the inclusive ethos they sought to cultivate within their classroom communities. *Speaking-with*, on the other hand, implies a deep emotional engagement between partners. The interpretations stemming from this stance are not predictable, but are always predicated on privileging the agency and complexity of the actor's experiences. In that regard, it subsumes not only an acknowledgment of voices historically absent in schools, but also requires an understanding of those voices.

One could argue that speaking-for efforts should always be predicated on a commitment to speak *with* the person; however, this has not always been reflected in the words and efforts of those who have represented the experiences of oppressed groups (Fielding, 2004). When well-intentioned advocates misrepresent the complexities within the experiences of marginalized peoples, they are less likely to be effective in their aims. *Speaking-with* has been described as a dialogic alternative that avoids an uncritically essentialist approach to the experiences of oppressed peoples (Fielding, 2004; Lodge, 2005). To what extent did the interpretive efforts of Stephanie and Jessica accomplish the speaking-with that might signal a more dialogic relation between students and teachers? What roles can either form of interpretation play in teachers' efforts to alter the narratives of ability/disability in the classroom? Can teachers engage in both forms to enhance accessibility in their classroom?

Monitoring Norms in Speaking-for

The interpretive work of both Stephanie and Jessica to a large extent drew on a form of speaking-for that was clearly intended to accomplish a certain kind of classroom where differences were normalized and where the shared commonalities of being 1st-grade students were emphasized. In that regard, it clearly benefited students with disabilities whose standing in the room as valued members might otherwise have been jeopardized, adversely affecting their overall development. They were readily drawn into the life of the classroom and participated in its academic and social life to the greatest extent they could. Additionally, such speaking-for stimulated the social–emotional conditions whereby peers could engage in various kinds of relations with their disabled peers and in that process learn about themselves and their peers. For example, Gabby's realization about Harry, "I didn't think I was going to like working with him, but now I really do!" (Naraian, 2008a, p. 106), may not have occurred in the absence of such speaking-for. To the extent that teachers' speaking-for offered such narrative resources for peers that might have been unavailable outside their classrooms, it clearly could (and certainly did) trigger new and more empowering stories of their disabled classmates. Many families in both classrooms delighted in the kinds of stories that they were hearing from their children regarding their relationships with disabled peers in the classroom.

In their anxiety to create an inclusive climate, teachers were also less attentive to the norms that accompanied their speaking-for activity. Thus they were unable to perceive that notions of personhood that they used to help students gain access to each other still remained bound to norms of ability. When Jessica instructed peer students to say to a student who might display alarming behaviors, "'I know you are angry; why don't you go to the safe place?" she was seeking to supply peers with linguistic tools that would sustain an inclusive climate. Her solution was to offer a strategy that could replace peers' fear and/or anxiety with a sense of control. The dictum that "everybody needs different things" on which Jessica's family narrative was based, justified a peer response that invited the student with disabilities to remove himself to the "safe place." Yet, by privileging peer students' need for stability, it implicitly suggested that some students' needs did not fall within the normal range of learners. In other words, the norms that governed the community could remain untouched while a student who seemed to behave differently needed to be regulated, albeit in a respectful manner.

Peers as Resources for Speaking-with

Such a continual suspicion of the "ideology of ability" (Siebers, 2008) in representing students to each other requires a vigilant monitoring that may be extraordinarily difficult to accomplish at all times. Can teachers realistically reconcile the competing priorities of supporting diverse learners (which implies the questioning of norms) as well as create safe communities for learning (which often requires norms)? Clearly, both Jessica and Stephanie, who were committed to inclusion, struggled to do so. One route to engaging in this difficult work might be to rely on *peers*. To stimulate alternate representations of a student's nonnormative behavior, teachers can privilege *peers'* interpretation of what the student might be communicating rather than a teacher-centered desire to restore normalcy and control in the classroom. How do peers make sense of this student? What would be their interpretation of the actions of a disabled student?

These questions would require a form of speaking-with that neither Jessica nor Stephanie might have been able to accomplish on their own. After all, the emotional engagement on which it was predicated required extended time and attention that is typically unavailable to teachers charged with enabling the participation of 25–30 students. Yet it was precisely such engagement that students were already actively seeking to accomplish with their disabled peers. The evolving narratives of students like Mark or Gabby or Andrea (Naraian, 2008a, 2008b), who sought to engage Harry in a variety of ways, testified to their compelling desire to *know* him deeply; they were already engaged in the process of narrativizing. The speaking-with that Jessica or Stephanie could not accomplish on their own, therefore, might be pursued by actively inviting peer narratives. It might then be interesting to consider these questions: What values do such peer interpretations reflect? How are they different from adult stories and why is that important?

Teachers' interpretive work in these classrooms laid the ground for this work. When Stephanie offered an interpretation of Trevor to the group, she not only gave him access to his peer community, but also allowed peer students to think of him in more expansive ways. To accomplish the speaking-with that remained largely outside the scope of her own activities, Stephanie could then systematically draw students into increasingly complex narratives about disability by continually inviting their interpretations about Trevor and evaluating their collective growth in understanding him. In keeping with its narrative roots, the validity of such peer interpretations would not stem from some "truth" about Trevor (or Harry) that may ultimately remain unavailable. So, for instance, it would be irrelevant to ask, "Is that what Trevor *really* thinks?" Instead, it was more important that the interpretations offered by the peer community should be *truth-like*. It should make sense to them as reasonable explanations. The *plausibility* of these interpretations would be derived from the strength and durability of students' interactive practices with their disabled peers.

Titchkosky (2011) suggests that one way of defining *access* is to think about it as the means to disclose "the gap between what is and what ought to be" (p. 24). Teachers' interpretive work offers evidence of how that can be translated in the classroom. It additionally suggests that the utility of *accessibility* as a construct to facilitate the inclusion of students with disabilities and create classrooms for diverse learners may ultimately rest on the capacity of instructional practice to establish meaningful connections between its members (Naraian, 2014).

CHAPTER 5

Working for Community
The Role of Families

Almost from the start and always without doubt, inclusive education has been associated with the notion of *community*. Students with disabilities can genuinely participate in inclusion only when the general education classroom community is itself based on the principles of care and equity (Lawrence-Brown & Sapon-Shevin, 2014; Sapon-Shevin, 2007; Villa & Thousand, 2000). This understanding of classroom "management" is based on recognizing the importance of learners' social–emotional development and their need to experience belonging before they can make academic gains in the classroom. Additionally, the project of making classrooms hospitable to learners whose social histories reflect marginalization by dominant groups calls for the creation of just communities where subjugated knowledges are honored and where different forms of diversity are valued (Kluth et al., 2003). Such communities are seen as nurturing the democratic values that sustain our society and fostering goals of citizenship that lie at the heart of public schooling.

Even as educators implicitly understand and accept this intertwining of commitments to community and inclusion, its implementation remains less deeply understood. The call to create caring communities has generally not considered the complexities of doing so alongside the multiple competing commitments that teachers have to take up simultaneously. Such competing priorities might include districtwide mandates to raise student scores on standardized tests, or it might mean a school's decision to sort students by ability to reach school improvement goals. There may also be the lack of supports for teachers to engage with students who experience difficulty in conforming to the behavioral demands of school. In any case, inasmuch as the requirement to implement community is integral to inclusion, identifying the challenges to such implementation may be equally necessary to understand how it can remain beneficial to all students. It is particularly important to understand the dilemmas that teachers encounter in this process. What kinds of communities do teachers implement? What do such communities tell us about their goals and beliefs? What makes it difficult to implement community?

One tension that I observed across school sites (and which was introduced in Chapter 4) is that even as the notion of community seeks to embrace diversity in different forms, it can just as easily be based on norms that work *against* a positive affirmation of differences (Berry, 2006; Linehan & McCarthy, 2001). After all, teachers require a shared set of expectations that can establish the platform on which learners can come together. As Chapter 4 illustrated, communities that were welcoming of students with a range of different learning profiles were almost always tethered to norms of behavior. For instance, in Stephanie's class, the concept of *community* seemed to have substituted for a form of classroom management. The discourse of classroom management, however, lies at some odds with the notion of community (Danforth & Smith, 2005). The former clearly uses behavioral norms to determine appropriate classroom interactions: Students are expected to demonstrate respectful behaviors in interacting with their peers and teachers that can help the smooth functioning of the classroom. A notion of community, on the other hand, respects and values learner differences. When teachers' enactment of community is intertwined with academic and behavioral norms, it will remain susceptible to the weaknesses that are inevitable when contradictory purposes are brought together. How can these weaknesses be mitigated?

One way to address these weaknesses is to understand these communities through the lens of family engagement. While researchers underscore the significance of families as partners for achieving strong educational outcomes (Epstein, 2007; Mac Iver, Epstein, Sheldon, & Fonseca, 2015), they rarely represent them as *necessary* for the successful implementation of community in the classroom. As a result, though research shows the need for a critical approach to family–school relations where family insights and experience are valued (Auerbach, 2007; Lightfoot, 2004), there have not been many descriptions of how this facilitates the creation of classroom community. In the chapters so far, we have learned about the different ways in which teachers implemented community in the classroom. In this chapter, I will attend specifically to the relations with families that marked the communities created by Jessica, Stephanie, and Anita and Maria. In doing so, I suggest that *teachers' implementation of community is deeply linked to their practice with families.* Subsequently, in a deliberate twist, I move away from the classroom to share the story of a parent coordinator who sought to support families in her school. I do so to illustrate the significance of *listening* to families in complex ways.

My purpose in this chapter is to present teachers/educators as engaged in the continuous work of defining and refining their understandings of community. In that regard, there is much in their approach that can be readily absorbed into an inclusive pedagogy. Simultaneously, their struggles provoke new directions for imagining the work of creating communities. My goal, therefore, is twofold: First, I seek to disclose the immense complexity within the concept of *community,* whose meanings are often assumed to be self-evident. My hope is that in understanding these complexities, educators will be more likely to recognize the process of community building as an endeavor that defies simplistic formulas. There are many ways it can be implemented with varying effects on multiple groups (students, families, and teachers). Each attempt at community is a step toward greater understanding of how we can be responsive to differences in a classroom. Second, I utilize the experience of these educators to remind us that even as schooling structures continually present a model of teacher ability that is individualistic, self-contained, and independent of the social context, working with families for community can permit teachers to become *more* effective in implementing this concept. It takes up a notion of *ability* as distributed across people rather than as located solely within the person (Lave, 1993; Lave & Wenger, 1991).

DEVELOPING COMMUNITIES FOR INCLUSION...
WITH OR WITHOUT FAMILIES

Arranging and planning for community work in the classroom preoccupied the educators I studied across sites. In their respective enactments of such community, there were many common elements that reflected their concern for preserving communitarian notions of mutual respect, collective work, and shared responsibility for the welfare of one's peers. Recognizing an emotionally safe place as a prerequisite for academic learning, these educators did not hesitate to mediate conflicts and controversy in the classroom through children's literature and/or exhaustive dialogues with students. With some direction from administration but no institutionally sponsored opportunity for collective self-reflection, these educators took up the full responsibility of choreographing their communities. As we saw in Chapter 4, their pedagogical approaches to implementing forms of community were not dissimilar: a firm reliance on rules of group and individual behavior and the likelihood of a top-down approach that prohibited student questioning of such norms. Each of their efforts was undertaken in the context of specific family–school relations that were reflected both in the classroom and in the larger school setting.

Jessica: Families as Resources for Student Achievement

During the period immediately preceding the time of the study, Jessica's suburban school, with a significant percentage of White middle-class families, had begun to recruit more students from the inner city, from Black low-income families, to maintain a district-sponsored percentage of minority students per school. The principal candidly reported the resistance of the families in the school to welcoming these students unconditionally. Her efforts to educate families about the racist character of existing cultural habits and practices in schools had accomplished very little. The PTO continued its traditions of cocktail party fundraisers and ice cream socials that drew few families of color and that left the divisions between them untouched. Within her own classroom in this building, Jessica directed and arranged various occasions for families to attend her classroom, such as publishing parties, and made herself available to them when required. However, she clearly did not invite their involvement; when mothers asked for opportunities to volunteer in the classroom, she could not identify spaces for them within the classroom where they could help. She noted matter-of-factly that her procedures for running the classroom community appeared to be functioning smoothly, thereby eliminating the need for any family assistance.

The members of the classroom "family" that Jessica sought earnestly to create did not therefore include the families of her students. She assumed responsibility for ensuring that her students felt safe and that they were imbibing the values of collective citizenship. It made sense, therefore, for her to welcome students with a range of abilities/disabilities into the academic life of her classroom and to prepare herself adequately to be supportive of their learning needs. It was also consistent that she would learn Spanish to communicate with a recently immigrated working-class parent. Neither was it surprising that she spoke about meeting the mother of Harry, a student with significant disabilities, before the school year began to obtain her perspective and realize in that process that he was "just like every other child." She realized that families of students with disabilities "have hopes for them like every other child." Given the value she placed on creating an emotionally safe learning place for her students, Jessica clearly understood the significance of family for understanding and being responsive to her students.

Jessica's practices serve as a reminder of the many simple ways to be welcoming of families. The learning she sought from families served an important, if instrumental, purpose; it was the kind of engagement with families that schools actively support, because it improved educational outcomes for students. Schools must solicit involvement of families because students' academic achievement is directly or indirectly linked to such engagement (Ferguson, Hanreddy, & Ferguson, 2014). In other words, "schools get more assistance in doing the job of teaching students" (Ferguson, Hanreddy, & Ferguson, 2014, p. 775). This widely circulating narrative of family–school relations is premised on understanding family experiences and schooling priorities as separate, discrete elements that may be brought together in the interests of the student, though they can also collide.

Jessica's participation in this larger family–school narrative was not at all unusual. She created and maintained connections with families, but in describing her experiences with families, it was clear that such encounters left her position as the teacher untouched; her engagement with them did not appear to, nor was it expected to, bring about shifts in her own thinking, teaching, learning. It was elicited to ensure that she fulfilled her professional commitment to provide a satisfactory education to her students. It was not expected to alter the ways she conceptualized her professional commitments.

The difference lies in the fact that while one objective sees families as resources to be used, the other goes beyond that to require educators to see every encounter with a family as an opportunity to question the values and beliefs that underlie their own practices. This is the stance of *cultural reciprocity* (Harry, Kalyanpur & Day, 1999) that positions families as significant to the growth of the classroom community.

As long as families were regarded as resources to be used to facilitate student achievement, family actions could always remain at risk of being evaluated as supporting or not supporting school-based priorities. In this context, it is not surprising that Jessica found family support unnecessary in the classroom. Families, by themselves, could not enrich her instruction. It might even mean that family actions that lay outside the scope of the values and priorities of the classroom, could be perceived as questionable. This was exemplified in Jessica's relations with her student Mark and his family. As hinted in the previous chapter, Mark seemed to question from the very beginning the "truth" value of the family narrative in the classroom, particularly in relation to Harry. While other students appeared willing to take up the community ethos to regard Harry as an equal member, Mark doubted Harry's ability to perform classroom tasks, suggesting that he really did not have the capacity to understand. Mark's responses both to Harry and other peers was interpreted by an outraged Jessica as a reflection of the individualistic streak in a White middle-class family. In describing Mark's "policing" of other students as a personality trait, she noted, "Mark is very intelligent; he wants everybody to know it, and then he is trying to control every situation, and I think Mom is also that way. You know, just by her coming in and kind of sitting at the table . . . it's like, control, you know." Families' participation could only be understood within the given parameters of family–school relations that required Mark's mother to either demonstrate a supportive orientation toward school or be perceived as combative.

Jessica's largely top-down approach to implementing this family narrative that we witnessed earlier clearly created an accepting ethos in the classroom, which may well constitute a necessary first step in many buildings. It may not have been significant to her at this time that students had fewer opportunities to explore how they could relate it to their own experiences. Nor might it have occurred to her that in the absence of such opportunities, students' learning about differences might be transient and/or fragile. In the immediate satisfaction of witnessing peers supporting Harry in her classroom (and noting, perhaps, Mark's own gradual process of change in attitude toward Harry), Jessica might not have had cause to question the ability of this community to have a sustained impact on students' understanding of difference in spaces beyond this classroom. *That* would have prioritized the circulation of new narratives of disability (discussed in Chapter 4) rather than the unquestioning acceptance of difference.

Stephanie: Parents as Challenging

Stephanie's urban school was located in a neighborhood with a similarly high percentage of White middle-class families who were actively involved in supporting the school's goals. In this building however, the halls bustled with families during morning drop-off and afternoon pick-up, though they could also be seen cleaning up after a classroom party, sitting with their children during Morning Meeting, or bringing supplies to classrooms. In this urban context where issues of equity were singularly pronounced in public discourse, the rhetoric of diversity put forth by the administration and the school community was stronger and more persistent than where Jessica worked. Leaders within the family community were more likely to actively seek the participation of all families. Some of the practices of the family community were still not dissimilar to those observed at Jessica's school—fundraising events such as auctions at notable venues in the city that required tickets for purchase. The school was well known in the city for its willingness and capability to receive students with significant physical and communication disabilities. Special and general educators taught collaboratively in many of these classrooms that were generally likely to have 3–5 adults (including paraprofessionals) supporting students with and without disabilities. The high ratio of adults to students in these classrooms meant that families, regardless of whether their child was disabled or not, clamored for the placement of their children within them.

Stephanie taught in one such collaboratively taught classroom where the ratio of students with and without disabilities was maintained at 40 to 60 percent. Unlike Jessica, Stephanie clearly, if not enthusiastically, acknowledged the linkage between families and the implementation of community in her classroom. When asked to identify the main challenge to implementing community in her classroom, she unhesitatingly replied, "Parents!" Her descriptions of the families in her classroom suggested a fragmented community where parents routinely failed to uphold the principles of care that she sought to implement within the classroom. They brought complaints about other families to her and seemed to encourage their children to take up *un*caring approaches toward peers whom the parents deemed suspicious. Reporting on one parent's reaction to a student, Stephanie observed:

> She [the parent] said, "He [her son, Aaron] is not to be anywhere around Ramona. I don't agree with the way that her parents are raising her. They really need some intervention. I think some calls should be made. People should visit the family." And I was just—I think my mouth just like hanged open for a little bit, and in my brain I was just like, "Do you realize what you're saying to Aaron? Like what is the pattern of working with people? What's the pattern of community that

you're giving him? I don't like somebody, therefore I can be mean to them?" And that totally works against what we're talking about in the classroom and what we're trying to build. And she really looks down on that family, and she's been talking to other families.

Stephanie clearly perceived family behaviors as contradicting the messages that she tried to send her students. She thought families' responses to students with disabilities in the classroom "smacked of pretentiousness," and she was clearly skeptical of their ability to mediate their children's understanding of these students. Indeed, she suggested that children's learnings from her classroom actually spread outward to parents, who, she claimed, had often made inappropriate comments about children and other families. As someone who believed strongly in modeling community for children, she did not appear to believe that the family community was supporting her efforts to do so.

Recognizing their role in sustaining the community in the classroom, she considered calling a meeting of the families. While her intention was to use the pretext of a curricular reason to justify the event, it was clear she intended to focus on educating families about appropriate community norms. Stephanie recognized that families might feel "attacked" by her for questioning their values. Still, she remarked confidently: "I think when they take a step back and they really think about it, they're going to want to be better people." Implicitly critiquing the norms of middle-class families, Stephanie suggested that if parents were going to teach their children that it was permissible to shun someone who was not from their social category, then this school was not appropriate for them; they needed to enroll them in a private school. Her own approach, instead, was to support families who were "stressed," calling for the need to "wrap our arms around them."

Stephanie saw her students as inevitably located within communities that existed outside her classroom and school. In that regard, her vision of community was more expansive than Jessica's. Both educators privileged their own understanding of *community*, which was premised on notions of fairness, equity, and belonging. When the understandings displayed by families countered those notions (directly or indirectly), they were seen unproblematically as deficient and, in Stephanie's case, as requiring to be educated to know better.

Anita and Maria: Cultural Insiders

The focus on community brought by Anita and Maria to their classroom more sharply reflected the broader institutional emphasis on accountability as well as the priorities of the predominantly working-class, Latino family community in which their students were embedded. Like Jessica and Stephanie, their efforts too were premised on some behavioral norms, though they were more likely to emphasize the significance of this for learning outcomes. For instance, they worried that Sam and Marcelo, two students with learning and emotional disabilities, needed to modulate their emotional responses so that they could be considered ready for other grade-appropriate experiences, now and in future years. While Marcelo lacked the confidence to speak for himself, Sam reacted unpredictably with emotional outbursts that hindered his ability to learn. Still, in the descriptions of the kind of classroom Anita and Maria sought to create, they were less likely to talk about desired student behaviors and more likely to dwell on maintaining their own strength against the pressures of testing, so as not to allow that to defeat their ability to create "playful" learning spaces.

Anita and Maria relished the context in which they found themselves. Not only did they share a common belief system for supporting dual-language learners with other educators in the building, they also shared similar cultural origins. Such origins further matched that of the community of families that made up this school. Working within a professional context that strongly resembled the family community was liberating in that it allowed the teachers to connect more readily with families. As Anita remarked, such freedom was exemplified in "the way I don't have to second guess how I'm going to phrase something or how it's going to be interpreted." An idiom could be immediately translated into Spanish "and the parent gets it." Such confidence was also borne out of a shared understanding of the significance of education for this largely immigrant, working-class community and the "tangible outcome" that it was likely to produce. It meant that the expectations of learning they brought as teachers to these students were guided by this shared perception of the political and economic status of this community in larger society.

The expectations of families that Anita and Maria held seemed largely similar to traditional notions of family involvement where parents were expected to come in for school-based events such as parent–teacher conferences and to cooperate with teachers in school-based processes such as signing forms and responding to teacher calls. Thus they were not quite sympathetic to a mother who was repeatedly unable to come to school to meet with them and wondered why she could not make time from her work to do so. In a separate conversation with me, this mother did worry that she had not been able to visit her son's school and was hoping that when she changed her job, she might be able to do so. While the teachers were aware of some of the specifics of her situation (e.g., she was divorced and had an older son with autism), they did not appear to draw significantly on her experiences when seeking to understand her son Marcelo.

Their identification as "cultural insiders" allowed them to presume that the norms of their classroom community did not conflict with the life experiences of the students. Their instructional approach, for instance, reflected a strong emphasis on explicit instruction that required students to demonstrate sustained engagement for long periods and be willing to follow directions closely (Archer & Hughes, 2011). It arose from the pressing requirement to help students succeed in high-stakes measurements of achievement for which the teachers had little regard. At the same time, they also refrained from upsetting the norms within this community. When asked about the impact the family community had had on their literacy instruction, Anita responded "Community? To be honest, I don't think about that when I make a curricular decision. More maybe like what I *wouldn't* bring in." She would *not* choose literature, for instance, that might offend their values, or take up practices like yoga that did not align with some religious leanings in the community. Recognizing this community as somewhat "conservative," they were careful about not offending their beliefs. Anita's comment attested both to her determination to be responsive to their values and also to the confidence in her own capability to understand the norms within this community.

Anita and Maria, like Stephanie, worked within a district where the expectations on teachers to produce proficient student scores on standardized tests had become more and more intense. Along with the rest of the school, they participated in test preparatory activities, even as they worked hard to mitigate some of its effects. They clearly felt troubled by the kinds of instructional practices triggered by the concerted focus on tests and the costs to student's learning that were entailed in this process. Yet, despite these pressures, they continued to create a community where students were invited to participate in the creation of learning supports, where their understanding of *ability* was stretched through literature, where collective learning was valued over independent activities, and where impromptu occasions to share out-of-school experiences were not uncommon. It was not surprising that classroom meetings on the rug that often stretched for more than 40 minutes were marked by vigorous participation and sustained engagement of all students.

LOCATING SELF, STUDENTS, AND FAMILIES: DISTRIBUTED LEARNING AND NARRATIVE COMPLEXITY

Within their classroom communities, teachers needed to create arrangements that inculcated values unlikely to be measurable (e.g., care, equity, kindness), while simultaneously adopting instructional practices to generate results that would be measured with heavy consequences for themselves and their students (Ravitch, 2013). In other words, a communitarian pedagogy had to coexist with a more individualized focus on student learning. Not surprisingly, some of these educators' accounts of *community* were intermingled with talk of "individual accountability" and "documentation" to "prove that kids are learning," alongside their concerns for their social–emotional growth and collective responsibility. Accomplishing these competing aims while creating communitarian environments meant, as we have seen thus far, that such communities remained vulnerable to behavioral norms and a pedagogical approach that might be authoritative rather than participatory. It was not surprising that Stephanie remarked ruefully in the middle of the year that students appeared "not to have internalized the kindness."

In an era of standardization and school accountability, where teacher competence has become a hotly contested public matter, how does a consideration of families support the implementation of communities in the classroom? In the following paragraphs I examine why the exclusion of families in these "family communities" may be significant for educators. I begin by looking at the ways teachers understood their own capacity for crafting community.

Shifting the Locus of Control for Choreographing Communities

From Jessica's perspective, keeping families at a distance did not appear to have hindered the kind of community she desired. Indeed, she noticed several occasions when children in the classroom made comments to her or to each other that seemed to confirm that the inclusive ethos in her class was working. Such noticeable effects reinforced the locus of control for implementing community within her own abilities to do so. In the event that these effects were troubling or did not reflect inclusion, she could then readily attribute their causes to factors within the children. Hence, Mark's initial resistance to Harry arose from an inherited streak of individualism; or if previously friendly nondisabled peers were beginning to drift away from Harry, she saw this as inevitable because they were advancing developmentally in ways that made such distance "natural." Families in this choreography were required to be "silent supporters," neither seen as directly influential within her community-building efforts nor as detracting from her ability to do so successfully. After all, if Mark's words and actions did not take up *her* family narrative, there was nothing she could do about *his* family values. It did not reflect on her ability to carry out her everyday work.

Stephanie's perception of her role in the community-building process might have been somewhat different, but no less contingent on her own inherent abilities. Immersed in a school environment where the strong physical presence of families in the school was considered its singular attraction, her everyday contact with families was far more numerous and intense. Unlike Jessica's school, where family movement in the building was more restricted, families in Stephanie's school moved freely inside and outside classrooms. Their influence on Stephanie's everyday reasoning and decisionmaking in the classroom was therefore understandably stronger. As a result, it was not surprising that she could perceive herself as needing to influence the families in ways that could support her vision of community in the classroom. To build and sustain her own capacity to implement a successful community, she needed to change the kinds of values families seemed to be instilling in their children that did not serve her vision.

Anita and Maria, too, clearly placed full expectations on themselves when considering their classroom community. As they reflected on inclusion and tried to unpack the conundrums posed by some of the students with disabilities, Anita and Maria worked with their own professional understandings, rarely mentioning families as a source of knowledge. For instance, in their struggles to identify the most appropriate placement for Sam, a student with emotional and learning difficulties, they thoughtfully debated a range of options, none of which seemed satisfactory. The only role his family seemed to have played in their deliberations was the recognition that his mother needed to be informed about her options. Perhaps Anita and Maria, in perceiving themselves both as cultural insiders and as advocates for Sam and his family, assumed that they were more knowledgeable about the system. Or, equally important, they might have considered that it was their professional responsibility to evaluate the outcomes on behalf of the family, who may not have the skills to negotiate with a complicated bureaucratic system.

In all these instances, teachers operated from the assumptions that the success or failure of the communities they implemented was contingent on the abilities *they* possessed. The implementation of community presented an opportunity for educators to develop their abilities to deliver inclusively oriented practice. Excluding families from their efforts may have simply allowed them room to achieve greater control over their own learning. In any event, even as their inclusive practices implicitly recognized the importance of the relational context for their students' learning, they seemed to perceive their own skill as choreographers of classroom communities as residing solely within their own learning rather than distributed across other adults, including families.

The premise of learning/intelligence as *distributed* is that abilities do not reside only *within* individuals (Lave & Wenger, 1991). They are, instead, spread across people (and things) collectively contributing to the achievement of desired outcomes. Individuals *experience* their abilities through interactions with others. Attributes such as intelligence or memory, then, may be understood as accomplishments that are *achieved* rather than as qualities that are *possessed*. During classroom participation, for instance, students' ability to complete a jointly executed task may be distributed across the group of learners as well as the artifacts that are used in the process that mediate such learning (Gomez, Schieble, Curwood, & Hassett, 2010). It means that no one member can claim sole authorship over the result. As Lave and Wenger (1991) point out, "Learning is a process that takes place in a participation framework, not in an individual mind. This means, among other things, that it is mediated by the differences of perspective among co-participants. It is the community, or at least those participating in the learning context, who learn under this definition. Learning is, as it were, distributed among co-participants, not a one person act" (p. 15).

Across the cases described above, the teachers did not view their capacity to create inclusive communities as emerging from the experience of supporting children's growth that they jointly shared with families. The outcome teachers and families desired—children learning to live and work in community—may not be attributed to either one or the other. It was accomplished from the collective efforts of both teachers and families, the texts that were used by each, the types of activities that mediated notions of community within each classroom and family context, and the interactive practices that marked each experience. In that regard, it was neither the teacher's capability nor families' incapability that produced a classroom community. Instead, it may be considered a joint accomplishment distributed across both classroom and family practices and the multiple tools, texts, and tasks they invoked.

Recognizing ability as distributed rather than localized within individuals could have some important implications for teachers in implementing community, as follows:

- Classroom norms would be collectively determined not only with students but also with families.
    » What priorities for social-emotional growth do families bring?
    » How can these priorities merge with teachers' objectives for the classroom?
    » Additionally, what specific experiences can generate such information—home visits, interviews, phone calls, interest inventories, focus groups, or other?
- Classroom arrangements would be created that acknowledge the diversity within family experiences.
    » What are the family experiences that stimulate their specific priorities?
    » How can these experiences influence classroom routines, such as Morning Meeting, or curricular experiences, such as designing learning projects?
    » How can that alter the opportunities afforded to families to participate in the classroom?
- Relations with families would be different from the typical middle-class notions of parental involvement where families help with fundraising, celebrations in the classroom, or serving as chaperones on fieldtrips (Lareau & Horvat, 1999). Opportunities for participation for families could be both curricular (e.g., support in content area work) and ancillary (e.g., obtaining resources, organizing parties), but offering many entry points would permit different forms of involvement to suit different family profiles.
- A commitment to the empowerment of the students and families from marginalized groups would require an openness on the part of educators to both receive and be changed by new and unfamiliar experiences that would then inform how they might implement community.

When Community Obscures Complexity: On Hearing Family Narratives

Notions of equity, fairness, and belonging that form the basis of any caring inclusive community may be insufficient if they obscure the complexities that inhere in any human experience. For example, Stephanie's resistance to middle-class values played a strong role in her decision to hold a meeting to remind families of the effects of their actions on the classroom community. It also presumed that families have one-dimensional lives where their children's school-based concerns occupy center-stage at all times. Or, Jessica's dismissal of Mark's "bossy" tendencies could have been interpreted differently by consulting with his mother, who described him (in a separate interview with me) as feeling compelled to play by the rules and expecting others to do so. Such instances draw attention to the complexities within the experiences of members of a *community* and underscore that the term itself comes fraught with tensions that cannot be wished away with feel-good notions of bringing diverse learners together in a single space. Any type of community always brings many complex and evolving subjectivities; the most well-intentioned, responsive forms of classroom practices are still likely to be experienced by each group and its constituent individuals in ways that are never fully predictable.

Families offer an important means of accessing those subjectivities. For example, Stephanie considered Abdul, a nondisabled learner, as a socially and academically successful student in the classroom. Yet, in my conversation with his mother, Halima, she disclosed that *his* experience of this community was much more complicated (Naraian, 2011a). She believed that Abdul yearned for deeper contact with his peers and that his reading proficiency granted him an opportunity, perhaps the only opportunity, to offer something valuable to his social partners—teachers and peers. His academic skills could make him a desirable peer as well as a favored student. A first-generation immigrant who had experienced exclusion herself, she remained frustrated by teachers' interpretations of Abdul's school participation as "fine," his lack of close friends as indicative that "he can just sit with anybody" or that he was simply "floating." At home, she could only hear Abdul's desperate cry, "Nobody's paying attention to me!" Abdul's experience of the tensions within community life in this classroom could not be available to Stephanie without Halima's interpretation. Listening to such interpretation in turn might require Stephanie to reconsider the ways in which she enacted community. She might need to draw on other norms of behavior that might then eventually inform the basis for this community.

These and other individual student narratives hint at experiences that remained outside the scope of values permitted in these classrooms, but which were often available to families. Even if families did not arrive with broader and more explicit considerations of equity, their experiences could continually disclose to the critical educator ways by which this focus could be sustained.

In other words, a narrow focus on their own children does not preclude a responsibility on the part of teachers to listen to families' stories for themes of care and justice. For example, Carolyn, a White middle-class parent, spoke to me about feeling the need to be physically present in the classroom to allow her daughter's voice to emerge. Her experiences not only suggested the advantages accrued to those families who could afford to be present in the classroom during the school day, but also the limitations of classroom practices where a seemingly "advantaged" student can appear to lack agency. In another instance, the narratives of a parent of a physically disabled child might explain her son's sudden decision to withdraw permission given to his peers to describe his disabled finger affectionately as his "stubby." For his baffled teacher, Stephanie, attending to such narratives might draw attention to norms of physical appearance in the classroom. Regardless of their exclusive focus on a single child, these stories bore traces of issues of equity, difference, and normalcy that can inform the work of community in the classroom.

Listening to such stories also surfaces the contradictions that are inevitable when considering that people occupy multiple positions simultaneously along dimensions of race, class, ability/disability, linguistic status, and so forth. Abdul's experience as the son of a first-generation Egyptian immigrant might hint at some marginalized social experiences, but his superior academic abilities conferred a privileged status upon him in the classroom. The location of Trevor, a multiply disabled wheelchair student who used a communication device, within a White middle-class family, allowed him to experience multiple trips to Europe as well as to the White House for a meeting with the vice president of the United States. Rafael, another physically disabled wheelchair user, was able to meet grade-appropriate goals with supports. His mother, who delivered newspapers, could not speak English and craved supports for herself to increase her son's reading proficiency.

Each family narrative bears elements that complicate idealized notions of social justice used to foster a commitment to principles of care and equity. Even as these notions are crucial to the project of inclusion, the implementation of community may require teachers to "hear" student and family experiences in a way that continually surfaces the many competing values that are inherent within them. Recognizing such contradictions may allow for forms of community that are premised less on abstract norms and more on the immediate needs of students and families. Even Anita and Maria, comfortably situated as they were in a cultural context they felt deeply connected to, drew on lofty, if simplified, concerns that prioritized the socioeconomic progress of the community. They were less likely to look for learnings in family stories that could enrich their knowledge of the everyday negotiations, anxieties, and resistances of families that informed their relations with school. When his mother sent 10-year-old Sam by himself in a taxi because she was running late, what were the conditions that she struggled with that necessitated this course of action? Such questioning, in turn, might have urged the teachers to draw on family experiences to introduce curricular materials that built on, and extended, the expectations of that community. For example, their commitments to social justice notwithstanding, there were few, if any, elements in their curriculum that could deliberately foster a critical consciousness in students toward the inequities that characterized their own lives.

In striving for a community that can benefit from family knowledges, I have suggested that educators need to "hear" family stories differently. Such listening, I argue, can surface the complexities of their lived experience that require educators to respond not with finalizing judgment but with a stance of compassionate inquiry.

LEARNING TO LISTEN

To further illustrate the significance of "hearing" family stories, in this section I describe the efforts of a parent coordinator in a school who sought to advocate for the families in the building against an administration that seemed to hold an adversarial stance toward them (see also Naraian, 2015, for more detailed information). I present her story as an instance of how the struggle for equity, in this case for families, demanded a form of listening that could attend to specificities of experience to (re)configure efforts toward equity.

Melanie's Story

A Black woman who had spent many years in schools in varying capacities, Melanie Wilson held the position of a parent coordinator at an elementary school within a large metropolitan district, Bell City School District. This position had been recently created in the district to promote better relations between schools and families. The role of the parent coordinator, broadly speaking, was to build relations with families and the local community, facilitate family involvement in schools, and serve as a resource for them. This might include disseminating information to families, hosting workshops for them, and working with school staff to address family concerns. The early excitement generated by this position, however, appeared to have given way to an inexplicable opposition from school personnel. Melanie reported: "The teachers thought we were spies and we were going to be spying on them, and the APs [Assistant Principals] and the principals thought we were going back *telling*, you know, what the school wasn't doing." Particularly frustrating and demoralizing for Melanie was the impasse between her and the principal in her school. The principal clearly appeared to mistrust her and remained stubbornly unwilling to engage in any form of relations with her that would help Melanie advocate for the families in her school. According to Melanie, the principal seemed to want her to clearly distinguish herself as being "on the side" of the administration rather than "on the side" of families. Melanie's professional integrity demanded that she keep confidential the information shared with her by families, and so she refused to adopt the position her principal sought.

Melanie's vision of supporting families was predicated on a deep empathetic engagement with their experiences. To that end, a significant portion of her work certainly entailed offering emotional support to families in distress, but it also lay the groundwork for the conflict with the administration. An empathetic approach to families meant that Melanie had access to the many small yet incredibly powerful stories that families shared about their situations. This drew her inevitably into many spheres of their lives besides the educational outcomes of their children in school. The latter, however, still remained the most consequential and significant marker for the administrators who may not have held the holistic conceptions of family contexts that Melanie was able to generate in the course of her interactions with families.

Melanie's willingness to empathetically acknowledge the experiences of families derived from her conviction that one should be capable of walking in the other's shoes. "I put myself in the parents' place and say 'how would I feel as a parent?' That means struggling sometimes with the language barrier, or coming from another country and not understanding, you know, the things that go on here, and you don't know how to speak up for yourself." So Melanie sought earnestly to find ways to educate families usually through workshops and invited speakers, about laws, systems, procedures, and options of which they may not have had prior knowledge. It also meant that the strategy she applied in working with families was never premised on confrontation. She acknowledged that she tried to "pacify" them and even laughingly noted that others thought that she tried to "pamper" them, but she was convinced that it was necessary to work with them in accomplishing resolution. To her, if a parent balked at the suggestion that their child needed special education services, it was completely logical because "what parent wants to hear that there is something wrong with their child?"

Melanie was simultaneously under no illusion that her empathetic stance could accomplish everything for families. She was fully cognizant that families had to take initiative in educating themselves about the system so that they could advocate for their children. So even as she was committed to empowering them through dissemination of resources and other means, she did not hesitate to hold them accountable for obtaining publicly available knowledge. This stance of accountability with support was always informed by the simple recognition that "if I lose their trust, what do I have?" Melanie, therefore, brought her intimate knowledge of families to the ways she designed her workshops, relying on interactive engagement rather than long talks or lectures and ensuring that there was always sufficient time for families simply to talk to each other. "They have all their business to talk about and I don't want to interrupt their business."

She was convinced that administrators did not want to talk to families, and when they did, they talked down to them. Unlike Melanie, these administrators had little familiarity with or connections within the community in which the school was located. Melanie's close connections to individual families and their unique experiences also meant that she carried a wealth of narratives that often defied a systemic response. For instance, she described the story of a deeply troubled parent battling economic and personal woes, whose children posed challenging behaviors in school. Melanie's concern led her beyond the scope of labeling the children as *disruptive* to supporting the mother by helping her find a home and raising her sense of self-esteem.

Melanie clearly made a distinction between serving the administration and serving families. She could see herself supporting the administration in the joint commitment to building a school community, but her moral and ethical commitment was to families. One might argue that it was the very immersion in family stories that also locked her into an oppositional relation with her school administrators. Ultimately, while those stories may have greatly supported Melanie's own growth and learning, it is unclear how much they accomplished for students and their families, since Melanie could not advocate on their behalf with the administration in the local school context. Indeed, within Melanie's own accounts, there were few reports of how she successfully helped resolve conflicts for families.

Complex Listening for Learning from, and with, Families

Melanie's emotional connection to families left her with little recourse other than to locate the problem within the administration and accomplish few meaningful changes for families. In a sense, her anger against the administration sustained the very conditions that provoked her sense of injustice. It produced no means to break the impasse between her and the administration. Implicit within her efforts to engage the administration was the conviction that her own position was morally unquestionable. For Melanie, steeped in soliciting an empathetic climate for her families in this building and secure in her ideological stance, there were few other ways to address the impasse. It seemed unlikely that her professional preparation to be a parent coordinator had equipped her with the tools to avoid such an ideological impasse, which could have improved the experiences of the families she supported.

The relations of teachers (discussed earlier in this chapter) with the families of their students occurred on a different terrain. They were not privy to, nor were they expected to learn about, the details of families' lives that Melanie garnered in her interactions with families. *It was the presumed cultural location of families as largely peripheral to the world of schooling that served as the common frame of experience for both.* Melanie's position required that she work directly against this narrative; teachers' roles as inclusive educators also required that they do the same. For both, however, it seemed that the scope of their professional practice simultaneously left them unable to accomplish this in any easy manner. For Melanie, it was the juxtaposition of her role as parent coordinator with her location as a representative of the school that complicated her relations with the school administration, leaving her less than effective in accomplishing results for families. For teachers, their concern for the well-being of their students ironically placed them in some opposition to their families, making the production of an inclusive community a complicated, contradictory affair.

How could Melanie and the teachers bring qualitative changes to the experience of schooling for families as well as uphold their commitments to equitable education? While the contextual specificities of each schooling context may suggest different trajectories of practice, I focus here on the kind of *listening* that professionals can extend to families that can lead to accomplishing goals of equity. It calls for an ability to bracket one's own ideological stance to remain open to multiple perspectives. For instance, even as Melanie learned about the many events in families' lives, her listening could not be solely based on their marginalized status as mostly immigrant and working-class families of color in a school system that typically granted little opportunity for families to participate on equal terms in schooling processes. Like Anita and Maria, her stance toward families, compassionate and empathetic as it was, did not include an assessment of the skills and resources available *within* families. Not doing so runs the risk of simplifying the breadth of family experiences.

Instead, to "hear" for complexity, one has to continually ask oneself, "What do I *not* know about this family's experience that can help me understand it differently?" or "What learnings has this family derived from their own experience, and how does that change my understanding of their story?" While such questions might have deepened the capability of Anita and Maria to implement a critically conscious 4th-grade community, it would also have provided clues to Melanie on what kind of issues to take up to support families. She might then have been spurred to build alliances with other professionals within the building that might then have led to different kinds of relations with the administration. For Stephanie and Jessica, it might have offered possibilities for new norms for their classroom community that could create genuinely authentic spaces of learning for their students. For all educators, such questions can continually serve as a reminder that the transformation of classrooms into inclusive communities is premised on an educator's openness to be transformed by the diverse experiences that are constituted within it. This kind of listening permits the contradictions that are inevitable within students' and families' experiences to be incorporated within pedagogical practice without compromising commitments to equity.

The requirement for teachers to create communities in an era of accountability and standardization means that their commitment to inclusive pedagogies is continually under threat. It must be negotiated against institutional practices that seek to reduce not only student learning but also teachers' own performance to objective scores on standardized tests (Cochran-Smith, Piazza, & Power, 2013). One of the markers of teacher competence valued in schools is the facility to demonstrate order and control in the classroom (Danielson, 2013). This means that inclusively oriented teachers are presented with a fundamentally contradictory task—implement community to support diverse learners *and* display professionally appropriate forms of classroom control (that are at odds with the notion of *community*). The argument in this chapter has been that understanding families as *jointly* engaged with teachers in the development of community in the classroom is one way to address this tension. Such a joint production of community can affirm student and family experience while advancing teachers' commitments to equity, care, and social justice.

CHAPTER 6

Shifting Perspectives
Teachers as Teacher Educators

Preservice and novice teachers newly inducted into the commitments and practices of inclusive education almost always lament the gap between their own visions and that of their colleagues and mentors. Some novice teachers may even look for different opportunities with like-minded colleagues to sustain these commitments (Naraian & Schlessinger, in press). The quest to bring about changes in other teachers' perspectives to benefit student learning may be an important aspect of the work of inclusive pedagogy. Research has explored forms of professional development for general educators to support students with disabilities (Bai & Martin, 2015; Brusca-Vega, Alexander, & Kamin, 2014; Herner-Patnode, 2009; Streiker, Logan, & Kuhel, 2012; Weiner, 2003). However, the role of adult education *within* teacher practice has merited much less attention as a potentially important dimension to inclusive education. The experiences of the teachers in this chapter attest to the skills required for this work as well as serve as a reminder that they are uniquely positioned to have an impact that may be different from, but complementary to, university-based teacher educators.

Schools have historically used teachers' proficiency in particular domains of instructional and curricular practice by inviting them to share such acquired knowledge for the benefit of other teachers. The hope is that through such support the other teachers will improve their own capacity in the specific instructional area. It has become increasingly common across school districts, therefore, for teachers to adopt the role of instructional coaches (Thurston, Ryan, Agarwal, & Hanselman, 2015). Such coaching, like other forms of professional development, is generally focused on subject matter content and how students learn that content (Desimone, Smith, & Phillips, 2007). Its purpose is to improve teachers' practices in specific curricular areas. It is also an opportunity to move away from traditional models of professional development that have relied on the dissemination of discrete chunks of knowledge offered in a decontextualized manner that lead to a fragmented learning experience (Spillane, 2002). The premise of coaching seeks instead to privilege the teacher as learner through guided and ongoing opportunities for growth.

Centered on subject area/instructional emphases, such coaching is still different from the kind of shift in mindset that inclusive educators seek when engaging with their colleagues. The foundational premise of inclusive education requires a recognition of how notions of ability/disability have become ingrained in standard routines and practices in schools. There is much less precedence in the professional development literature, however, that can encompass curricular activity as well as the disruption of normative beliefs of student learning, and also remain situated within the local context (Herner-Patnode, 2009; Naraian & Oyler, 2014; Weiner, 2003). In the aftermath of legal action against school systems that have failed to address the needs of students with disabilities, some large districts have taken up reform measures to bring about changes in procedures and practices (e.g., Hehir et al., 2005; Walcott, 2011). For the most part, however, the spread of inclusive supports across school systems has been reliant on the committed efforts of individual leaders who bring strong social justice commitments (Theoharis, 2007). Teachers' roles within this process, therefore, while certainly a daunting endeavor, can also be an opportunity for the kind of coaching that has been largely missing in schools.

This chapter looks at the work of a few educators who found themselves engaged in this form of coaching with their colleagues. I begin with Elena, whose domain of professional support included navigating special education procedures in her school. I follow this with a brief exploration of Paul's efforts to shift the attitudes of his colleagues toward the role of families in inclusive schooling practices. I devote the bulk of the remainder of the chapter to describing the efforts of two specialists, Julie and Blair, who engaged in a multiyear, multisite program of individualized coaching to help teachers support students with difficult behaviors within their classrooms (Naraian, Ferguson, & Thomas, 2012). I particularly highlight three important skills that these teachers brought as teacher educators: presuming the competence of their colleagues; taking an empathetic stance toward the beliefs and dispositions presented by colleagues; and having a willingness to shift in their own thinking to bring about a shift in the thinking of their colleagues

TEACHERS SUPPORTING COLLEAGUES

Giving Back to the School: Elena

At the time of my study, Elena Moreno was a speech therapist in a middle school in Bell City, a large metropolis served by several hundred schools. Elena's school chose to participate in a pilot program initiated by the city's Board of Education to support students with disabilities within their home schools. Educators within pilot schools were encouraged to participate in professional-development activity whose purpose was to collectively build the capacity of the schools to create inclusive environments where students with disabilities could be supported to achieve the same educational outcomes as their nondisabled peers. As a member of a pilot school, Elena took up the opportunity for such professional development. Like Paul, she volunteered for the strand of professional development that centered on building family–school connections. The following description of Elena is based on my interactions with her during the yearlong professional development experience as well as through three interviews with her during the course of the same year. At the time of the research, Elena had already begun to assume additional responsibilities conferred on her by the school administration; she was working closely with the school IEP teacher; and she had started to offer workshops to small groups of teachers. She still remained deeply attached to her work as a speech therapist, especially given the number of students to whom she had been assigned in recent months. But on the whole, Elena seemed to be in the midst of gradually but surely reconfiguring the parameters of her professional identity, so that providing related services to students could coexist comfortably with burgeoning relationships with administrators and mentoring/development activities with teachers around supporting students with disabilities.

Understanding Teachers Through "Involvement." Central to Elena's conception of her professional role(s) was her preoccupation with being "involved" in her school. She clearly sought to identify and build connections with her colleagues. Given her status as related service provider, she was only too aware that she could easily be regarded as "someone who just picks up the kids and takes them to their little room and does their little thing." She worked actively against this perception, getting more involved with teachers and linking her own lessons with students to the curricular goals of classroom teachers. She gradually developed strong relationships with teachers, feeling strengthened herself as she recognized that teachers were more receptive to her, coming to perceive her as a support rather than as a mere source of interruption in their classrooms. The synergy from her own raised levels of confidence and a recognition of teachers' growing regard meant that she received with greater willingness the additional responsibilities that the administration began conferring on her. These responsibilities placed her more officially in the role of a support professional for teachers, leading to greater opportunities for building trust with them, while simultaneously complicating the boundaries of her role.

Perhaps it was her role as an adjunct professional in the classroom that provided Elena a unique window into the particular complexities of being a classroom teacher. She described teachers in deeply empathetic ways, even as she recognized the gaps in their perspectives or experiences. She noted the insecure and punitive climate within which they worked, the stringent evaluative practices that determined tenure decisions, and the administrative pressures to implement curriculum in specific ways. She also recognized that many of them required extensive levels of support in meeting special education procedural requirements. But above all, she seemed convinced that teachers were fundamentally responsible and professional. "They truly *are* caring of the kids, I have to say. The teachers that I have worked with, that I've gone to the classrooms and sat with the student in their class, they *do* try, the teachers *do* try. They just want someone to come in and say, (pause) *this* is how you do it, this is a *different* way of doing it." She did not hold any illusions that *all* teachers would readily fit this description, but she remained optimistic about the rest.

Elena's understanding of her colleagues clearly countered stereotypical notions of teachers as not only uncaring but as unable to benefit from professional development. She was also keenly aware of the discrepancies in levels of competence among teachers, which necessitated greater or lesser amounts of support. Newer teachers, particularly, required extensive mentoring in this area. But in the final analysis, it seemed less important to identify those who needed greater support as much as to offer a systemic means of support to *anyone* who needed it. Additionally, she seemed to recognize the particular means by which professional development could more likely effect changes in practices. For instance, she saw the significance of timing as crucial given the differing loads that weighed on teachers at different times of the year. She simultaneously recognized the importance of acknowledging teachers' existing practices when introducing new ones. "I think once they are made aware that 'Oh, this is something I already do' they'll be more comfortable and more open to it."

Elena valued the learning that collaborative activity among teachers brought in its wake. During our final interview in the fall of 2011 (after completion of the yearlong PD sequence), she expressed her deep regret in losing the weekly informal meetings on Friday afternoons when teachers, general and special education, would meet to discuss the progress of students with labeled disabilities, assess the need for any paperwork for them, and assist each other in the entering of data. These informal meetings were taken away during the 2011–2012 academic year when the school abandoned its policy of dismissing students early on Friday to permit professional development activity. She saw this change as a huge setback for the professional community in the school. "Okay, you just come to work Monday through Friday but you never get together as a group even to discuss any new changes or what is going on or upcoming things that are happening; that is something that the teachers definitely want. Makes you feel like you are part of the community."

Elena strove to facilitate a community of support, seeking to sustain a web of connected professionals rather than individuals struggling by themselves. On a pragmatic note, such support also meant that teachers could be held more accountable for completing the required paperwork, which made it less likely that the school could be deemed as "out-of-compliance." Elena recognized that teachers did not always pursue their IEP goal writing in a collaborative manner as intended by the law. Her empathetic stance notwithstanding, Elena was not hesitant about expecting teachers to implement the procedures with fidelity, but her stance was clearly inclined toward offering them generous, just-in-time supports to be able to do so.

As Elena began to assume greater nonpedagogical responsibilities, her connections with the administration deepened. She was called upon to assume a leadership role in managing student issues related to special education, as well as in creating supports for general education staff. For instance, it was she who would first receive information that an IEP had been determined to be out-of-compliance; or, if the district authorized a family's use of an outside agency for the delivery of related services, it was Elena who would receive that letter of authorization. She then had the responsibility of communicating that decision with the accompanying documents to the family. Elena felt very comfortable in the relationship that she had begun to develop with the administration that had been very supportive of her own professional development needs. Indeed, her decision to sign up for the PD experience on family–school connections was partly derived from wanting to "give back to the school" because "they have been good to me."

Still, she was both careful and cautious in sustaining these relations. For instance, when the administration requested that she attend an information session about a new documentation process (developing portfolios for students at risk of failure), she recognized that it would be to her advantage to have a colleague accompany her. Sure enough, following that session the administration asked her, with only a day's advance notice, to implement a workshop for the general education teachers on the portfolio process. Though Elena took this on as a challenge (and actually implemented it with a different colleague), she was fully aware that it may have been a strategic decision on the part of the administration to enlist her participation in the hope that school staff would be more receptive to the new process when offered by Elena and her colleague.

Elena as Positioned for Change. Elena's greatest asset may probably have been her proficiency in the procedural elements of special education that she seemed to regard as being separate from the pedagogical work of teachers. For many teachers (new or experienced) the formal procedures related to the documentation and implementation of special education practice is an enormous distraction from the more creative activity of designing curricular experiences for their students and developing deep relationships with them. Elena's assessment of teacher need in this area surfaces a critical area of support for teachers to broaden the parameters of their existing practices and move, albeit slowly, toward greater inclusive classroom environments. Her approach to teachers presumed their basic competence, which was unaffected by their inability to complete formal procedures with fidelity. In representing her colleagues to me, Elena offered no judgment, but an empathetic awareness of the scope of their activities. One might well argue that Elena's devotion to supporting teachers in the implementation of procedures was uncritical and merely perpetuated the status quo. Yet, as a teacher educator, Elena seemed to draw on a mix of knowledge, empathy, and strategy that could enlist teacher support more readily than perhaps other forms of professional development initiated by the administration. Clearly, administrators recognized the particular skills she brought when they used her to deliver a potentially difficult message to the teachers, as in the new, additional tasks entailed in the portfolio process.

Elena displayed the skills to serve as an intermediary between the administration and the teaching staff. Through her own related service work and her empathetic posture with teachers, she remained grounded in the experiences of students in classrooms. Simultaneously, her out-of-classroom responsibilities brought her more directly in contact with both administrative and family experiences. Elena was strategically suited, therefore, to bring about shifts in thinking within various sectors of school practice. The growth she sought for herself, however, centered on her capacity to be an effective source of support for teachers, not on bringing about fundamental shifts in response to ability/disability. The changes in belief she desired in teachers revolved around building *their* sense of self-efficacy in relation to struggling learners. She tried to accomplish this through both schoolwide workshops on classroom practices for diverse learners and individualized supports to teachers in managing special education procedures. To the extent that inclusive education practice implies a continual reconfiguration of teacher identity and teacher competence (see Chapter 3), she was engaged in important inclusive education work. After all, unless teachers could engage competently with existing procedures and practices that would be used to document their own proficiency as capable certified professionals, they might be less likely to mitigate its effects on children and their families.

Can the facility to embrace an intermediary position that called for straddling multiple, even competing priorities suffice to provoke or stimulate dramatic shifts in others' beliefs about learning ability? What does this space of "being in the middle" entail if it must actually bring schools closer to the vision of spaces where all forms of ability are welcomed? I turn now to a brief glimpse into Paul's attempt to engage his colleagues in shifting their deficit orientation to families.

Shifting Lenses of Self and Colleagues: Paul

In this section I offer a brief glimpse of Paul's approach to the learning of colleagues that was similarly supportive rather than evaluative, even as it went beyond subject matter content or school-based procedures. Like Elena, Paul enrolled in the same professional development opportunity to understand family–school relations within inclusive schooling practices. Unlike Elena, who sought a shift in teachers' understanding of their self-efficacy but did not describe experiencing this shift within herself, Paul's starting point was in understanding his own journey.

At the beginning, Paul's approach to family–school relations was dominated by legal issues—how should he conduct himself with a family in a legally responsible manner befitting a professional within the school system? He recognized that cultural differences between schools and families were inevitable. Yet, in the absence of legal guidelines that supported risk taking on the part of educators in this area, he fell back on the standard procedures established in schools to engage with families. So, for instance, he approved of the role of the counseling team at the school to control how information about the students' families was disseminated to teachers. He interpreted their authority to do so as a form of protection for himself since there was no guarantee that the school would provide institutional backing for his actions.

Yet, through participating in PD experiences, Paul began to view such relations differently. Reporting on how the process of doing interviews and a home visit led him to see both a student and her family differently, he described his amazement at discovering that this family presented such an important resource for other families in the school. He discovered "all the other dimensions that made Talia's mother an entire person, as opposed to only being the mother of one of my students." Paul's understanding emerged partly from recognizing that the questions schools typically asked families reflected narrow objectives. He came to realize that the goal of interviewing families was not merely to learn more about the student in relation to school; it was to understand the family in deeper ways and then figure out what that would mean for his own practice. In other words, to shift his thinking from families as merely supporting the work of schools, to schools as playing an important role in strengthening families (and by extension the entire community), he would need to adopt a posture of "I want to learn *from* you" (please tell me your story) rather than "I am a professional sent to learn *about* you" (I am collecting information about you). Engaging with the family in this way disclosed different ways to interact with this student and her family that Paul had not considered before.

Following the home visit/interviews with this family, Paul excitedly contemplated many options about connecting families with each other so that they would benefit from each other's expertise and knowledge. Additionally, as part of his project within the yearlong PD, he decided to conduct a workshop for his own colleagues in school to encourage them to view families in the ways he had now begun to take up. Beginning where he knew most teachers in his school would be comfortable—data about student performance in school—he shared his experiences with them and the changes in understanding the role of families that he had undergone. He received a range of responses from his colleagues; some offered a positive affirmation of his experience, while others were less certain that it was appropriate for teachers to engage so directly with families in the absence of specialized professional knowledge to do so. Paul's reaction to this was measured, though optimistic. He did not expect teachers to run out and do interviews with families right away. But consciously applying the concept of *presuming competence* (Biklen & Burke, 2006) to his colleagues, he was able to extend an empathetic understanding of their inability to enter his vision at that time and think *with* them. So, for instance, his response to teachers' apprehensiveness to the concept of home visits was to suggest creating a database of families who express willingness to participate in interviews with teachers (this would, of course, be preceded by a survey of families for this purpose). He also concretized the shift in thinking demanded of teachers by embedding it in their routine work. So, for instance, he suggested that the questions to be asked during a home visit could become the first part of the vocational assessment that educators were already required to conduct with students.

Paul was not unlike Elena in that he located teachers' presumed inabilities within the everyday struggles of their work. But Paul's understanding of his journey positioned him differently from Elena for bringing about deeper and more fundamental shifts in thinking. Elena's stance reflected the support of a more competent peer for greater success in achieving school-based outcomes. In that way she could scaffold their learning in this area, but she did not seek to bring about deep changes in how teachers approached schooling. Paul's vision, in this regard, was more expansive. The outcomes he desired were more *transgressive* in the likely effects that they might have on family–school relations within his building. Such radical outcomes necessitated that Paul take up an empathetic rather than evaluative response to his colleagues' tempered reaction to his own momentous learning experience. This empathetic posture would be a notable characteristic of the kind of painstaking, extensive support that the educators whom I describe next provided to teachers as they embarked on reducing classroom referrals of students with behavioral challenges to alternative settings.

TAKING THE LONG ROAD: DIFFERENTIATING SUPPORT NEEDS FOR PEER DEVELOPMENT

In this section, I describe the systematic process undertaken by two educators—Julie, a behavior specialist, and Blair, a social worker—in the Midwest School District (MSD), an urban school district. Collectively, these educators were charged with the implementation of a model to support teachers in engaging with students who demonstrated challenging behaviors in school. During the period of the study (2005–2007) MSD comprised about 8,000 students and 800 certified teachers within nine elementary schools, two middle schools, and one comprehensive high school. The student body was predominantly Black (97% in 2007), with 77% receiving free or reduced-price lunch.

Historically, MSD had used a traditional pull-out model for addressing the needs of students with social, emotional, and behavioral challenges. As student behavior came to take an important place in district concerns, the newly instated leadership at the time of the study decided to implement a new model that could support students in inclusionary ways. Julie and Blair, who had significant experience with students with emotional and behavioral needs, were recruited to implement this model across multiple elementary schools. The premise of this model was to eliminate a pull-out structure for support that located the problem within children. Instead, it sought to improve the school environment through a thoughtful and systematic understanding of the immediate context. By working directly with individual teachers for prolonged periods, the specialists implementing the model were able to determine priorities for professional development that emerged organically from the particular school context. In that regard, the model did not prescribe a sequence of predetermined objectives for professional development and instead prioritized spaces for collaborative inquiry for all participants including the specialists themselves. Rejecting the expert–novice relationship within traditional PD, the emphasis was on the transformative processes that occurred within both teachers and specialists when engaged in an agenda of and for change. (For more details about the model, see Naraian et al., 2012.)

In the following paragraphs, I focus particularly on how the teacher educators supported the learning and development of the teachers with whom they worked. My hope is that their efforts can disclose not only the particular skills that are required to enable this process, but also the unique advantages accrued to their positions as school-based educators when seeking to support shifts in peer-teachers' perspectives.

Understanding the Local Context

By the time Julie and Blair began to work at MSD, they had already initiated innovative approaches to working with such students in other schools and collaborated with teachers to implement those new ways of responding to the needs of these students. Their shared commitment to an ecological approach to understanding the needs of students with emotional and behavioral difficulties had resulted in a strong personal and professional partnership.

In past efforts, they had drawn primarily on their expertise and worked with children and youth, modeling and explaining their work to other teachers. This new endeavor at MSD was different; it required them to assist teachers to think and act differently about their students rather than just showing and telling what teachers should be doing. The model specifically excluded them from working directly with students to bring about a change in their behaviors—the "fix the child" approach. Instead, the aim of the model was to provide teachers with the tools to create classroom environments where students would be supported to learn, and perhaps change their behaviors.

As outsiders to the district, Julie and Blair had to understand the unique conditions available to teachers and students in these schools. The relations between teachers, between teachers and students, and between the administration and staff in these schools seemed to collectively create a pervasive climate of tension and dissatisfaction. Like many urban schools, these schools were characterized by a scripted approach to teaching and learning, a continual anxiety about student scores, and a punitive evaluative process that prohibited teachers from adopting more creative approaches to teaching. Not surprisingly, in most of these buildings teachers held students accountable to stringent rules of appropriate behavior. Students who violated such rules were punished mostly through the withdrawal of privileges. Additionally, teachers were generally unwilling to relax those standards for students who might require other supports or interventions.

Within this context, the project of shifting teachers' mindsets was daunting. Julie and Blair understood that many teachers disliked their work intensely or were consumed in merely maintaining order in their classrooms. The objective of enabling teachers to establish nurturing and caring classrooms seemed remote indeed when teachers saw students as problems and as the cause of their own dissatisfaction. After a few months, Julie and Blair gradually came to understand teachers as battling an oppressive context that placed enormous burdens on them and that spilled over into the classroom. If they were going to be successful in supporting these teachers, they needed to make this the grounding premise of their work with them. This is supported in recent research that has begun to acknowledge the role of emotional knowledge as contributing significantly to the curricular and instructional decisions that teachers make (Zembylas, 2007).

The Process of Facilitating Change

From the very beginning Julie and Blair maintained an empathetic stance with teachers, acknowledging the constraints under which they operated and validating their grievances and concerns in working under stressful conditions. They viewed this empathetic position as necessary for achieving the kinds of relations with teachers that would enable them to bring about eventual changes in their thinking. It seemed appropriate, then, that the very first thing that Julie and Blair set out to do was to build relationships with the teachers. They implicitly recognized that teachers' emotional responses to stressful conditions within which they worked required a forum for expression and validation. Without that, it would be difficult to make deeper sense of complex and challenging school/classroom events. They found ways to engage with the teachers by adopting an empathetic stance so that they could build strong relations with them. As Julie remarked, "I feel like a lot of what I have done with the push-in is just to be supportive in any way I can, just to tell them, you know, kind of bend my ear, just to say 'Gosh, it looks like you are having a rough morning today and how can I help you?' because I don't feel like they get a lot of support."

Enacting an Empathetic Approach. This empathetic posture would then dictate the ways they introduced teachers to their own roles, planned collective opportunities for teachers, and supported them in the use of different strategies. During weekly professional development sessions or individual coaching sessions, they never failed to recognize the pressures that the teachers faced. With some groups they found that such acknowledgment helped teachers move quickly to building new skills; they were more receptive to reflective exercises that would help them understand their own practice differently. Zembylas (2007) notes that teachers' emotional knowledges that are constituted on several different planes—individual, relational, and sociopolitical—collectively influence the ways teachers interact with students and the climate they sustain within the classroom. Julie and Blair's decision to directly acknowledge and utilize the teachers' emotional experience as a means to bringing about change in their practice reinforces these strong connections between emotions and pedagogy.

They also soon realized the challenges of working with adult learners. As Julie noted, it was easier to work with students. "They [kids] are much more flexible and willing to try things and they'll say, 'that kind of works.' As an adult, it's like, if I admit your way was better or that it worked, then it would also [mean] having to say what I was doing didn't work and that's a much more bitter pill." Bringing about fundamental shifts in thinking in adults was not easy. They learned that when teachers have become accustomed to receiving methods and strategies that they are told would fix the problem, they are less likely to begin to see the connections between the problems they encounter and their own practice.

To elicit and sustain trust, as well as to engage teachers in the process of transformation, Julie and Blair had to be thoughtful about the supports they provided. At the outset, this meant that they had to devise strategic ways to gain entry into teachers' classrooms and feel welcomed by them. Thus, even though the model required them to work with teachers rather than students, they might begin with the latter if that meant being able to elicit the trust of the teacher. Both modeled ways of teaching and interacting with students that they hoped would eventually be used by the classroom teachers as well. They offered their assistance in the classroom, sometimes merely observing, at other times assisting individual students within the room. They opted to allow the teachers to set the agenda for the professional development sessions by asking them what they needed. Then, regardless of whether they thought it was appropriate, they would bring them the resources they needed. By beginning with the teachers' definitions of their situation, their needs, and possible solutions, Blair and Julie could build the trust to introduce newer ideas and strategies that might be comfortable for the teacher to adopt.

This stance of inviting teachers to share their own descriptions of the class, and probing for more details about those descriptions and how teachers felt about them, became an important means not only to elicit trust but also to begin the process of reflection that is integral to initiating change. For example, when beginning a conversation with one teacher, Mr. Adams, regarding a particularly challenging student in his classroom, Julie was observed asking, "What behaviors do *you* want from Joe?" Julie might empathize with Mr. Adams that as far as this student was concerned, the teacher was clearly on his own and did not have any other support. She might also make sure that she acknowledged his efforts by noting, "I liked how you . . . ," when debriefing an interaction between the teacher and Joe. Julie and Blair gleaned a wealth of information through such conversations that they used when consulting with teachers about their practice. They could better anticipate the responses of the teachers with whom they had already begun to form a relationship. They could also then thoughtfully plan questions to ask that would assist teachers to reflect on their own practice and discuss alternate interpretations and approaches to the class and/or student. It was not so much Julie's or Blair's assessment of the situation but the teachers' that made all the difference in what might be possible for them to do in response. In the end, they might offer them some strategies to consider, but those suggestions had to fit the teachers' definition of the situation and teaching style rather than their own.

Julie and Blair saw these individual debriefing and coaching sessions as particularly necessary for teacher growth. It allowed them to understand teachers' motivations and actions so that they were better able to tailor their supports for each. So, even as debriefing sessions might inevitably revolve around particular students, by persistent probing on overall classroom practice, they were able to draw the attention of the teacher to the teaching–learning environment within the classroom as a whole. Not surprisingly, teachers began to generate their own solutions rather than depend on Julie and Blair for them. At first, it seemed teachers did not appear to prioritize this part of their relationship. They seemed to be happy to have another adult to help them in the classroom with students, but shared little interest in joining Julie and Blair in a quest to think differently about the students and their practice. Yet Blair and Julie persevered in their commitment to supporting teachers despite their reservations about the instructional methods used by teachers. Eventually, several teachers did come to recognize the importance of collectively reflecting on the events in their classrooms.

Effects on Teachers. The emotional support provided to teachers clearly brought benefits to them. As Mr. Adams shared in a separate interview with researchers, "I really enjoy having her [Julie], because it's somebody else, an objective third party to give me some advice and all that on how we can best help him [Joe]." However, more than the immediate support for the student, he also experienced a shift in his own capacity to feel competent as a teacher.

"I just feel that since I've talked to her, since I've started working with her, I am a little bit better, a little bit more able to deal with the discipline in the classroom, because that is something that I struggled with the first two years teaching and this is my 4th year, and it's been a huge difference. I was improving already as the year started, but once I started to work with Julie I feel that I have improved more. She's helped me be able to figure out some different things to just think about when I am working with the kids."

This teacher took pride in the fact that he had built a relationship with Joe, something that no one else in the building had been able to do thus far. This in turn allowed him to feel confident that he could manage issues of discipline in the classroom and "adapt better" to its conditions.

This teacher had been open and willing to participate in the reflection–inquiry process with Julie. However, there were other teachers who felt certain in the validity of their own instructional practices and continued to regard students with difficult behaviors as interfering in their ability to run classrooms smoothly. In these cases, it was a struggle for Julie and Blair to focus purposefully on the teachers who might well believe that they did not need any assistance from them. Instead, they focused on creating opportunities for such teachers to develop deeper relationships with their students. This might, for instance, entail taking over the class, while that teacher had the opportunity to interact individually with a student. They hoped that such one-on-one moments might assist the teacher to acquire an understanding of the student that went beyond the confines of the classroom. In fact, this method of releasing teachers from routine classroom responsibilities to do the activities that would make them less dependent on external "expert" knowledge by deepening their own understanding of students, represented a key element of the methodology adopted by Julie and Blair.

Self-Reflection as Teacher Educators: Julie and Blair

As much as they sought to help teachers reflect on their practice, Julie and Blair also had to continually reflect on their own. They had to continually be vigilant about their tendency to fix the problem for the teachers rather than allow them to arrive at the solutions themselves. They had to do this even as they focused on building the relationships that would allow them to eventually assist teachers to engage in deeper inquiry and learning. Given their own expertise in working with students with difficult behaviors, they had to consciously avoid offering the strategies or methods of intervention that occurred so readily to them. In actual fact, however, they were not always able to refrain from doing so. Both struggled personally to change their own instructional behaviors.

For both of them, it was the reflective space provided to them by the district superintendent, Nora, who had initiated the model in the district and had recruited them to implement it, that would remain a critical part of their practice. Discussions facilitated by Nora and the university researchers continually made them aware of their tendencies to offer solutions to teachers and the ways they could modify their assistance so that they were actually helping the teachers build their own capacity to generate solutions, rather than directly offering them the solutions. Julie and Blair began to articulate this support dynamic on which they depended. "I could walk in and just say you got to do this, this, and this, but you know Nora has made it clear that it's the process, . . . it's not about product" (Julie). Helping teachers develop their own inquiry into their practice so that they could confidently solve their own problems was the real outcome. As Blair quoted Nora more than once, "'I don't care if you solve any kind of problem' . . . . She says it's not about that. That end product is irrelevant." It was assisting teachers to go through the process of investigating their own practice that was distinctive about this model of professional development.

The emphasis, adopted by Nora, on teacher reflection as critical to the process of professional growth, has been well documented in teacher education research. Teacher education scholarship is replete with injunctions to engage teachers in thoughtful self-reflective processes to bring about changes in practice (e.g., see Cochran-Smith & Lytle, 2001; Zeichner & Liston, 1996). As these scholars point out, teachers are continually engaged in problem solving in the course of their practice. Within this process, teachers use their own practical theories based on particular belief systems to frame the issues and dilemmas they have confronted in their classrooms. A reflective stance would involve making visible some of these tacit forms of knowledge that could then allow teachers to begin reconstructing their practice. The task Julie and Blair took up was not simply about facilitating changes in teachers' craft, but in finding the ways by which teachers could reframe their experiences with students in new ways.

As they assisted teachers to reframe their practice, they could not help but wonder about how their own effectiveness was being assessed by the teachers with whom they worked. Working with the group at one elementary school, for example, made them feel more successful, even as it simultaneously made them acutely aware of their inadequacy at a different elementary school. During the early days of the model implementation, when they were providing greater pragmatic assistance in the classroom, the feedback received from teachers was less about changes occurring in their thinking and more about the usefulness of the assistance they provided in the classroom. At that time they might have attributed this to the failure of those teachers to recognize that they needed help. In the early stages of this work, Julie commented, "Part of the problem is that the teachers that really need the most help in terms of changing how they deal with behaviors in the classroom are the ones that don't have insight into the fact that they need help, which [might be] too threatening." More than a year later, they were acutely conscious of the fact that it was *they*—Blair and Julie—who seemed to be unable to gain credibility in the eyes of some of the teachers. Coming to understand teachers differently was itself a significant dimension of their reflective practice.

The assessment of their (in)effectiveness prompted them to further develop their own activities in ways that could both meet the needs of the teachers and perhaps enable them to acquire a different perspective on their students. It was not simply the goals of the model, that is, a shift from exclusionary to inclusionary practice that could guide their progress. It was also the perception of teachers about the service Julie and Blair provided that would be necessary to gauge how effectively they were able to accomplish the goals of the model. So, when they were unable to get teachers to locate part of their struggles within their own practice, their efforts were directed to helping reduce their levels of frustration against a faceless, punitive system. Increasingly, Blair and Julie were "really able to center on them [the teachers]. . . . It's really hard to change kids. But our goal is 'how can we help you maybe do something different so that you don't get so frustrated and you don't get so upset.'" (Julie). The well-being of the teacher remained a critical route to supporting the implementation of more inclusively oriented practices in the classroom.

SHIFTING MINDSETS: LEARNING FROM ELENA, PAUL, JULIE, AND BLAIR

The change in focus from student to teacher learning that Julie and Blair had to undertake does not diminish the importance of meeting the educational needs of the student. It simply recognizes that within the project of moving schools to more inclusive practices, teachers too must be conceptualized as learners who are always situated within their contexts and require unique supports (Borko, 2004). In this regard, the four educators described in this chapter were able to uphold three important commitments when supporting their colleagues. I suggest that the adequacy of efforts to support and encourage teachers to take up more inclusive stances in their approach to schooling may need to consider these commitments, as discussed below.

Presuming Peer-Teacher Competence

A central premise that has grounded the work of scholars in the field of a disability studies–informed teacher education is the notion of presuming competence (Biklen & Burke, 2006). Such a stance requires educators to assume that students are capable of growth and learning, in the absence of reliable information to the contrary. It means that when an educator is unable to determine whether a student can accomplish a skill or task, he or she must presume that the student is capable of participating in that activity that might then lead to the development of that skill. In other words, students' learning can never be fully predicted and so the least dangerous assumption (Donellan, 1984) is to provide an opportunity for the students to demonstrate their capability. This might mean that when teachers wonder if students with certain types of disabilities can succeed in a classroom, they must first presume that the students can benefit from this experience before determining how their participation can be structured. When students react to a teacher in ways that are seen as disrespectful, inappropriate, or offensive, the educator must first presume that the students bear a story, even if presently unavailable, that can explain such behavior. While this concept has been the cornerstone for encouraging teachers to facilitate inclusive experiences for students with disabilities, it has been used less in the work of teachers and teacher educators educating teachers.

In the experiences described in this chapter, it seemed fairly clear that Elena, Paul, Julie, and Blair were beginning with the assumption that teachers were capable of change and growth.

As teachers themselves already immersed in schooling routines and practices, they brought deeply shared understandings about the conditions within which instructional practice had to be accomplished. They could speak from within the composite of obligations, pressures, freedoms, constraints, and joys that made up the everyday context of teaching for the members of their professional communities. This served as their strongest asset in enlisting teachers in change toward greater inclusivity—the likelihood of trust and credibility with their colleagues that each presumed but never took for granted, and that enabled them to take the risk of adopting, however temporarily, a different relationship with their peers. The presumption of teacher competence that emerged from such shared understandings allowed Julie and Blair to continue supporting teachers regardless of the punitive climate they saw being enforced in classrooms, giving the teachers instead the time and space to rethink their practice. It was also this stance that permitted Paul to conduct the workshop for his colleagues while still holding tempered expectations of its effects on them.

Adopting a Posture of Empathy

If these educators presumed the competence of their colleagues to grow, they also intuitively recognized the importance of a climate of emotional support for that learning to occur. While that was made most clearly visible in the work of Julie and Blair, it was no less evident in the work of the others. Elena was unwilling to see her colleagues judged harshly by the administration or by others, if they were not given the supports to become proficient in mandated procedures. She understood that teachers were more likely to adopt new practices when they were shown as being connected with what they were already doing in the classroom. She recognized the pressures under which teachers worked and took satisfaction in relieving some of that for them. Paul's empathetic stance emerged in his refusal to judge his colleagues for their actions.

The significance of emotional support emerges from the recognition that teaching itself constitutes significant emotional labor (Hargreaves, 2001; Isenbarger & Zembylas, 2006). Using the frame of "emotional geographies of teaching," Hargreaves (2001) describes the moral, political, and sociocultural distances that often exist between teachers', students', and families' experiences. Such distances impact the ways teachers respond emotionally within their teaching–learning contexts. For instance, in the schools where Julie and Blair worked, teachers had little or no control over the kinds of instructional expectations that were placed on them. Their distance from such policymaking meant that they experienced anxiety and helplessness in remedying the situation. Such anxiety was then exacerbated in the face of student actions that threatened to damage their own sense of professional self-worth. When Julie and Blair listened to teachers and allowed *them* to describe the situation in their classrooms, they were, in a sense, offering an avenue not just for validating feelings of anger but as an opportunity to grow from it. Similarly, when Elena lamented the loss of opportunities for collective problem solving among teachers each Friday afternoon, she was registering the importance of that space for learning that could permit teachers to alter, albeit briefly, the "emotional geography" of their day by engaging with their colleagues to develop deeper understandings of students.

As deeply implicated in identity processes (Boler & Zembylas, 2003), teachers' emotions are an integral part of their competencies as educators. A feminist perspective on emotions understands them not as individualized or medicalized phenomena, but as always entangled with social arrangements (Ahmed, 2004; Boler, 1999). The emotional validation offered to their colleagues by the empathetic stance of these four educators appeared to corroborate this point. They implicitly recognized that the social conditions within which teachers worked played a significant role in their abilities to be effective as educators and to perceive themselves as such.

Mirroring the Process of Transformation Through Self-reflection

For the four educators described in this chapter, the process of supporting their colleagues to shift in their thinking was not separate from their own willingness to do the same. While Paul used the collaborative space of the professional development opportunity to engage with, and question, his assumptions and beliefs with other participants, Julie and Blair did the same with the administrative leaders and university researchers who supported their work. It was within these nonthreatening, collegial, and intellectually stimulating spaces that they could come to understand how they approached their own practice and the implications this had on what they sought in others. For instance, through these reflective discussions with others, Julie and Blair were able to identify the unique ways each of them took up the charge of supporting teachers and the differential impact that it had both on themselves and on the teachers. In becoming aware of these differences, they were then better able to adjust their own practice to more efficiently implement the model of professional development. Each meeting with the administrators and researchers was an opportunity to revisit the main goals of their work and parse out its meanings for their own practice as specialists supporting teachers.

For Paul, his engagement in self-reflection may have emerged from his natural inclination to do so continually as well as from the collective opportunities for reflection encouraged within his own school by his principal. Not surprisingly, he could freely comment on how the opportunity to visit a family's home debunked his stereotypical assumptions about public housing environments. As he encountered literature and ideas that disclosed assumptions in routine schooling practices that devalue family knowledges, he engaged honestly with these arguments, both challenging them and recognizing the ways in which such practices have become accepted in schools. Paul remained continually critical of his own and others' practices. Still, even as he spoke about seeking to bring about changes in thinking among his colleagues, he remained cognizant of the many ways their practices could be interpreted. It was not surprising, then, that he reacted to his peers' responses to his workshop without judgment but with understanding.

Elena did not directly afford me a glimpse into the process of change that she might have experienced. In some ways her own engagement with the professional development opportunity in which she participated mirrored the kind of participation she seemed to be seeking in the teachers she supported. In other words, in not privileging a shift in thinking but focusing more on the procedural forms of support, she might have avoided the discomfort entailed in creating and participating in such inquiry spaces. Her form of support then, while no less important, may have lacked the potency latent in the work of Julie and Blair, as well as that of Paul. The efforts of Paul, Julie, and Blair were significant in the type of shifts they were seeking to bring about and whose success depended on the experience of change that they had themselves experienced. In the absence of an overtly self-reflective stance on this process of growth, Elena's work, while significant in its own way for the teachers she supported, may have been less generative for bringing about enduring change within the building.

CHAPTER 7

Learning from Teachers' Work
Toward Inclusion as a Pedagogy of Deferral

General and special educators all over the world are situated in the midst of competing discourses of ability/disability that they must negotiate carefully to facilitate inclusive opportunities for their students with disabilities. The objective of this book has been to attend to their struggles in accomplishing this charge. In this chapter, I explore new concepts and theories evoked for me by the experiences of educators described in this book, which, in conjunction with the theoretical foundations presented in the Introduction, can direct us to new ways of understanding the work of doing inclusion. My purpose is to solidify the fundamental premise of this book, that is, principles of doing inclusion emerge not only from visions of equity and justice, but also from a careful study of teacher practice.

THE INTERPRETIVE STANCE TOWARD TEACHER PRACTICE REFLECTED IN THIS BOOK

Researchers may adopt different interpretive lenses to make sense of the practices of the participants within their studies. For instance, my location as a researcher within the disability studies tradition (described in the Introduction) affords me certain lenses for interpreting how disability and learning are described and enacted in schools. I have also consciously made other decisions in the ways I have approached the narratives of teachers. These decisions, described below, are equally integral to my interpretive stance toward teacher practice. They have been critical for a more expansive theorizing of the complex work of doing inclusion.

Rearticulation as an Investigative Approach

One important decision I have made is reflected in my use of *rearticulation* (Collins, 2000) as an approach to understanding teachers' experiences. In her work, Patricia Collins consciously seeks to situate herself in the everyday lived experiences of ordinary Black women rather than rely exclusively on Black women intellectuals. In describing Black feminist thought, she argues that it "affirms, rearticulates, and provides a vehicle for expressing in public a consciousness that quite often already exists. More important, this rearticulated consciousness aims to empower African American women and stimulate resistance" (p. 36). A careful rearticulation of the stories of educators, which I have attempted in this book, not only counteracts stereotypes of teachers as colluding passively with oppressive systems; it can also disclose potential sites of resistance that may otherwise be unavailable.

The deficit-based discourses within which teachers' experiences are inevitably grounded no doubt remain a threat within this process, and any researcher or educator must monitor this vigilantly. But such rearticulation also allows a more nuanced understanding of teachers' work and their capacity to recognize the potential of systems to dehumanize their students. Indeed, the pervasive influence of schooling discourses that regulate teacher and student performance disclosed through the process of rearticulation suggests that any understanding of inclusive pedagogy will be partial, at best, and ineffective, at worst, if it does not in some manner account for them. In that regard, by valuing the efforts of teachers who are compulsorily situated within these constricting discourses, a rearticulation of the lived experiences of school personnel seeking to support students with disabilities inclusively, would also make the process of reform more dialogic. It does so by affording a mechanism to escape the "theory–practice divide." Reflecting a stance of solidarity with teachers, the practice of rearticulation establishes their (and other school personnel's) work as necessary for continually refining a concept of inclusive education.

As the teachers' experiences described in this book suggest, the discomfort that inclusive education scholars experience in negotiating with discourses that are not cleanly aligned with constructivist, empowering, and expansive notions of schooling, disability, and learning is not theirs alone. Teachers, too, experience the same misgivings and unease when taking up positions that contradict their commitments to equity. However, situated in the midst of compulsory school routines, they have little recourse other than to negotiate with such uncomfortable positions to accomplish a synthesis that can then restore their ability to function effectively as caring teachers.

This deliberate attention to teacher experiences, whether critical, unreflective, thoughtful, or flawed, does not minimize the wealth of scholarly knowledge gleaned in the past two decades from the careful analysis of how schools function to sort, categorize, and objectify the learning differences that are inevitable among students (e.g., see Brantlinger, 2006; Gallagher, 1998; Skrtic, 1995; Ware, 2010). Rather, such experiences can deepen our understandings of how we can better equip teachers to work toward inclusion, particularly in schooling contexts that are either ambivalent about it or reluctant to understand its implications for *all* of schooling. This conscious focus on teacher experience requires us to extend to school personnel the same stance of presuming competence that we desire teachers to extend to students. It provokes us to imagine teacher work for inclusion in ways that can straddle multiple, competing ideologies. It directs us to think about theoretical frames that can help us hold such competing visions together without losing our own identities as inclusive educators.

It may surprise readers that in surveying teacher practices across sites, this book has not attended to instructional frameworks that are typically considered to support an inclusive pedagogy such as differentiated instruction (Tomlinson, 2014) or Universal Design for Learning (Rose, Meyer, & Hitchcock, 2006). I do not seek to minimize the significance of drawing on these to implement instruction that can accommodate the needs of diverse learners. Many important books have been written about the utility of such frames for inclusive education. My purpose, however, was to develop some markers of inclusive pedagogy that emerged from teachers' practice rather than to investigate the extent to which their practice supported or drew on such instructional frameworks. The latter would be an important research question; it was not, however, the focus of this book. My presumption in this book has been that the implementation of any instructional framework must contend with contextual specificities that inevitably transform abstract principles in unpredictable ways. It is the intersection of such specificities and the fundamental tenets of inclusive education that I have sought to examine in this book.

Interlocking Theory and Practice

Not surprisingly, as I investigated the experiences of educators, an important question that arose for me was this: How can the rearticulation (Collins, 2000) of teachers' experiences generate theoretical frames and concepts that will interlock readily with the conditions of schooling in which they (teachers) are situated? My use of the term *interlock* is intentional. The Merriam-Webster dictionary defines *interlock* as "to connect so that the motion or operation of any part is constrained by another" (www.merriam-webster.com/dictionary/interlock). In using such a *machine* metaphor, I depart from my own expressed views on how such metaphors can be unhelpful to an understanding of disability (Danforth & Naraian, 2007). One may argue that it works directly against the narrative principles that have been a core premise of this book. I deliberately take up this contradiction both because of its relevance to the work of teachers and also to participate for a moment in the world of competing visions in which teachers are necessarily situated. As a narrative inquirer, I seek to privilege the ways in which actors come to understand the worlds they inhabit (Clandinin, 2013). As a scholar committed to supporting teachers' efforts to advance inclusion in schools, I can also appreciate a conceptual framing of practices that may obtain greater currency in schools. Like many of the teachers in the book who worked creatively with instructional tension (Stillman,

2014), my hope in this chapter is to reconcile these conflicting paradigms in ways that can be generative for the field.

My assumption, therefore, is that the concepts and theories scholars offer teachers in their efforts toward inclusion must *interlock* with existing practices in ways that can not only alter the directions in which they operate, but also strengthen the intensity with which they are delivered. My argument is that without such *engagement* (another machine metaphor) inclusion will continue to be understood in narrow, restrictive ways, remaining distant from the vision of multisector transformation of schooling systems that spurs the work of scholar-activists and activist-practitioners. My intent is to begin that process in this chapter. The rearticulation of teacher experience that I have tried to accomplish in this book occurred in the midst of my interest in exploring U.S. Third World feminist scholarship. This scholarship has generated new meanings of resistance that lie at the heart of teacher work in implementing inclusion. It has simultaneously offered new ways of thinking about the "doing" of inclusion that can encompass a dual commitment to equity for students with disabilities and their families as well as to the complex lives of teachers in schools.

NEW CONCEPTS FOR INCLUSION:
THE AFFORDANCE OF U.S. THIRD WORLD FEMINISM

Sandoval (2000) has suggested that within the writings of U.S. Third World feminists lie the core principles of a methodology of resistance that can be taken up by any social justice movement. Like other feminists of color, she has drawn on the experiences of marginalized people around the world to offer a "methodology of the oppressed" that can be generative for educators as they negotiate oppressive systems and structures in the struggle for inclusion. According to these writers, the unique location of women of color in the United States and Third World contexts leaves them marked by a "simultaneity of oppression" invoking skills that distinguish them as "urban guerillas" (Hurtado, 1996). As these women grapple with the everyday structures and relations of domination, their resistance occurs in the small everyday practices rather than through publicly organized forms. Their daily struggles require movement through multiple ideological positions that can leave their individual subjectivities diffused and ambiguous.

The conceptual premises of this body of work and the constructs it has generated resonated with my understanding of the struggles of all actors, including teachers, within the project of inclusion. It offered a way to conceptualize the *process* of doing inclusion that went beyond specific curricular methods, offering instead a rationale for decisionmaking when taking up such methods. In the following sections, I articulate a few concepts that may assist teachers when embarking on the journey to inclusion (Nguyen, 2015).

Inclusive Education as Borderland

For educators, the contradictory experiences of engaging with oppressive systems may disturb their sense of professional belonging or identity. If they are inclusive educators, can they take up special education practices? If they take up behaviorist practices such as direct instruction, does that mean they are no longer constructivists? If they prepare their students to be successful in standardized testing, are they being complicit with exclusionary forces? Such dilemmas imply that teachers must have a stable intellectual "home" whose boundaries are fixed and known. One's identity and professional worth (as educator, scholar, activist), we assume, is derived from remaining faithful to the intellectual boundaries of one's home.

U.S. Third World feminists, however, complicate the notion of home as they draw on the struggles of marginalized people around the world. Exploring the experiences of immigrants and refugees of color, Minh-Ha (2011) observes that the static concept of *home* may refer to an illusory place; home itself has no fixed boundaries. "The meanings of here and there, home and abroad, third and first, margin and center keep on being displaced depending on how one positions oneself" (p. 39). This conception of *traveling* between states (literally and figuratively) reconfigures meanings of *home* or *dwelling*. Traveling itself becomes a form of dwelling or a state of home—a state of in-between, of neither here nor there, but elsewhere within here and elsewhere within there. For educators who are typically socialized into ideological positions that characterize their professional identity such as general educator, special educator, or inclusive educator, this means that forays into forms of practice that are outside the boundaries of such pregiven identities do not suggest a betrayal of professional values. Rather, such forms of practice permit a more fluid concept of inclusion.

To *travel* (or *practice*) in this manner means leaving one's self with no fixed boundaries. For Anzaldua (2007), this state of being reflects the consciousness of the *borderland*s, whereby surrendering notions of safety, one begins to develop a new consciousness, the *mestiza* consciousness. Such a consciousness has a high tolerance for contradictions, for ambiguity, and for the capacity for assuming new forms. It supports a continual process of stretching and remaining flexible where "nothing is thrust out, the good, the bad, and the ugly, nothing rejected, nothing abandoned" (p. 101). Oppositional activity that reflects the consciousness of the borderlands moves between and through multiple ideological positions. Like the survival strategies adopted by Third World peoples, such a movement requires the practitioner to read each situation of power and carefully select the best ideological position that can work against the forces of power (Sandoval, 2000).

While the movement between competing visions and positions can be profoundly unsettling, it can also be a potentially empowering practice. One develops the ability to tune oneself to any environment. This empowering potential of the consciousness of the borderlands emerges from the state of "middleness" that does not imply compromise or a weak selling-out. "A median position, on the contrary, is where the extremes lose their power; where all directions are (still) possible; and hence, where one can assume with intensity, one's freedom of movement" (Minh-ha, 2011, p. 70). The release from categorical positions—the "home" locations—deposits the educator within a space of practice where one has to become comfortable with ambiguity. In acknowledging such ambiguity, English (2005) describes those who work across differences and categories as inhabiting a necessary hybrid space; they are Third-Space practitioners. Such Third-Space practitioners are deeply attuned to issues of power in different contexts, but do not allow their practice to be fully shaped by it. They embrace the contradictions that must arise as they continually readjust their practices to render them most effective. In the struggle for inclusion, teachers too can be Third-Space practitioners.

Advocating for inclusive practices implicates not only resistance to oppressive discourses of difference, but also a simultaneous engagement with them and with other problematic discourses on schooling and learning. In compelling one to undertake a dialogue across differences, such a coalitional approach is no less a form of oppositional practice. In blurring boundaries to work across differences, educators privilege the multidimensional experiences of all actors (teachers, students, and families), leaving themselves open to the possibility of change while always committed to equitable schooling. Such careful navigation means that the scope of inclusive practices can never be fully known—it remains unpredictable, unfinished, and changing—rendering inclusion a "principled, unending process" (Booth, 2009, p. 126).

Situated Agency

Fundamental to the preparation of teachers for inclusive education is the premise that teachers will act as change agents to push schools toward greater equity and inclusivity. As schools are framed as hosting inequitable conditions that marginalize some learners, teachers are implicitly socialized into understanding that change in schools is contingent on the actions they take up to work against those conditions. Framing agency in teaching for social justice as resistance to inequitable schooling conditions automatically triggers certain kinds of questions:

- What are the forms of resistance in which teachers engage?
- Who resists, and who doesn't?
- What elements of teacher practice constitute resistance to inequitable schooling conditions and practices?

Such questions imply that agency is a stable internal property that teachers simply transport from one context to another. It also evokes a deficit model of understanding teacher actions; teachers are seen either as heroically confronting systems or as passively colluding with them (Achinstein & Ogawa, 2006). These notions of teacher agency may acknowledge the significance of the social context in nurturing teachers' sense of efficacy in undertaking teaching for social justice, but they still remain largely located within the individual (Agarwal, Epstein, Oppenheim, Oyler, & Sonu, 2010; McClean, 2008; Naraian & Schlessinger, in press; Peters & Reid, 2009; Rice, 2006).

A struggle for equity that invokes a borderland consciousness means that oppositional agency is never stable. Instead, it remains a fluid, shifting concept that develops over time and is intertwined with the contexts of practice. The many readings of power accomplished as one negotiates across multiple ideological positions to arrive at an instructional decision implies that oppositional agency can be unpredictable, even contradictory (Mohanty, 2003). Such decisionmaking is inseparable from teachers' evolving identities that are formed in the midst of the culture and priorities of each schooling context (Priestly et al., 2012). Situated therefore within the local struggles that inform their everyday contexts of practice, teachers' actions are improvisational, as they draw collectively on past experiences and future projections (Priestly et al., 2012; Sloan, 2006). Teachers assess the choices available to them differently depending on how their unique histories permit them to build on the material and social conditions in which they carry out their practice. What may seem an appropriate set of actions in one context may not be pursued in another. Additionally, what may seem appropriate to one teacher in a given context may not be pursued by another.

The experiences of the teachers described in this book also suggest that, situated within the complex environments of schools, teachers cannot rely solely on abstract ideals of equity and social justice to guide their decisionmaking when taking up inclusive practices. The common interests of groups may differ from the needs and desires that distinguish members *within* such groups (Mohanty, 2003). The students with disabilities and their families whom teachers support occupy different positions along the axes of class, gender, race, and other social categories. The meanings of disability experience, then, are not self-evident. Teachers have to be responsive to the unique needs and wishes of each type of family or, as in the case of Anita and Maria, to the larger goals of the family community.

Such responsiveness might mean deploying practices that don't fit neatly with an inclusive philosophy, but yet might positively transform the experience of schooling for *that* student and/or the family. As teachers reflect on such practice, they might be able to identify the *ideology of ability* that is implicated within the requirement to take up such a stance. For instance, the preparation for standardized testing clearly draws on ability-based norms to distinguish slow/fast, high achieving/low achieving, competent/incompetent categories of learners. Yet, in privileging the narrative of empowerment that families within their school community derived from the successful completion of schooling by its students, such preparatory practices by Anita and Maria can still further the project of inclusion. And herein lies the space of creativity that teachers may take up in many different ways. In the case of Anita and Maria, their privileging of student subjectivities alongside their commitments to student success, transformed their pedagogy from a mere combination of competing methods to a unique implementation of "real" reading (Naraian, 2016b). For Paul, it was the creative configuration of students, teachers, and classrooms in his building that could minimize the threat of ability-based grouping. Teachers' agency, like the project of inclusion itself, remains situated, unpredictable, and fluid.

World-Traveling Through Narrative

This book has privileged a narrative approach to understanding the experiences of teachers in schools. In that regard it has followed an important methodological stance within my scholarship as well as that of many disability studies–informed inclusive education scholars (e.g., see Connor, 2008; Ferguson & Ferguson, 1995). Within Third World feminist work, the significance of the narratives of marginalized people is recognized not because of its "truth" power but because of the complexities they disclose that may otherwise be unavailable in larger political debates. The narratives of Chicana feminist writers, for instance, has allowed them to both understand and disclose the multiple and competing ways in which women experience their oppression. Their experiences are rooted in a "theory of the flesh . . . where the physical realities of our lives—our skin color, the land or concrete we grew up on, our sexual longings—all fuse to create a politic born out of necessity" (Moraga, cited in Moya, 2000, p. 93). The influence of historically experienced material contexts on the judgments and choices that individuals make confer deep significance to narratives.

As a case in point, we have often heard that schools are beleaguered with requests from families to provide specialized treatment to students with autism. Yet there are fewer narratives that can surface the complex decisionmaking of families who seek this support; that is:

- What were the particular conditions within which such decisions came to assume a reasonable status?
- What were the multiple themes circulating within their rationale that collectively gave it credibility?
- What social institutions are implicated in families' decisionmaking?
- What are the relations between specific groups/individuals and these institutions?

When the social locations of individuals predispose them to understand the workings of power in different ways, we are obliged to acknowledge that.

It might well be true that their narratives register the circulation of stereotypical cultural discourses of ability/disability. Yet the breadth of their meanings is severely circumscribed, if those are the only ways they are read.

Narratives, therefore, are particularly significant to educators as they begin to navigate the ambiguities inherent in the doing of oppositional work. It registers a particular way of *hearing* people's experiences, calling for what Maria Lugones (1987) describes as "world-traveling." Lugones draws on the experiences of women of color who are positioned as outsiders to the mainstream and move between different "worlds," thus seeing themselves and others in multiple ways. Lugones argues that the flexibility gained with this kind of movement between dominant and nondominant worlds allows one to perceive individuals in "loving" rather than in "arrogant" ways. Such "loving perception" requires that we identify *with* individuals within those worlds. An "arrogant" perception, on the other hand, allows the speaker's world to remain untouched by the individual whom she or he is describing. Lugones notes: "We are fully dependent on each other for the possibility of being understood and without this understanding we are not intelligible, we do not make sense, we are not solid, visible, integrated, we are lacking. So traveling to each other's 'worlds' would enable us to *be* through *loving* each other" (p. 8).

Such world-traveling requires that the listener–educator seek to locate herself within the complex life histories of actors in schools (students, families, and other groups). This means that regardless of the overwhelming circulation of discourses of normalcy and fixed-ability thinking, educators (and researchers) remain open to the stories of students and families without characterizing them as deficient, heroic, or passive. It means extending an openness to understanding the meanings of disability in school even if that may sit at odds with more progressive notions of inclusive schooling that are premised on rejecting an ideology of ability. A receptivity to such narratives can disclose new ways of understanding student experiences and, by extension, help identify new forms of support. When Paul conducted a home visit and discovered the range of experiences within the family of his student, not only was he filled with ideas for facilitating parent networks in his school, but the ways in which he could relate to his student were also shifted, enabling him to mediate her peer relations in ways that he might not have used before.

As a researcher, I too recognize the necessity for world-traveling. For instance, when I first entered Stephanie's classroom, I noticed that she allowed *any* student, if they felt unable to speak, to use a portable communication device procured especially for Trevor. My immediate response was outrage at the lack of respect extended to him. However, it took an openness on my part as a participant-observer in the classroom over an extended period of time to understand her rationale and come to see it as inseparable from her desire to have an open, transparent community (Naraian, 2011b). My world-traveling as a researcher required that I remain open to Stephanie's narrative of experience in this classroom. Such a stance, for researchers and practitioners alike, confers validity to the decisions made in the interest of inclusion and evokes many unpredictable sites for resistance and empowerment in everyday schooling.

Diaspora

Notions of traveling suggested within Third World feminist conceptions of home also invoke the experience of diaspora. The concept of *diaspora* might implicitly suggest a "homeland," but recent scholarly work has questioned this focus on geographical boundaries and emphasized instead the relations between peoples who express different histories, even as they inhabit the same geographic space (Brah, 2003). Members of a particular diaspora, for instance, cohabit the same spaces with members of other historically formed and dispersed communities. Rather than a bounded group, therefore, diaspora references a location where "multiple subject positions are juxtaposed, contested, proclaimed, or disavowed" (Brah, 2003, p. 631). With a focus on identities of all groups rather than on borders, diaspora has come to signify a kind of consciousness. Such a consciousness engages with dislocation and movement and is always informed by relations of power (Brah, 2003; Brubaker, 2005). Diaspora affords a way to think about places in such a way that, rather than assume fixed boundaries, they can be conceived as fluid and changing (Larsen & Beech, 2014).

A diasporic sensibility (Kooy & de Freitas, 2007) may already reflect the experience of many special educators who are dispersed throughout a school system in various roles, spaces, and configurations that imply different relations between professionals and other school personnel. Stephanie's experience as a special educator (with a dually certified status) in a collaboratively taught team was one such location where multiple professional identities intersected within inequitable relations. As a special educator with considerable influence in schoolwide arrangements, Paul experienced a different configuration of relations that evoked a different range of identity-making practices. Other special educators may perform even more diffuse roles when their services and encounters with school professionals locate them across many sites within and outside a single building.

As several chapters have illustrated, the disciplinary home of educators (general or special education) may grant them a specific status in schools, but the nature of everyday practice required a continual movement between knowledge boundaries that inevitably influenced how they came to see themselves as educators. For both general and special educators, this means that besides a requirement to grow comfortable with uncertainty and ambivalence (English, 2005), their professional identities are constantly being negotiated across multiple configurations of people and places. A general educator's identity when coteaching with a special educator may evolve in completely different ways than when collaborating with a general educator or when teaching alone. Or a special educator such as Stephanie who is dually certified, may experience, as she clearly did, both general and special education quite differently when placed in the role of a general educator (Naraian, 2010a). Or an educator's partnership with families may challenge the foundations of one's professional practice. Each encounter can be experienced as a dislocation because it pushes up against pregiven notions of competency and professional knowledge domains. Yet it can also be understood as an invitation to move across those boundaries and stimulate new configurations of people and identities.

As we saw in Chapter 2, such movement across boundaries often centered on deciphering student learning need. The privileging within Third World feminism of the material conditions of experience allows teachers to straddle both *social constructionist* (learning disability does not reside within individuals but is socially constructed) and *realist* (learning disability is a real phenomenon that originates at least partially within the individual) orientations. A student's learning need therefore may be socially constructed—after all, without an official category such as Learning Disabled, a student might not be understood as such—but, it is not *only* socially constructed (Moya, 2000). The qualitatively different ways the student encounters the physical world may originate in a bodily difference. This means that when a teacher makes the determination that in-depth instruction with a small group of students may be necessary to support their skill development in preparation for testing, it may not reflect an exclusionary or deficit-based approach; it may still be justifiable as part of an inclusive pedagogy. The criterion is the teacher's recognition that the determination of such needs refers outwardly to a pervasive ideology of ability in schools that requires students to show evidence of learning via successful performance in examinations.

This orientation to needs as materially experienced but always referencing outwardly to social inequities is well suited to a diasporic sensibility. It means that special educators can certainly draw on their professional knowledge domains to engage directly with the needs as presented by the students, offering them the supports that they may be well qualified to provide. Yet they can only do so by acknowledging the inequitable relations within the system that are spawned by an ideology of ability. For general educators, it leaves the privileged location of the general education space fragile and unstable. If learning needs are always contingent on a student's location across multiple axes of class, gender, ethnicity, linguistic status, and so forth, for whom is the general education space designed? How does one decide who can be in, or out? In other words, it complicates any easy referral to an alternative system such as special education that is perceived to address special learning needs. For both types of educators, a diasporic stance that recognizes professional boundaries as always shifting and permeable permits greater scope for imagining new places of learning and new networks of people and places.

Each of the constructs discussed in this section can be generative for understanding the work of teachers in schools and for preparing novice teachers to take up inclusive pedagogy. Collectively, they offered theoretical support for reenvisioning inclusion so as to register its complexity and its location within the contextual specificities of schools.

INCLUSION AS A PEDAGOGY OF DEFERRAL

The movement across professional boundaries, the straddling of competing frameworks of learning, the partial application of discourses of normalcy, the pursuit of learning needs—none of these practices would be identified as indicators of an equity pedagogy. Yet they collectively subsumed, informed, and constituted the "doing" of inclusion undertaken by teachers described in this book. Such inclusion was grounded in the material specificities of schooling contexts, which both shaped and were shaped by the efforts of teachers. This rearticulation of teachers' experience suggests that a politics of polarity (inclusion versus exclusion) may be insufficient to meet the complicated demands of enabling inclusivity in practice. Drawing on the experiences of teachers in this book, I suggest that inclusion as an act of *deferring* may be more elastic to accommodate both material conditions and commitments to equity.

Enacting a Pedagogy of Deferral

Inclusion as a pedagogy of *deferral* begins with the recognition that time conceptualized linearly is a structural element within schools. Time occupies an irrevocable, unremitting status in schools that clearly constrained teachers' abilities to envision inclusion. As we explored in Chapter 2, it compels educators to evaluate students against predetermined expectations about their learning and achievement (Metcalfe & Game, 2007). Students are unquestioningly expected to meet certain standards within a prespecified period of time. Seeking to restore the agency of educators, Orlikowski and Yates (2002) instead suggest the concept of *real-enough time* (versus *real time*) that minimizes this notion of time as given, objective, and unchangeable. It begins when educators decouple *expectations* of learning from their pedagogy and instead privilege the *potential* of the student. By recognizing the potential of the student as always in process, unfolding, and unfinished, they *defer* the outcome of student performance.

As a form of "living in the future," such deferral continually privileges the unobserved and unfinished capacity of the student:

- What can the student do/know that he or she has not demonstrated yet?
- What kinds of activities might disclose such learnings?
- What elements of this student's identity are likely hidden?
- How can they be surfaced?

In seeking to *know* a student, teachers need not discount objective measurements such as test scores, but they would recognize them as only a part of a project where the outcome has *not yet* been realized. Although scores do indicate something, they are insufficient by themselves to assess student potential, which always remains located in the future. In other words, the learnings shown at the present time may represent something about the learner. When projecting into the future, however, such understandings are inevitably partial and always in flux. In taking up such a stance, educators reconfigure the movement of time and its relationship with certainty; they are now in real-enough time.

A pedagogy of deferral, therefore, acknowledges that the meanings of student responses are never complete in themselves and always signal unspoken utterances and hidden forms of being. In their quest for inclusion, the teachers described in the book were engaged in this process to various degrees. When Stephanie offers an interpretation of Trevor to establish his connectedness to the group, she is engaging in a form of deferring that notices present action, reorients it to the future through an articulation of possibility, and draws on past experiences with the student to offer an interpretation that can be believable (see Chapter 4). Trevor becomes recognizable to his peers who can now invest in understanding him further. Similarly, a practice of deferring might offer educators the opportunity to support the connectedness of students who present behavioral challenges with peers. It would call for the teacher to offer an explanation or commentary to the group that would reorient the student to his or her peers in a manner that preserved community relations. In thus imbuing a student's actions with recognizable meanings, the teacher allows the student's potential to remain unfinalized and unfinished both for the student's peers and also for the teacher.

Such a pedagogy can take other forms as well. For example, the simultaneous focus brought by Anita and Maria on both the immediate needs as well as long-term outcomes for students may be understood as a form of deferral (see Chapter 3). Their recourse to instructional methods that were contrary to constructivist orientations to learning emerged from a conscious decision to maximize potential for student success. In other words, even as the demands of the present (i.e., the necessity to use forms of explicit instruction to raise students' achievement scores) required a response that might not sit neatly with visions of an inclusive learning environment, the commitment to the same students as future citizens of a presently disadvantaged community rendered such response both necessary and ethical (Delpit, 1988). Similarly, Paul's decision to take up a "flexible" tracking was stimulated by a desire to ensure that his students' futures were not limited by arbitrary definitions of success handed down by the district through meaningless IEP diplomas (see Chapter 3). Problematic as the grouping of students by ability might have been, the ways in which he configured arrangements of students, teachers, and classes acknowledged their continually evolving identities as learners and their relationship to the school community.

A pedagogy of *deferral* can also be meaningful for special educators who may facilitate inclusion in schools and/or who may seek to address the "functional" performance of a student with disabilities. When considering the utility of a setting (self-contained or general) for a student's learning, they would need to reject a focus on the capacity of such a setting to support skill acquisition (i.e., the "time" within a self-contained setting may permit greater ability to acquire skills of independent living). Instead, they have to privilege the potential of that setting to generate opportunities for the student to *practice* skills that might be usable in a variety of future environments, permitting new forms of learning. It was clear that the academic model of identity that Stephanie tried to create for Trevor in the classroom understood his potential differently than a more "institutional" model of identity that Kristine unwittingly subscribed to, when she focused on present skills that could support a future where Harry would be able to independently "count pills."

For all educators, general or special, the collaborative work involved in the enactment of inclusion must itself instantiate a pedagogy of deferral. This was much more visible in the work carried out by Julie and Blair (see Chapter 6) than perhaps in the relations that Stephanie might have had with her general education coteacher. When Julie and Blair pursued mentoring relations with teachers who clearly subscribed to deficit understandings of their students and dismissed the inadequacy of their own practice as contributing to student behaviors, Julie and Blair were practicing a form of deferral. Decoupling their expectations of what teachers *should* be doing from their status as learners who could grow, Julie and Blair instead privileged relationships with teachers that might disclose their capability to understand students differently. So, by focusing on the needs of the moment—emotional validation and strategies that could raise teachers' levels of confidence—Julie and Blair left open the possibility that these teachers would eventually develop new ways of thinking about learners and schools.

Occupying a Half-Half Position

A pedagogy of deferral is rooted in the contradictions and conflicts that characterize the everyday work of teachers. It acknowledges the space of ambiguity within which teachers must necessarily carry out their work. It is also derived from an understanding of disability that is not categorical. Titchkosky (2011) uses the term *half-half* to describe the status of persons with disabilities as they negotiate socially conferred meanings of disability stemming from perceived needs (e.g., the labels of *dyslexia, visual impairment, deafness*) with embodied experiences within social environments. Deploying a "politics of wonder" that interrogates the assumptions behind mainstream practices that exclude the difference of disability, she illustrates access as the means to disclose "the gap between what is and what ought to be" (p. 24). Even as one adopts the labels of disability conferred by others, one is still free to continually stretch and reconfigure its meanings.

When Anita and Maria selected a book about a girl with significant disabilities to help shift student perceptions of difference within their classroom (see Chapter 3), they began the process of engaging with this "half-half" position. The book served to stretch the meanings of inclusion for themselves and their students. As they mulled over student responses to the book during their planning, they drew on their understandings of students' prior knowledge to introduce new meanings of participation. Their conversations on inclusion in the classroom could therefore avoid didactic tellings in favor of an approach that resembled a dialogue to a greater extent, as they tried to identify and expand their "band of normal" (Anita). The teachers described their hope for their students that having "loved this character so much," perhaps they might leave this classroom thinking about "why don't I get to know a person first before I judge them." In doing so, they were using the "realistic" goals that they ascribed to the experience of reading to complicate students' notions of normalcy.

Such conversations on normalcy and inclusion were, no doubt, still situated within a classroom practice where students were grouped largely according to their abilities for book groups and where choice, by the teachers' own admission, remained restrictive, even if it "mimicked" real life. To the extent that the selection of this book stimulated student thinking around notions of inclusion and participation, Anita and Maria were enacting their commitments to equity in the present. They also temporarily relinquished notions of ability levels to enable student understanding; students were not placed in book groups for this experience. Teachers' *expectations* of students in this case were linked not to their demonstrated levels of learning but to their *potential* as thoughtful future citizens whose capacity for understanding difference could be fostered by this book. Still, in reverting to ability-based grouping for other literacy experiences, they remained located within the present demands of school that required objective evidence for the development of skills that would influence those same futures. They were in a sense occupying a "half-half" position that required them to work within commonplace, fixed meanings of ability/disability even as it simultaneously permitted them to stretch the boundaries of the same.

A pedagogy of deferral acknowledges the deficit-based discourses that frame teachers' practice, but it simultaneously affords them the opportunity to respond agentively to them. Each act of deferring, whether in interpreting student action to mean more than presently conveyed, or in the planning of educational experiences that assume student potential as never fully revealed in the present, serves as an occasion for the educator to improvise a response that will work to minimize the gap between what is and what could be. To the extent that such improvisations carry the risk of being subsumed within deficit discourses of learning and disability, such a pedagogy needs to be applied thoughtfully. Yet such risks also mimic the unpredictability already inhering within schooling environments that call for teachers to take up multiple, often contradictory positions. The reflective process that informs such practice and generates a rationale for it ensures that such pedagogy can still remain in sync with the core beliefs of inclusive education.

IN SUM...

The work of inclusive education is as complex as the theories that underlie such work. This book emerged from a need to understand such complexity while always presuming the competence of teachers. In that regard, it represents a desire for a humanizing approach toward those who are engaged in the pragmatic work of doing inclusion. The teachers portrayed in this book neither displayed heroic forms of resistance to troubling practices of schooling nor did they take them up uncritically. There was nothing particularly extraordinary about their practice any more than the work that all teachers do is extraordinary within the current climate and within similar material contexts. This rearticulation of their experiences, therefore, does not hold them up as exemplars. While any attempt to do so would represent a vision of inclusion as *finished* that is contrary to the meaning of inclusion suggested in the book, it also does not reflect its primary intent. Rather, I hope that their stories can serve as the beginning of the process of thinking about inclusion from the ground up, as it were. What would inclusion look like if we thought *with* teachers rather than *for* them? How would that influence what we would come to expect from schools and from teachers? What kinds of coalitions would that evoke for us as researchers and teacher educators?

As teachers increasingly come under attack within popular discourses on public education and are subject to greater state scrutiny and censure (Cochran-Smith, Piazza, & Power, 2013; Ravitch, 2013), a humanizing approach as represented in this book may be important, if we are to enlist them in the project of inclusion and help them sustain their commitments. It offers researchers a means to better understand and describe the tensions that frame teachers' attempts to create equitable opportunities for all students, including students with disabilities. It permits a recognition of teacher capacity as situated rather than as fully internal; it is as equally interwoven with the social context, as is student learning. Such an understanding of inclusive practice that can work from the ground up may confer greater elasticity to our theorizing and strengthen the capacity for inclusion to acquire traction in a variety of schooling contexts.

References

Achinstein, B., & Ogawa, R. T. (2006). (In)Fidelity: What the resistance of new teachers reveals about professional principles and prescriptive educational policies. *Harvard Educational Review, 76*(1), 30–63.

Agarwal, R., Epstein, S., Oppenheim, R., Oyler, C., & Sonu, D. (2010). From ideal to practice and back again: Beginning teachers teaching for social justice. *Journal for Teacher Education, 61*(3), 237–247.

Ahmed, Sara (2004). *The cultural politics of emotion*. New York, NY: Routledge.

Anastasiou, D., & Kauffman, J. M. (2011). A social constructionist approach to disability: Implications for special education. *Exceptional Children, 77,* 367–384.

Anzaldua, G. (2007). *Borderlands, la frontera: The new mestiza* (3rd ed.). San Francisco, CA: Aunt Lute Books.

Archer, A. L., & Hughes, C. A. (2011). *Explicit instruction: Effective and efficient teaching*. New York, NY: Guilford Press.

Au, W. (2013). What's a nice test like you doing in a place like this? The edTPA and corporate education "reform." *Rethinking Schools, 27*(4). Retrieved from www.rethinkingschools.org/archive/27_04/27_04_au.shtml

Auerbach, S. (2007). From moral supporters to struggling advocates: Reconceptualizing parent roles in education through the experience of working-class families of color. *Urban Education, 42*(3), 250–283. doi: 10.1177/0042085907300433

Baglieri, S., Bejoian, L. M., Broderick, A. A., Connor, D. J., & Valle, J. W. (2011). [Re]claiming "inclusive education" toward cohesion in educational reform: Disability studies unravels the myth of the normal child. *Teachers College Record, 113*(10), 2122–2154.

Bai, H., & Martin, S. M. (2015). Assessing the needs of training on inclusive education for public school administrators. *International Journal of Inclusive Education, 19*(12), 1229–1243.

Berry, R. A. W. (2006). Inclusion, power, and community: Teachers and students interpret the language of community in an inclusion classroom. *American Educational Research Journal 43*(3), 489–529.

Bessette, H. J. (2008). Using students' drawings to elicit general and special educators' perceptions of co-teaching. *Teaching and Teacher Education, 24,* 1376–1396.

Biklen, D. (2005). *Autism and the myth of the person alone*. New York, NY: New York University Press.

Biklen, D., & Burke, J. (2006). Presuming competence. *Equity & Excellence in Education, 39*(2), 166–175.

Bogdan, R. C., & Biklen, S. K. (2007). *Qualitative research for education: An introduction to theory and methods* (5th ed.). Boston, MA: Pearson.
Boler, M. (1999). *Feeling power.* New York, NY: Routledge.
Boler, M., & Zembylas, M. (2003). Discomforting truths: The emotional terrain of understanding difference. In P. P. Trifonas (Ed.), *Pedagogies of difference: Rethinking education for social change* (pp. 110–136). New York, NY: Routledge.
Booth, T. (2009). Keeping the future alive: Maintaining inclusive values in education and society. In M. Alur & V. Timmons (Eds.), *Inclusive education across cultures: Crossing boundaries, sharing ideas* (pp. 121–134). New Delhi, India: Sage Publications India.
Booth, T., & Ainscow, M. (2011). *Index for inclusion: Developing learning and participation in schools* (3rd ed.). Bristol, United Kingdom: Center for Studies on Inclusive Education.
Borko, H. (2004). Professional development and teacher learning: Mapping the terrain. *Educational Researcher, 33*(8), 3–15.
Brah, A. (2003). Diaspora, border, and transnational identities. In R. Lewis & S. Mills (Eds.), *Feminist postcolonial theory: A reader* (pp. 613–634). New York, NY: Routledge.
Brantlinger, E. (2006). Who benefits from special education? Remediating (fixing) other people's children. Mahwah, NJ: Lawrence Erlbaum.
Browder, D. M., & Spooner, F. (2006). *Teaching language arts, math, & science to students with significant cognitive disabilities.* Baltimore, MD: Brookes.
Browder, D. M., Wakeman, S. Y., Flowers, C., Rickelman, R. J., Pugalee, D., & Karvonen, M. (2007). Creating access to the general curriculum with links to grade-level content for students with significant cognitive disabilities. *Journal of Special Education, 4*(1), 2–16.
Brubaker, R. (2005). The 'diaspora' diaspora. *Ethnic and Racial Studies, 28*(1), 1–19. doi:10.1080/0141987042000289997
Bruner, J. (1986). *Actual minds, possible worlds.* Cambridge, MA: Harvard University Press.
Bruner, J. (1990). *Acts of meaning.* Cambridge, MA: Harvard University Press.
Brusca-Vega, R., Alexander, J., Kamin, C. (2014). In support of access and inclusion: Joint professional development for science and special educators. *Global Education Review, 1*(4), 37–52.
Cazden, C. (2001). *Classroom discourse: The language of teaching and learning.* Portsmouth, NH: Heinemann.
Clandinin, D. J. (2007). Preface. In D. J. Clandinin (Ed.), *Handbook of narrative inquiry: Mapping a methodology* (pp. ix–xvii). Thousand Oaks, CA: Sage.
Clandinin, D. J. (2013). *Engaging in narrative inquiry.* Walnut Creek, CA: Left Coast Press.
Clandinin, D. J., & Connelly, F. M. (1996). Teachers' professional knowledge landscapes: teacher stories—stories of teachers—school stories—stories of schools. *Educational Researcher, 25*(3), 24–30.
Cochran-Smith, M., & Dudley-Marling, C. (2012). Diversity in teacher education and special education: Issues that divide. *Journal of Teacher Education, 63*(4), 237–244.
Cochran-Smith, M., & Lytle, S. L. (2001). Beyond certainty: Taking an inquiry stance on practice. In A. Lieberman & L. Miller (Eds.), *Teachers caught in ac-*

tion: Professional development that matters (pp. 45–58). New York, NY: Teachers College Press.

Cochran-Smith, M., Piazza, P., & Power, C. (2013). The politics of accountability: Assessing teacher education in the United States. *The Educational Forum, 77*(1), 6–27.

Cochran-Smith, M., Villegas, A. M., Abrams, L., Chavez-Moreno, L., Mills, T., & Stern, R. (2015). Critiquing teacher preparation research: An overview of the field: Part II. *Journal of Teacher Education, 66*(2), 109–121.

Collins, P. H. (2000). *Black feminist thought.* New York, NY: Routledge.

Connor, D. J. (2008). *Urban narratives: Portraits in progress.* New York, NY: Peter Lang.

Danforth, S. (Ed.). (2014). *Becoming a great inclusive educator.* New York, NY: Peter Lang.

Danforth, S., & Gabel, S. (2006). *Vital questions facing disability studies in education.* New York, NY: Peter Lang.

Danforth, S., & Naraian, S. (2007). Use of the machine metaphor in autism research. *Journal of Developmental & Physical Disabilities, 19*(3), 273–290.

Danforth, S., & Naraian, S. (2015). This new field of inclusive education: Beginning a dialogue on conceptual foundations. *Intellectual and Developmental Disabilities, 53*(1), 70–85.

Danforth, S., & Smith, T. (2005). *Engaging troubling students: A constructivist approach.* Thousand Oaks, CA: Corwin Press.

Danielson, C. (2013). *The framework for teaching: Evaluation instrument* (2013 ed.). Princeton, NJ: The Danielson Group.

Delpit, L. D. (1988). The silenced dialogue: Power and pedagogy in educating other people's children. *Harvard Educational Review, 58*(3), 280–298.

Desimone, L. M., Smith, T. M., & Phillips, K. J. R. (2007). Does policy influence mathematics and science teachers' participation in professional development? *Teachers College Record, 109*(5), 1086–1122.

Donnellan, A. (1984). The criterion of the least dangerous assumption. *Behavioral Disorders, 9,* 141–150.

Dudley-Marling, C. (2004). The social construction of learning disabilities. *Journal of Learning Disabilities, 37*(6), 482–489.

Dudley-Marling, C., & Gurn, A. (2010). Troubling the foundations of special education: Examining the myth of the normal curve. In C. Dudley-Marling & A. Gurn (Eds.), *The myth of the normal curve* (pp. 9–23). New York, NY: Peter Lang.

English, L. M. (2005). Third-space practitioners: Women educating for justice in the global south. *Adult Education Quarterly, 55*(2), 85–100.

Epstein, J. L. (2007). Connections count: Improving family and community involvement in secondary schools. *Principal Leadership, 8*(2), 16–22.

Ferguson, D. L., Hanreddy, A. N., & Ferguson, P. M. (2014). Finding a voice: Families' roles in schools. In L. Florian (Ed.), *The SAGE handbook of special education* (pp. 763–784). Thousand Oaks, CA: Sage.

Ferguson, P. M. (2002). A place in the family: An historical interpretation of research on parental reactions to having a child with a disability. *Journal of Special Education, 36*(3), 124–130.

Ferguson, P. M. (2003). Winks, blinks, squints, and twitches: Looking for disability and culture through my son's left eye. In F. R. Devlieger & D. Pfeiffer (Eds.),

Rethinking disability: The emergence of new definitions, concepts, and communities (pp. 131–147). Antwerp, Belgium: Garant.

Ferguson, P. M. (2007). The doubting dance: Contributions to a history of parent/professional interactions in early 20th century America. *Research and Practice for Persons with Severe Disabilities, 33*(1–2), 48–58.

Ferguson, P. M., & Ferguson, D. L. (1995). The interpretivist view of special education and disability: Deconstructing the conventional knowledge tradition. In T. M. Skrtic (Ed.), *Disability and democracy: Reconstructing (special) education for postmodernity* (pp. 104–121). New York, NY: Teachers College Press.

Ferguson, P. M., & Nussbaum, E. (2012). Disability studies: What is it and what difference does it make? *Research and Practice for Persons with Severe Disabilities, 37,* 70–80.

Fernandez, M., Wegerif, R., Mercer, N., & Rojas-Drummond, S. (2001). Re-conceptualizing "scaffolding" and the zone of proximal development in the context of symmetrical collaborative learning. *Journal of Classroom Interaction, 36*(2), 40–54.

Fielding, M. (2004). Transformative approaches to student voice: Theoretical underpinnings, recalcitrant realities. *British Educational Research Journal, 30*(2), 295–311.

Fosnot, C. T. (2005). *Constructivism: Theory, perspectives, and practice.* New York, NY: Teachers College Press.

Frank, A. W. (2010). *Letting stories breathe: A socio-narratology.* Chicago, IL: University of Chicago.

Freire, P. (2000). *Pedagogy of the oppressed* (30th anniversary ed.). New York, NY: Continuum Press. (Original work published 1970)

Gabel, S. (2005). Introduction: Disability studies in education. In S. Gabel (Ed.), *Disability studies in education: Readings in theory and method* (pp. 1–20). New York, NY: Peter Lang.

Gallagher, D. (1998). The scientific knowledge base of special education: Do we know what we think we know? *Exceptional Children, 64*(4), 493–502.

Gallagher, D. (2004). Entering the conversation: The debate behind the debates in special education. In *Challenging orthodoxy in special education: Dissenting voices* (pp. 3–26). Denver, CO: Love Publishing.

Gallagher, D. (2006). If not absolute objectivity, then what? A reply to Kauffman and Sasso. *Exceptionality, 14,* 91–107.

Gee, J. P. (2000–2001). Identity as an analytic lens for research in education. *Review of Research in Education, 25,* 99–125.

Gomez, M. L., Schieble, M., Curwood, J. S., & Hassett, D. (2010). Technology, learning, and instruction: Distributed cognition in the secondary English classroom. *Literacy, 44*(1), 20–27.

Graham, L. J., & Slee, R. (2008). An illusory interiority: Interrogating the discourse/s of inclusion. *Educational Philosophy and Theory, 40*(2), 277–293.

Gray, S. L. (2004). Defining the future: An interrogation of education and time. *British Journal of Sociology of Education, 25*(3), 323–340.

Haager, D., & Vaughn, S. (2013). The Common Core State Standards and reading: Interpretations and implications for elementary students with learning disabilities. *Learning Disabilities Research & Practice, 28,* 5–16.

Halverson, R. R., & Clifford, M. A. (2006). Evaluation in the wild: A distributed

cognition perspective on teacher assessment. *Educational Administration Quarterly, 42*(4), 578–619.
Hargreaves, A. (2001). Emotional geographies of teaching. *Teachers College Record, 103*(6), 1056–1080.
Harry, B., Kalyanpur, M., & Day, M. (1999). *Building cultural reciprocity with families: Case studies in special education.* Baltimore, MD: Brookes.
Hehir, T., Figueroa, R., Gamm, S., Katzman, L. I., Gruner, A., Karger, J., & Hernandez, J. (2005). *Comprehensive management review and evaluation of special education.* New York, NY: New York City Department of Education.
Herner-Patnode, L. (2009). Educator study groups: A professional development tool to enhance inclusion. *Intervention in School and Clinic, 45*(1), 24–30.
Heshusius, L. (1989). The Newtonian mechanistic paradigm, special education, and contours of alternatives: An overview. *Journal of Learning Disabilities, 22*(7), 403–415.
Holland, D., Lachiotte, W., Jr., Skinner, D., & Cain, C. (1998). *Identity and agency in cultural worlds.* Cambridge, MA: Harvard University Press.
Holland, D., & Lave, J. (Eds.). (2001). *History in person: Enduring struggles, contentious practice, intimate identities.* Santa Fe, NM: School of American research Press.
Holquist, M. (2000). *Dialogism: Bakhtin and his world.* London, United Kingdom: Routledge.
Horner, R. H., & Carr, E. G. (1997). Behavioral support for students with severe disabilities: Functional assessment and comprehensive intervention. *The Journal of Special Education, 64*(2), 167–180.
Hurtado, A. (1996). *The color of privilege: Three blasphemies on race and feminism.* Ann Arbor, MI: University of Michigan Press.
Isenbarger, L., & Zembylas, M. (2006). The emotional labour of caring in teaching. *Teaching and Teacher Education, 22,* 120–134.
Jaeger, P. T. (2012). *Disability and the Internet: Confronting a digital divide.* Boulder, CO: Lynne Rienner.
Jaruszewicz, C. (2005). Responsible eclecticism: Using a structured analysis process to facilitate curriculum discourse with graduate preservice early childhood students. *Journal of Early Childhood Teacher Education, 26,* 361–375.
Kauffman, J. M., & Sasso, G. M. (2006). Toward ending cultural and cognitive relativism in special education. *Exceptionality, 14,* 65–90.
Kliewer, C., & Biklen, D. P. (2007). Enacting literacy: Local understanding, significant disability, and a new frame for educational opportunity. *Teachers College Record, 109*(12), 2579–2600.
Kluth, P., Biklen, D. B., & Straut, D. M. (Eds.). (2003). *Access to academics for all students: Critical approaches to inclusive curriculum, instruction, and policy.* Mahwah, NJ: Lawrence Erlbaum.
Knight, J. (2002). Crossing boundaries: What constructivists can teach intensive-explicit instructors and vice versa. *Focus on Exceptional Children, 35,* 1–16.
Kooy, M., & de Freitas, E. (2007). The diaspora sensibility in teacher identity: Locating self through story. *Canadian Journal of Education, 30*(3), 865–880.
Lalvani, P. (2015). Disability, stigma, and otherness: Perspectives of parents and teachers. *International Journal of Disability, Development, and Education, 62*(4), 379–393.

Lareau, A. (1987). Social class difference in family–school relationships: The importance of cultural capital. *Sociology of Education, 60*(2), 73–85.

Lareau, A., & Horvat, E. M. (1999). Moments of social inclusion and exclusion: Race, class, and cultural capital in family–school relationships. *Sociology of Education, 72*(1), 37–53.

Larsen, M. A., & Beech, J. (2014). Spatial theorizing in comparative and international education research. *Comparative Education Review, 58*(2), 191–214.

Lave, J. (1993). The practice of learning. In J. Lave & S. Chaiklin (Eds.), *Understanding practice* (pp. 3–32). Cambridge, United Kingdom: Cambridge University Press.

Lave, J., & Wenger, E. (1991). *Situated learning: Legitimate peripheral participation.* Cambridge, United Kingdom: Cambridge University Press.

Lawrence-Brown, D., & Sapon-Shevin, M. (2014). *Condition critical: Key principles for equitable and inclusive education.* New York, NY: Teachers College Press.

Lightfoot, D. (2004). "Some parents just don't care": Decoding the meanings of parental involvement in urban schools. *Urban Education 39*, 91–107.

Linehan, C., & McCarthy, J. (2001). Reviewing the "community of practice" metaphor: An analysis of control relations in a primary school classroom. *Mind, Culture, and Activity, 8*(2),129–147.

Lingard, B., & Gale, T. (2010). Defining educational research: A perspective of/on Presidential Addresses and the Australian Association for Research in Education. *The Australian Education Researcher, 37,* 21–49.

Linton, S. (1998). *Claiming disability: Knowledge and identity.* New York, NY: New York University Press.

Lodge, C. (2005). From hearing voices to engaging in dialogue: Problematising student participation in school improvement. *Journal of Educational Change, 6*(2), 125–146.

Lugones, M. (1987). Playfulness, "world"-traveling, and loving perception. *Hypatia, 2* (2), 3–19.

Mac Iver, M. A., Epstein, J. L., Sheldon, S. B., & Fonseca, E. (2015). Engaging families to support students' transition to high school: Evidence from the field. *High School Journal, 99*(1), 27–45.

Massey, D. (1994). Double articulation: A place in the world. In A. Bammer (Ed.), *Displacements: Cultural identities in question.* Bloomington, IN: Indiana University Press.

McLean, M. A. (2008). Teaching about disability: An ethical responsibility? *International Journal of Inclusive Education, 12*(5–6), 605–619.

Mercer, N. (2002). Developing dialogues. In G. Wells & G. Claxton (Eds,), *Learning for life in the 21st century: Sociocultural perspectives on the future of education* (pp. 141–153). Malden, MA: Blackwell.

Merriam, S. B. (2009). *Qualitative research: A guide to design and implementation.* San Francisco, CA: Jossey-Bass.

Metcalfe, A., & Game, A. (2007). Becoming who you are: The time of education. *Time Society, 16*(1), 43–59. doi:10.1177/0961463X07074101

Michalko, R. (2002). *The difference that disability makes.* Philadelphia, PA: Temple University Press.

Minh-ha, Trinh T. (2011). *Elsewhere, within here: Immigration, refugeeism, and the boundary event.* New York, NY: Routledge.

Mohanty, C. T. (2003). *Feminism without borders: Decolonizing theory, practicing solidarity*. Durham, NC: Duke University Press.

Moya. P. (2000). Post-modernism, "realism," and the politics of identity: Cherrie Moraga and Chicana feminism. In P. M. L. Moya & M. R. Hames-Garcia (Eds.), *Reclaiming identity: Realist theory and the predicament of postmodernism* (pp. 67–101). Berkeley, CA: University of California Press.

Naraian, S. (2008a). "I didn't think I was going to like working with him, but now I really do!": Examining peer narratives of significant disability. *Intellectual and Developmental Disabilities, 46*(2), 106–119.

Naraian, S. (2008b). Institutional and self-stories: Investigating peer interpretations of significant disability. *International Journal of Inclusive Education, 12*(5), 525–542.

Naraian, S. (2010a). General, special . . . *and* inclusive: Refiguring professional identities in a collaboratively taught classroom. *Teaching and Teacher Education, 26*, 1677–1686.

Naraian, S. (2010b). "Why not have fun?" Peers make sense of one inclusive high school program. *Intellectual and Developmental Disabilities, 48*(1), 14–30.

Naraian, S. (2011a). Pedagogic voicing: The struggle for participation in an inclusive classroom. *Anthropology and Education Quarterly, 42*(3), 245–262.

Naraian, S. (2011b). Seeking transparency: The production of an inclusive classroom community. *International Journal of Inclusive Education, 15*(9), 955–973.

Naraian, S. (2011c). Teacher discourse, peer relations, and significant disability: Unraveling one friendship story. *International Journal of Qualitative Studies in Education, 24*(1), 97–115.

Naraian, S. (2014). Agency in real time? Situating teachers' efforts towards inclusion in the context of local and enduring struggles. *Teachers College Record, 116*(6), 1–38.

Naraian, S. (2015). Love's labor lost: Emotional agency in a school worker's story of family advocacy. *International Journal of Qualitative Studies in Education, 28*(1), 92–111.

Naraian, S. (2016a). Inclusive education complexly defined for teacher preparation: The significance and uses of *error*. *International Journal of Inclusive Education, 20*(9), 946–961.

Naraian, S. (2016b). "Real" reading: Reconciling explicit instruction with inclusive pedagogy in a fourth grade classroom. *Urban Education*. Advance online publication. doi:10.1177/0042085916648742

Naraian, S. (2016c). Spatializing student learning to re-imagine the "place" of inclusion. *Teachers College Record, 118*(12), 1–46.

Naraian, S., Ferguson, D. L., & Thomas, N. (2012). Transforming for inclusive practice: Professional development to support the inclusion of students labeled as emotionally disturbed. *International Journal of Inclusive Education, 16*(7–8), 721–740.

Naraian, S., & Oyler, C. (2014). Professional development for special education reform: *Re-articulating* experiences of urban educators. *Urban Education, 49*(5), 499–526.

Naraian, S., & Schelssinger, S. (in press). When theory meets the "*reality* of reality": Reviewing the sufficiency of the social model of disability as a foundation for teacher preparation for inclusive education. *Teacher Education Quarterly*.

Naraian, S., & Surabian, M. (2014). New Literacy studies: An alternate frame for preparing teachers to use assistive technology. *Teacher Education and Special Education, 37*(4), 330–346.

Nguyen, X. T. (2015). *Journey to inclusion*. Rotterdam, The Netherlands: Sense Publishers.

O'Neill, S., Geoghegan, D., & Petersen, S. (2013). Raising the pedagogical bar: Teachers' co-construction of explicit teaching. *Improving Schools, 16*(2), 148–158.

Orlikowski, W., & Yates, J. (2002). It's about time: Temporal structuring in organizations. *Organization Science, 13*(6), 684–700.

Peters, S., & Reid, D. K. (2009). Resistance and discursive practice: Promoting advocacy in teacher undergraduate and graduate programmes. *Teaching and Teacher Education, 25,* 551–558.

Polkinghorne, D. E. (1988). *Narrative knowing and the human sciences*. Albany, NY: State University of New York Press.

Poplin, M. (2011). Valuing a plurality of research methodologies and instructional ideologies in classroom research. *Learning Disability Quarterly, 34,* 150–152.

Poplin, M., Rivera, J., Durish, D., Hoff, L., Kawell, S., Pawlak, P., & Veney, C. (2011). She's strict for a good reason: Highly effective teachers in low-performing urban schools. *Phi Delta Kappan, 92,* 39–43.

Poplin, M., & Rogers, S. (2005). Recollections, apologies, and possibilities. *Learning Disability Quarterly, 28,* 159–161.

Priestley, M., Edwards, R., & Priestley, A. (2012). Teacher agency in curriculum making: Agents of change and spaces for manoeuvre. *Curriculum Inquiry, 42*(2), 191–214. doi:10.1111/j.1467-873X.2012.00588.x

Ravitch, D. (2013). *Reign of error: The hoax of the privatization movement and the danger to America's public schools*. New York, NY: Knopf.

Reid, D. K. (2004). The discursive practice of learning disability: Implications for instruction and parent-school relations. *Journal of Learning Disabilities, 37*(6), 466–481.

Rice, N. (2006). Promoting "epistemic fissures": Disability studies in teacher education. *Teaching Education, 17*(3), 251–264.

Ritchey, K. D. (2011). The first "R": Evidence-based reading instruction for students with learning disabilities. *Theory Into Practice, 50,* 28–34.

Rose, D. H., Meyer, A., & Hitchcock, C. (2006). *The universally designed classroom: Accessible curriculum and digital technologies*. Cambridge, MA: Harvard Education Press.

Sandoval, C. (2000). *Methodology of the oppressed*. Minneapolis, MN: University of Minnesota Press.

Sapon-Shevin, M. (2007). *Widening the circle: The power of inclusive classrooms*. Boston, MA: Beacon Press.

Schwartz, D. L., Lindgren, R., & Lewis, S. (2009). Constructivism in an age of non-constructivist assessments. In S. Tobias and T. M. Duffy (Eds.), *Constructivist instruction: Success or failure* (pp. 34–61). New York, NY: Routledge.

Scruggs, T. E., Mastropieri, M. A., & McDuffie, K. A. (2007). Co-teaching in inclusive classrooms: A metasynthesis of qualitative research. *Exceptional Children, 73*(4), 392–416.

Siebers, T. (2008). *Disability theory*. Ann Arbor, MI: University of Michigan Press.

Skrtic, T. (Ed.). (1995). *Disability and democracy: Reconstructing (special) education for postmodernity.* New York, NY: Teachers College Press.

Slee, R. (2011). *The irregular school: Exclusion, schooling, and inclusive education.* New York, NY: Routledge.

Sleeter, C. (1986). Learning disabilities: The social construction of a special education category. *Exceptional Children, 53*(1), 46–54.

Sloan, K. (2006). Teacher identity and agency in school worlds: Beyond the all-good/all-bad discourse on accountability-explicit curriculum policies. *Curriculum Inquiry, 36*(2), 119–152.

Soja, E. W. (1996). Thirdspace: Journeys to Los Angeles and other real-and-imagined places. Malden, MA: Blackwell.

Spillane, J. P. (2002). Local theories of teacher change: The pedagogy of district policies and programs. *Teachers College Record, 104*(5), 377–420.

Stillman, J. (2014). Teacher learning in an era of high-stakes accountability: Productive tension and critical professional practice. *Teachers College Record, 113*(1), 133–180.

Streiker, T., Logan, K., & Kuhel, K. (2012). Effects of job-embedded professional development on inclusion of students with disabilities in content area classrooms: Results of a three-year study. *International Journal of Inclusive Education, 16*(10), 1047–1065.

Strogilos, V., Nikolaraizi, M., Tragoulia, E. (2012). Experiences among beginning special education teachers in general education settings: The influence of school culture. *European Journal of Special Needs Education, 27*(2), 185–189.

Taylor, S. J. (2006). Before it had a name. In S. Danforth & S. Gabel (Eds.), *Vital questions facing disability studies in education* (pp. xiii–xxiii). New York, NY: Peter Lang.

Theoharis, G. (2007). Social justice educational leaders and resistance: Toward a theory of social justice leadership. *Educational Administration Quarterly, 43*(2), 221–258.

Thousand, J., Villa, R., & Nevin, A. (2007). Differentiating instruction: Collaborative planning and teaching for universally designed learning. Thousand Oaks, CA: Corwin Press.

Thurston, D., Ryan, L., Agarwal, P., & Hanselman, P. (2015). Professional sensemakers: Instructional specialists in contemporary schooling. *Educational Researcher, 44*(6), 359–364.

Titchkosky, T. (2011). *The question of access: Disability, space, meaning.* Toronto, Canada: University of Toronto Press.

Tomlinson, C. (2014). *The differentiated classroom: Responding to the needs of all learners.* Alexandria, VA: ASCD.

Troia, G. A., & Graham, S. (2002). The effectiveness of a highly explicit, teacher-directed strategy instruction routine: Changing the writing performance of students with learning disabilities. *Journal of Learning Disabilities, 35,* 290–305.

Tyack, D., & Cuban, L. (1995). *Tinkering toward Utopia: A century of public school reform.* Cambridge, MA: Harvard University Press.

Valle, J. W., & Connor, D. J. (2011). Rethinking disability: A disability studies approach to inclusive practices. New York, NY: McGraw Hill.

Vaughn, S., & Linan-Thompson, S. (2003). What is special about special education for students with learning disabilities? *The Journal of Special Education, 37,* 140–147.

Villa, R. A., & Thousand, J. S. (2000). *Restructuring for caring and effective education: Piecing the puzzle together* (2nd ed.). Baltimore, MD: Brookes.

Vrasidas, C., & Zembylas, M. (2004). Online professional development: lessons from the field, *Education + Training, 46* (6/7), 326–334.

Vygotsky, L. (1978). *Mind in society.* Cambridge, MA: Harvard University Press.

Vygotsky, L. (1986). *Thought and language* (A. Kozulin, Trans.). Cambridge, MA: MIT Press.

Walcott, D. M. (2011, November 29). Chancellor's memo. In *Principals' Weekly* (pp. 2–3). New York, NY: NYC Department of Education.

Ware, L. (2010). Disability studies in education. In S. Tozer, B. P. Gallegos, A. Henry, M. B. Greiner, & P. G. Price (Eds.), *Handbook of research in the social foundations of education* (pp. 244–260). New York, NY: Routledge.

Weiner, H. (2003). Effective inclusion: Professional development in the context of the classroom. *Teaching Exceptional Children, 35*(6), 12–18.

Wenger, E. (1998). *Communities of practice: Learning, meaning, and identity.* New York, NY: Cambridge University Press.

Wertsch, J. V. (1991). *Voices of the mind: A sociocultural approach to mediated action.* Cambridge, MA: Harvard University Press.

Wood, P., Bruner, J., & Ross, G. (1976). The role of tutoring in problem solving. *Journal of Child Psychology and Psychiatry, 17,* 89–100.

Wortham, S. (2006). *Learning identity: The joint emergence of social identification and academic learning.* Cambridge, United Kingdom: Cambridge University Press.

Yanchar, S. C., & Gabbitas, B. W. (2011). Between eclecticism and orthodoxy in instructional design. *Educational Technology Research and Development, 59,* 383–398.

Yell, M. L. (2012). *The law and special education* (3rd ed.). Upper Saddle River, NJ: Pearson.

Zeichner, K. M., & Liston, D. P. (1996). *Reflective teaching: An introduction.* Mahwah, NJ: Lawrence Erlbaum.

Zembylas, M. (2007). Emotional ecology: The intersection of emotional knowledge and pedagogical content knowledge in teaching. *Teaching and Teacher Education, 23,* 355–367.

Zigmond, N., & Kloo, A. (2009). The "two percent students": Considerations and consequences of eligibility decisions. *Peabody Journal of Education, 84*(4), 478–495.

Index

Ability
 as distributed, 102, 103
 focus on, 2
 separating students by, 9
Ability, ideology of, 3, 4, 13, 54, 135
Ability norms, 72, 90
Acceptance, 85–87, 88
Access/accessibility, 18. *See also* Participation; Voice
 defining, 91
 equality of, 73
 and interpretive work, 81–88, 91
 meanings of, 73–74
 as neccessary for promoting inclusion, 43
 physical, 74
 and special education, 44
Accountability, 101, 109
Achinstein, B., 135
Adequate yearly progress (AYP), 45–46
Adult education, 11–12, 121. *See also* Coaching; Professional development
Agarwal, R., 111, 135
Agency, 7
Agency, of teachers, 5, 71, 134–136
Agency, oppositional, 135
Ahmed, S., 127
Ainscow, M., 2
Alexander, J., 111
Ambiguity
 comfort with, 134
 of inclusive instructional practice, 69–72. *See also* Methodologies
Anastasiou, D., 2, 6
Andrews Children's School, 27–28

Angie (pseudonym), 66–67, 68
Anita (pseudonym), 9, 21, 35, 38, 40, 43, 44, 52, 53, 64, 69, 70, 98–100, 102, 105, 135, 136, 141, 143
 described, 32–33
 eclectic approach to methodologies, 71
 implementation of community, 109
 literacy instruction, 57–61
 and maneuvering place-time, 48–50
Anzaldua, G., 133
Archer, A. L., 56, 57, 100
Arrogant perception, 137
at risk label, 31
Au, W., 6
Auerbach, S., 11, 93
AYP (adequate yearly progress), 45–46

Baglieri, S., 5, 13
Bai, H., 111
Banking form of education, 57
Beech, J., 138
Behavior
 norms of, 87–88, 104
 Positive Behavioral Interventions and Supports, 24
 professional development centered on, 119–125
 rules of care, 84
 and student support, 119
Behavioral challenges, 30, 39
Bejoian, L. M., 5, 13
Bell City Academy of Arts and Culture, 28, 30–31
Benchmarks, and inclusion, 27
Berry, R. A. W., 93

Bessette, H. J., 39
Biklen, D., 4, 12, 13, 55, 75, 82, 118, 125
Biklen, S. K., 16
Binaries, ix, 13
Black feminist thought, 129–130
Blair (pseudonym), 35, 112, 118–125, 126, 127–128, 142
Bogdan, R. C., 16
Boler, M., 127
Booth, T., 2, 134
Border-crossing, 70
Borderlands, 133–134, 135
Borko, H., 125
Boundaries, movement across, 139
Brah, A., 138
Brantlinger, E., 130
Broderick, A. A., 5
Browder, D. M., 47, 54
Brubaker, R., 138
Bruner, J., 14, 15, 79
Brusca-Vega, R., 111
Burke, J., 12, 118, 125

Cain, C., 66, 76
Care, rules of, 84
Carr, E. G., 54
Cazden, C., 75
Change agents, teachers as, 134
Clandinin, D. J., 14, 64, 131
Classroom families, 11, 21–23, 85–88
Classroom management, and notion of community, 93
Clifford, M. A., 15
Coaching, 19, 111–112. *See also* Adult education; Professional development
Cochran-Smith, M., 13, 15, 110, 124, 144
Cognition, distributed, 11, 15, 102, 103
Collaboration
  among teachers, 114
  in Anita and Maria's classroom, 32–33
  inequitable relations in, 39
  and relations between general and special education, 66–67

Collaborative inquiry, importance of, 78
Collaborative learning opportunities, 15
Collins, P. H., 9, 129–130, 131
Communities, transparent, 25–27, 71, 81–85
Community
  and classroom management, 93
  complexities in, 93–94, 104–106
  and distributed learning, 103
  and families, 93, 97–98, 101, 103, 104–106
  implementing, 19, 81, 93, 97–98, 101
  implementing without family involvement, 94–95
  joint production of, 110
  and locus of control, 101–102
  and measurable values, 100
  and norms, 93, 94, 98
  notion of, and inclusive education, 92
  and shared cultural origins, 99–100
  speaking-with, 88
Community, logic of, 40
Competence, presuming, 12, 118, 125–126
Competence, teacher, 11, 116, 122–123
Connectedness, student, 39, 40–41, 42–44
Connelly, F. M., 14, 64
Connor, D. J., 4, 5, 74, 136
Consciousness, *mestiza*, 133
Consciousness, of borderlands, 133–134, 135
Constructivism, 54–55, 56
Constructivist pedagogies, 56–57
Coteaching
  in Anita and Maria's classroom, 32–33
  and relations between general and special education, 66–67
Cuban, L., 37
Cultural reciprocity, 96
Curriculum
  approaches to, 69
  emphasis on functional skills, 47
  ways of thinking about, 68
Curwood, J. S., 102

Index

Danforth, S., 4, 5, 93, 131
Danielson, C., 110
Day, M., 96
Decisionmaking, by teachers, 3–4, 7–8
Deferral, pedagogy of, 19, 140–144
Deficit-oriented approaches, 4, 6, 54, 143
De Freitas, E., 138
Delpit, L. D., 141
Democratic values, 4
Desimone, L. M., 111
Dialectical engagement, 65
Dialogue, importance of, 78
Diaspora, 138–139
Difference
　struggle to understand, 35
　understandings of, 74
Differentiated instruction, 5
Direct/explicit instruction, 9, 55, 56–57, 58, 59, 99
Disability
　peer understandings of, 76–78
　and power relations, 80
　social context of, 12–13
　as socially constructed, 2, 12
　and terminology, 81
　understandings of, 79–80
Disability studies in education (DSE), 12–13
Disability studies tradition, 2, 129
Disabled student, use of term, 3
Discipline, 24. *See also* Behavior
Distributed learning/cognition, 11, 15, 102, 103
Documentation, 115
Donellan, A., 126
Draper, Sharon, 60
DSE (disability studies in education), 12–13
Dual certification, 25, 66, 67
Dual vision, 61, 62
Dudley-Marling, C., 7, 13, 40
Dwelling, 133

Edwards, R., 52
Elmore, R., viii
Emotional geography, 127
Emotional labor, 127

Emotions, 127
Empathetic approach, 120, 121–122, 126–127
English, L. M., 134, 138
Epstein, J., 93, 135
Equal, vs. fair, 24
Equitable schooling, 7
Equity, 13. *See also* Social justice
　enacting commitments to, 15
　and listening to families, 106–110
Expectations, 140, 142, 143
Experience, privileging of, 55
Explicit/direct instruction, 9, 55, 56–57, 58, 59, 99

Fair, vs. equal, 24
Families
　at Andrews Children's School, 28
　and community, 19, 93, 97–98, 101, 103, 104–106
　and educational outcomes, 95
　exclusion of, 95
　experiences of, 104–106
　home visits, 118, 128, 137
　Jessica's relations with, 23
　listening to, 106–110
　professional development on building family-school connections, 113, 115
　at Riverside Heights School, 34
　Stephanie's relations with, 26–27
　teachers' relations with, 10–11
　understandings of disability, 11
　at West Creek Elementary School, 24–25
Families, classroom, 11, 21–23, 85–88
Feminism
　Black feminist thought, 129–130
　feminist perspective on emotions, 127
　Third World feminism, 19, 132–140
Ferguson, D. L., viii, 13, 16, 54, 95, 112, 136
Ferguson, P. M., 11, 13, 54, 55, 75, 95, 136
Fernandez, M., 15
Fielding, M., 89
Figured identities, 66
Figured worlds, 66

Fonseca, E., 93
Fosnot, C. T., 56
Frameworks, 131. *See also* Methodologies
Frank, A. W., 80
Freire, P., 57
Functional skills, emphasis on, 47

Gabbitas, B. W., 61, 64
Gabel, S., 4, 12
Gale, T., 61
Gallagher, D., 5, 13, 54, 130
Game, A., 140
Gee, J. P., 76
General education knowledge, privileging of, 25
Geoghegan, D., 57
Goals, and time, 45
Gomez, M. L., 102
Graham, L. G., 71
Graham, S., 55
Grammar of schooling, 37
Gray, S. L., 45
Gurn, A., 7

Haager, D., 54
Half-half positions, 142–143
Halverson, R. R., 15
Hanreddy, A. N., 95
Hanselman, P., 111
Hargreaves, A., 127
Harry, B., 96
Hassett, D., 102
Hehir, T., 112
Herner-Patnode, L., 111, 112
Heshusius, L., 54, 56
High need label, 31
Hitchcock, C., 131
Holland, D., 35, 52, 66, 76
Holquist, M., 76
Home, 133, 134
Horner, R. H., 54
Horvat, E. M., 11, 103
Hughes, C. A., 56, 57, 100
Human development, sociocultural perspectives on, 14–15
Hurtado, A., 132

Identities, figured, 66
Identity, 18. *See also* Voice
Identity, model of, 83
Identity, professional, 65–69, 133, 138
Identity, student, 75–76
Identity, teacher, 116
Identity processes, 55–56
Ideology of ability, 3, 4, 13, 54, 135
Inclusion. *See also* Inclusive education; Inclusive pedagogy
  attitudes toward, 32
  eligibility criterion for, 38
  meanings of, 2–3, 60, 72
  as place, 72
  research on, vii, viii
  teachers' contributions to developing meaning of, 5
  understandings of, 1–2
  unpredictability of, 7
  use of term, vii
Inclusive education. *See also* Inclusion; Inclusive pedagogy
  ambiguity of, 69–72
  premises of, 4–5
  principles of, 6–12
  progress in, vii–viii
Inclusive pedagogy, 54–55
Individualization, 45, 47
Inquiry, collaborative, 78
Instructional frameworks, 131. *See also* Methodologies
Interaction, appropriate, 22–23
Interpretation, peers,' 90
Interpretive work, 10, 18–19
  and acceptance, 85–87
  and accessibility, 81–88
  and implementation of community, 81
  narrativizing, 79–80, 90–91
  and norms, 87–88
  speaking-for, 88–90
  speaking-with, 89
  and student identity, 75–76
  and understandings of disability, 76–78, 79–80
Involvement, 113
Isenbarger, L., 127

Jaeger, P. T., 74
Jaruszewicz, C., 61
Jessica (pseudonym), 11, 35, 38, 40, 43, 46, 47, 77–78, 81, 89, 90–91, 94–96, 104, 109
   background, 21–23
   commitment to classroom family, 85–88
   view of families, 101
Julie (pseudonym), 35, 112, 118–125, 126, 127–128, 142

Kalyanpur, M., 96
Kamin, C., 111
Kauffman, J. M., 2, 5, 6
Kliewer, C., 82
Kloo, A., 47
Kluth, P., 4, 92
Knight, J., 56, 57
Kooy, M., 138
Kuhel, K., 111

Lachiotte, W., 66, 76
Lalvani, P., 11
Language, 3
   Stephanie's emphasis on, 26
   used to describe students, 63–64
Lareau, A., 11, 103
Larsen, M. A., 138
Lave, J., 11, 15, 35, 52, 74, 94, 102
Lawrence-Brown, D., 92
Learning
   collaborative learning opportunities, 15
   and participation, 102
   sociocultural perspectives on, 14–15
   transmission model of, 57, 78
   understandings of, 79
   zone of proximal development, 15
Learning, distributed, 11, 15, 102, 103
Learning needs, 39–40, 41–44, 47–48, 49
Lewis, S., 57
Lindgren, R., 57
Linehan, C., 93
Lingard, B., 61
Linton, S., 13

Liston, D. P., 124
Literacy instruction, 57–61, 71
Lodge, C., 89
Logan, K., 111
Loving perception, 137
Lucado, Max, 86
Lugones, Maria, 137
Lytle, S. L., 124

Mac Iver, M. A., 93
Maria (pseudonym), 9, 35, 38, 40, 43, 44, 52, 53, 64, 69, 70, 98–100, 102, 105, 135, 136, 141, 143
   described, 32–33
   eclectic approach to methodologies, 71
   implementation of community, 109
   literacy instruction, 57–61
   and maneuvering place-time, 48–50
Martin, S. M., 111
Massey, D., 37, 53
Mastropieri, M. A., 39
Mathematics, 28, 29–30, 50–51, 52, 64
McCarthy, J., 93
McClean, M. A., 135
McDuffie, K. A., 39
Mechanistic pedagogies, 56–57
Mercer, N., 15, 75
Merriam, S. B., 16
Messiness, of inclusive instructional practice, 69–72. *See also* Methodologies
Mestiza consciousness, 133
Metcalfe, A., 140
Methodologies, 131
   approaches to, 55, 56–65, 70–72
   dialectical engagement, 62–65
   eclectic approach to, 57–62
   straddling, 9–10
Meyer, A., 131
Michalko, R., 81
Millman, Isaac, 85
Minh-ha, T. T., 133, 134
Mohanty, C. T., 135
Moreno, Elena (pseudonym), 19, 35, 112–116, 118, 126, 127, 128
Moses Goes to a Concert (Millman), 85

Moya, P., 136, 139

Naraian, S., viii, ix, 2, 4, 5, 9, 16, 35, 39, 44, 47, 48, 56, 57, 66, 68, 74, 81, 88, 89, 90, 91, 104, 106, 111, 112, 119, 131, 135, 136, 137, 139
Narrative inquiry, 13–14, 131
Narratives, 79–80, 136–137
Narrativizing, 79–80, 90–91
Nevin, A., 73
Nguyen, X. T., 132
Nikolaraizi, M., 39
No Child Left Behind (NCLB), 30, 45, 47
Normalcy, 4, 5, 7
Norms
  and community, 93, 94, 98
  role of in family story, 87–88
Norms, ability, 72, 90
Norms, academic, 87–88
Norms, behavioral, 87–88, 98, 104
Nussbaum, E., 55

Ogawa, R. T., 135
O'Neill, S., 57
Oppenheim, R., 135
Oppositional agency, 135
Orlikowski, W., 140
Outcomes
  equal, 73–74
  and families, 95
  real, 60
  and time, 45
Out of My Mind (Draper), 60
Oyler, C., 9, 16, 112, 135

Paradigms. *See* Methodologies
Parents. *See* Families
Participation, 18, 82. *See also* Access; Voice
  explicit instruction coupled with, 58–59
  and learning, 102
  and student identity, 75–76
  by students with disabilities, 73–74
Paul (pseudonym), 19, 21, 35, 38, 52–53, 69, 70, 71–72, 112, 126, 137, 138–139, 141
  background, 28–30
  dialectical engagement with methodologies, 62–65
  empathetic approach, 127
  engagement in self-reflection, 128
  and maneuvering place-time, 50–51
  and math curriculum, 50–51
  participation in professional development, 117–118, 127
Pedagogies, mechanistic, 56–57
Pedagogy of deferral, 19, 140–144
People First movements, 3
Personhood, notions of, 90
Peters, S., 135
Petersen, S., 57
Phillips, K. J. R., 111
Philosophies. *See* Methodologies
Piazza, P., 110, 144
Place, 16, 37, 38
  and conceptions of whose learning matters, 38
  demands on students and teachers, 38–39
  differentially experienced, 46
  inclusion as, 72
  linkage with ability norms, 72
  and student competencies, 38
  and student connectedness, 40–41, 42–44
  and student distribution, 42, 51
  and student learning needs, 42–44
  in thinking about students and learning, 37
Placement, 8–9, 36, 52
Place-time
  differentially experienced, 46
  and learning needs, 47–48
  and mathematics instruction, 52
  negotiating, 18
  and placement, 52
  and student success, 48–53
Place-within-place, 39
Polkinghorne, D. E., 14
Poplin, M., 13, 55
Positive Behavioral Interventions and Supports (PBIS), 24
Potential, 140, 141, 143
Power, C., 110

Power relations, 80
Practice, interlocking with theory, 131–132
Practice, quality of, 9
Presuming competence, 12, 118, 125–126
Priestly, A., 52
Priestly, M., 52, 135
Professional development, 19. *See also* Adult education; Coaching
  for addressing behavior, 119–125
  on building family-school connections, 113, 115, 117–118
  and deferral, 142
  and empathetic approach, 120, 121–122, 126–127
  and presuming competence, 125–126
  reflection-inquiry process, 121–123, 124
  and self-reflection, 127–128
  and teacher growth, 122
Professional identity, 65–69, 133, 138

Rationales, 7
Ravitch, D., 6, 100
Real-enough time, 140
Realist orientation, 139
Real reading, 57–61
Rearticulation, 129–131
Reflection, 68–69
Reflection-inquiry process, 121–123, 124
Reid, D. K., 12, 135
Representation of students with disabilities, 82–83, 88
Research, on inclusion, vii, viii
Responsive literary context, 82
Rice, N., 135
Ritchey, K. D., 55
Riverside Heights School, described, 33–34
Rogers, S., 13, 55
Rojas-Drummond, S., 15
Rose, D. H., 131
Ross, G., 15
Rules of care, 84
Ryan, L., 111

Sandoval, C., 132, 133
Sapon-Shevin, M., 39, 92
Sasso, G. M., 2, 5, 6
Scaffolding, 50
Schieble, M., 102
Schlessinger, S., 111, 135
School-to-prison pipeline, 9, 32, 60
Schwartz, D. L., 57
Scruggs, T. E., 39
Self-reflection, 69, 123–125, 127–128
Self-renewal, 64
Sheldon, S. B., 93
Siebers, T., 3, 13, 54, 81, 90
Skills, emphasis on, 47, 57
Skinner, D., 66, 76
Skrtic, T., 13, 54, 130
Slee, R., 4, 9, 71
Sleeter, C., 40
Smith, T., 93, 111
Social constructivist orientation, 139
Social justice, 7, 13, 15, 32, 105–106. *See also* Equity
Soja, E. W., 37
Sonu, D., 135
Space, 37. *See also* Place
Speaking-for, 88–90
Speaking-with, 88, 89
Special education, mainstream, 54
Special education, traditional, 54
Special education practice. *See also* Methodologies
  coupled with inclusive education, 9
  implementation of, 115, 116
Spillane, J. P., 111
Spooner, F., 47
Standardization, 101, 109
Stephanie (pseudonym), 9, 11, 35, 38, 40, 41, 42, 43, 44, 46, 70, 71, 81, 89, 90, 91, 104, 105, 109, 137, 138, 141, 142
  background, 25–27
  commitment to transparent community, 81–85
  and concept of community, 93
  identity-making process, 66–69
  and implementation of community, 101
  view of families, 97–98

Stillman, J., 131
Straut, D. M., 4
Streiker, T., 111
Strogilos, V., 39
Student connectedness, 39, 40–41, 42–44
Student learning, 39–40, 41–44, 51
Student learning needs, 47–48, 49
Student with disabilities, use of term, 3
Support, for teachers, 114, 115
Surabian, M., 74

Taylor, S. J., 12
Teacher agency, 5, 52–53, 71, 134–136
Teacher competence, 11, 116, 122–123
Teacher growth, 122
Teachers
  as change agents, 134
  decisionmaking by, 7–8
  emotional labor of, 127
  empathy for, 120, 121–122, 126–127
  identity making by, 65–69, 138
  identity of, 116, 133, 138
  reflection-inquiry process, 124
  support for, 114, 115
  as teacher educators, 112–128. *See also* Coaching
  views of, 113–114
Technology, use of, 43
Testing, 33, 51, 53, 100, 110
Test preparation, 33, 59, 100
Theoharis, G., 112
Theory, interlocking with practice, 131–132
Theory-practice divide, 5
Third-Space practitioners, 134
Third World feminism, 19, 132–140
Thomas, N., 16, 112
Thousand, J., 73, 92
Thurston, D., 111
Time, 18, 44–48, 140. *See also* Placetime
  differentially experienced, 46
  and goals, 45
  and individualization, 45
  lack of, 36–37
  limitations of, 8
  linear conception of, 44–46
  organization of, 37
  in thinking about students and learning, 37
Time, general education, 45
Time, special education, 45
Titchkosky, T., 3, 73, 91
Tomlinson, C., 131
Tragoulia, E., 39
Transmission model of learning, 57, 78
Transparent communities, 11, 25–27, 71
Traveling, 133
Troia, G. A., 55
Tyack, D., 37

Universal design for learning (UDL), 5
U.S. Third World feminism, 19, 132–140

Valle, J. W., 4, 5, 74
Vaughn, S., 54
Villa, R., 73, 92
Villegas, A. M., 15
Voice, 18, 74, 75–76, 77. *See also* Identity; Participation
Vrasidas, C., 15
Vygotsky, L., 14, 15

Walcott, D. M., 112
Ware, L., 4, 130
Wegerif, R., 15
Weiner, H., 111, 112
Wenger, E., 11, 15, 74, 94, 102
Wertsch, J. V., 14
West Creek Elementary School, 23–25, 41, 42
Wilson, Melanie (pseudonym), 106–109
Wood, P., 15
World-traveling, 137
Wortham, S., 75, 83

Yanchar, S. C., 61, 64
Yates, J., 140
Yell, M. L., 73
You Are Special (Lucado), 86

Zeichner, K. M., 124
Zembylas, M., 15, 120, 121, 127
Zigmond, N., 47
Zone of proximal development, 15

About the Author

Srikala Naraian is an associate professor in the Department of Curriculum and Teaching at Teachers College, Columbia University and program director of the Elementary and Secondary Inclusive Education Programs. After many years of teaching as an itinerant teacher of students with visual impairments and blindness in public schools, mostly in the midwestern U.S., she received her PhD in Education from the University of Missouri-St. Louis. She locates herself in the disability studies tradition and is interested in investigating processes of inclusive education, teacher preparation for inclusive education, and the education of students with significant disabilities. Her research is centered on inclusive practices within schools; she draws on the experiences of educators, students, and families to investigate the production of inclusive classroom communities.

Additionally, Naraian has offered professional development to teachers in New York City schools on inclusive practices with a particular focus on strengthening family–school relations. She has prepared teachers for inclusive education in international contexts, particularly in Iceland and in India. She served as a Fulbright Specialist in Inclusive Education at Ravenshaw University, Odisha, India. She is presently a Guest Professor at the University of Iceland, where she co-teaches a course on autism. Her current projects include working collaboratively with a nonprofit agency in New York City, Parents for Inclusive Education, to document the initiatives taken by school leaders within New York City schools to support the inclusion of students with disabilities. She has published widely in many journals, including *International Journal of Inclusive Education*, *Teachers College Record*, *Anthropology and Education Quarterly*, *Curriculum Inquiry*, and *Teacher Education and Special Education*.